Shopper Marketing

Shopper Marketing

A How-To Business Story

Paul Barnett

BUSINESS EXPERT PRESS

Shopper Marketing: A How-To Business Story

Copyright © Business Expert Press, LLC, 2016.

First published in 2016 by
Business Expert Press, LLC
222 East 46th Street, New York, NY 10017
www.businessexpertpress.com

ISBN-13: 978-1-63157-357-6 (paperback)
ISBN-13: 978-1-63157-358-3 (e-book)

Business Expert Press Consumer Behavior Collection

Collection ISSN: 2163-9477 (print)
Collection ISSN: 2163-937X (electronic)

Cover and interior design by Exeter Premedia Services Private Ltd., Chennai, India

First edition: 2016

10 9 8 7 6 5 4 3 2 1

Printed in the United States of America.

This book is dedicated to my 3 lovely girls: Sheridan, Pia and Paige

Abstract

The book outlines a practical approach to shopper marketing in order to grow both revenue and brand equity. A story runs through the book in the first part of each chapter, so that it is easier to connect the theory and tools in the second part of each chapter, with a real-world scenario.

The book follows the story of the Big Beverage Company, who receive a call from their biggest customer one afternoon asking for their help in getting the coffee category growing again.

This sets the Big Beverage Company and their management team on a journey from being a brand-focused business, to one that understands how a broader emphasis on the category and its shoppers can lead to greater growth for themselves and their retail partners.

The book contains over 300 industry and academic references as well as numerous examples from the author's own experience.

Keywords

category management, digital marketing, FMCG, key account management, retail marketing, shopper insights, shopper marketing

Contents

Acknowledgments

The story in this book is a work of fiction. Any resemblance to actual persons, living or dead, or actual events is purely coincidental.

The characters in this book are a mash-up of the many people I have worked with over the years. These same people have also helped me develop many of the ideas, insights, and tools in this book. I owe all of them a debt of gratitude. And so in no particular order a special thanks to Stuart Crabb, Doug Cunningham, Max Johnston, James Mounter, Christopher Connor, Jennifer Rogers, Megan Parker, Tim Liong, Sarah Lacey, Philip Smiley, Paolo Lanzarotti, Lies Ellison-Davies, Wim Junge, Aravind Thippanaik, Carl Dempsey, Paul Linton, Jim Woolfrey, Gurkeerat Singh Virk, David Shlager, Alastair Cochrane, Michael Stewart, Nick Foley, Tom Bradley, Mario Montuori, Eugene Varricchio, Ian Barnes, Doug Brodman, and Gina Cook for the editorial help.

Introduction

I wrote this book for a 25-year-old me. It contains things I wish I had known when I started my career in the early 1990s.

"It is a novel approach of introducing each principle, by casting it in a real world scenario, so that the reader can not only see the principle, but how its implementation might actually occur in a major brand company."

Herb Sorensen, PhD, Shopper Scientist LLC
Author: *Inside the Mind of the Shopper*

"A must have read for Shopper Marketers combing real life tools for making your activities more effective as well as understanding some of the internal hurdles that need to be overcome. Paul uses his extensive experience to provide some easy wins and processes, a truly different take on how to become better at Shopper Marketing."

Chris Connor, Group Head of Shopper Capability, SABMiller plc

"A comprehensive overview of shopper marketing."

Nick Foley, President, SE Asia Pacific & Japan, Landor

"Shopper Marketing, many talk about it but few really get it. Paul does, and in spades. Moreover in these pages he provides a clear, practical, digestible and usable guide to doing it."

Paolo Lanzarotti, Managing Director, Plzensky Prazdroj, a.s.

"Paul passionately brings to life the importance (and challenges) of Shopper Understanding and Shopper Activation in today's business environment. His perspectives, observations and recommendations are clearly based on years of real-life application (not theory)—as an FMCG business leader and "Shopper" evangelist. His assessment is grounded and practical, and will no doubt help readers better equip themselves to tackling the Shopper/Category opportunities."

Jamie Knott, Category & Channel Sales Development (CCSD) Director, NESTLE POLSKA S.A.

"The book gives a comprehensive overview of the fundamentals of shopper marketing, and gives insight into commercial management as a whole."

Lies Ellison-Davis, Global Director Shopper Marketing, Friesland Campina

"Paul delivers a practical, engaging story on shopper marketing that can be embraced by all retail and supplier business people."

Doug Brodman, Senior Vice President Sales at Miller Brewing Company from 2002 to 2006

"Organisational storytelling at its best! A compelling practitioner's guide to demystify shopper marketing."

Tom Bradley, European Strategy Director at Bacardi

CHAPTER 1

The Key Points in This Chapter

- Without a compelling offer to the shopper, it is difficult for an organization's strategy to be effective.
- Retailers and suppliers can work together to create value through focusing on the needs of the shopper. This is the profit source that they share a common interest in winning.
- It is beneficial for suppliers to work with retailers on value creating projects as some strategies that retailers employ can be value dilutive for suppliers.

Part A: The Phone Call

They had closed the quarter by pulling forward as many customer orders from the next month as possible. This was the third quarter in succession that they had been required to do this in order to reach their target. This just created a circular problem for the next quarter and so no one enjoyed working this way.

"We got there, but is this sustainable?" asked Jamie to the other members of the sales leadership team. There was grumbled agreement.

"I agree that this isn't how we want to operate, but until we can get the new products to market, we're going to have to grind it out" replied the Sales Director, Ben, trying to focus the team.

Jamie was the business manager for the largest channel of customers; his energy was infectious, both positive and negative, and grinding it out through the summer, his last with his wife before their first child arrived, was not something he was looking forward to.

Leaning forward, he looked across to Simon, their Trade Marketing manager, and challenged him for more support, "Is there anything we can do to bring the new lines forward?"

"I'm trying to have Go-Jo," the project name for their new flavored milk powder, "ready two weeks early so we can sell the first orders in quarter four. I'm also pushing for a 1.5 kilogram pack of Choclo to be produced as a one-off promotional pack for everyone in September, but it's not looking good."

"I'm pushing where I can," he continued, "I've spoken to all the brand project teams and made them aware of the situation, but from their point of view, market share is stable and so they're reluctant to do anything that outside of the plan."

"If we keep spending on promotions the way we are, they will have a problem with profit before long," replied Jamie leaning back this time for emphasis, "my trade promotion spending is up 10 percent on last year; our baseline just isn't strong enough." Jamie's phone began to flash; "It's Amy, I better take this," and he stepped away from the room leaving the rest of the team to work through their plans again.

"Hi Amy, what's up?"

Amy was the buyer for their biggest customer, Shopmart. She was in her early thirties and a rising star at the company. She had taken on the hot beverages portfolio about six months ago after overseeing the return to profit of their seasonal confectionery range. In that role, she'd introduced allergy-free Easter eggs under their own private label, and worked with Cadbury to develop an exclusive range of Christmas products that reduced the need to price fight as regularly as they had been over the last decade. Hot beverages was one of the biggest categories at Shopmart; the profit per meter of trading space was one of the highest in the store. It was a category that a shopper would switch retailers for, so it was high profile and often on the front of their sales leaflets and featured in their TV slots.

The relationship between Jamie and Amy and their respective companies was a symbiotic one. The Big Beverage Company was 20 percent of the total hot beverages category, a group of products that included milk flavorings, tea, and coffee; and in turn Shopmart was 15 percent of the Big Beverage Company's total sales.

"Hi Jamie, I'm just out in stores; what are you doing?"

"Plotting ways to hit the sales target!"

"Funny, I was just thinking the same thing."

At least she isn't ringing to tell me off about our poor service levels again, thought Jamie.

"I'm at the Broadmeadows store to discuss the refurbishment it's about to get. You know we're trying to find more space for Health & Beauty. We had coffee at Starbucks before we went into the store though; have you seen the new coffee intrinsics material they have around the counter now?"

"Not lately, they're the competition so I steer clear!" and he said it as a joke but Amy did not laugh.

"You should check it out; it explains how coffee is grown and harvested and acts as re-enforcement to why you should pay $5 for a Latté."

"Anyway," she continued, "It got us wondering just how the total coffee market is performing and what we can do to win a bigger part of it. Could you come in next week and let us know what you have on this? We want to use the Broadmeadows store to test some future concepts?"

"Sure, we have heaps of stuff on that. I'll bring our Trade Marketing guy, Simon along."

"Great, does Thursday afternoon at 3 p.m. work? I'll ask my boss to come along too."

"See you then."

Jamie ended the call and walked back toward the boardroom. He could see Simon standing at the white board writing as the group called out ideas. In bold letters was *banded pack*! and *Sports bag offer*; the same stuff as last year he thought.

The meeting finished with a list of prioritized ideas that Simon committed to responding on within the next two weeks. He knew it was a long stretch that any of them could be commercialized; there was a great deal of energy already being invested in preparing for the upcoming new product launches. It was his job, however, to try and get the marketing and sales teams that planned the activities for each of the product portfolios focused on both the short- and long-term execution.

He had joined the Big Beverage Company 10 months ago after spending four years working with a small consulting company called Shopperscan that specialized in using shopper insight to help build category growth plans. The company was half owned by Shopmart who provided the data in return for client services for their buyers. Consulting had been a lot of fun; it had provided him with exposure to a wide array of companies, categories, and people. He had worked on projects with the leading beer companies to redesign the chilled beer section, with a large confectionery company to re-imagine the aisle and multiple others that had all involved collaboration between retailer and supplier with the express goal of improving sales by finding ways to win more purchases from shoppers. He had learnt more in those four years than he had in the prior six with Novartis where he had started as a graduate.

He had been hired by Ben with the intention of bringing the shopper closer to the front of their commercial agenda. This was not a change that happened overnight though, and he had to keep reminding himself of this every time he tried to get people interested in growth plans that were not solely brand oriented.

At the last sales leadership team meeting, he had been given a two-hour slot to talk about shopper marketing, and how they could use it as part of their regular interacts with retail customers. To illustrate his point, he used an exercise he had picked up from one of the more senior Shopmart buyers.

"OK Jamie, here is the task; Ben is the buyer at Dandy Supermarkets and you've got to talk to him about your plans to grow the Coffee category. You can't mention any of our brands though. Let's see how long you can go."

"Hi Ben," and he rose to shake his hand. "How's business?"

"Good Jamie, how about you?"

"Great, shares are up and business is strong."

"What's driving that?"

"The Grande Blend promotion we ran last quarter was one of our best ...." Ben sat down.

"Not bad Jamie, 30 seconds; longer than usual!" heckled someone from the back of the room. There was muted laughter from the group.

"It's clear we have a bit of work to do," had been Ben's blunt summation.

"Simon, Ben; you got a second?" asked Jamie as everyone shuffled out at the end of the meeting.

"That was Amy who rang before; she was visiting stores with John. They were in Starbucks and got to wondering what the broader coffee market is doing. She asked us to come in next week and give them some ideas on how to grow."

"Interesting, what did you say?"

"I said we had heaps of stuff," and he winked at Simon.

"Next week!" Simon groaned.

There was a brief pause before Ben broke the tension: "Maybe this is the exact situation we needed to instigate change?"

Part B: Joint Value Creation by Focusing on the Shopper

All businesses strive for the same thing, whether they are a large multinational or small local enterprise, they all want to create value for their shareholders. They have three high-level strategies they can employ to create this value:

1. Growth in revenue
2. Growth in profit
3. Improved efficiency

Most of the time, a business is employing all three with varying degrees of focus across the organization. However, without a compelling offer to the shopper, none of these strategies will be effective.

Table 1.1 High level strategy examples for a retailer

Growth in revenue	Growth in profit	Improved efficiency
Promotional campaigns	Increased fees and charges to suppliers	Inventory reduction
New stores	Lower purchase prices	Distribution optimization
Store refurbishments	Higher everyday prices	Warehouse cross-docking
Expanded range	Loyalty marketing to shoppers	Retail ready packaging
Increased marketing		

In this chapter, Amy is asking for Jamie's help in making sure that the Shopmart offer to the shopper is as good as it can be. At the same time, the Big Beverage Company and their sales management team is struggling for growth and starting to talk about how a broader emphasis on the category and its shoppers can lead to greater growth for themselves and their retail partners.

The consumer should always be at the heart of everything a manufacturer does, and the collective efforts of the business should be to generate demand that moves beyond trial to loyalty. However, when shopping people have specific attitudes and behaviors that are distinct from their consumption habits, these must be understood and served. When organizations can act on their shopper insights they maximize the relevance and effectiveness of their execution. And it's through this execution that operating cost is transformed into value and brand equity grows.

At Shopmart, Amy is hoping that the Big Beverage Company does indeed have sufficient insight into the broader needs of coffee shoppers, so that she may alter elements of her retail marketing mix to create value.

At the Big Beverage Company, Jamie is in turn hoping that they possess this insight and can turn it into a compelling shopper proposition with Shopmart, as failure to do that may mean that Amy looks for other ways of creating value, ways that may destroy value for them. For example, in the coffee category that Amy is managing, she could employ any or in fact all of the three strategic choices above. She could for example:

a. Try to grow coffee sales 5 percent more than Shopmart is at present
b. Negotiate for a 3 percent lower cost of goods
c. Increase fees and charges to suppliers by 10 percent

In this situation though, only one of them represents joint value creation for both Shopmart and the Big Beverage Company: option A; options B and C will mean transferring money from the Big Beverage Company's bottom line to Shopmart's. They would of course negotiate to attach counterparts to any increase in investment with Shopmart against demand generating initiatives, like increasing share of shelf or promotional support, but these concessions from Shopmart may only last for a year

Table 1.2 Shopmart value creation options table

	Base	A. +5% Sales	B. −3% COGS	C. +10% in Fees
Sales	$100.00	$105.00	$100.00	$100.00
Cost of goods	($78.00)	($81.90)	($75.66)	($78.00)
Gross profit	$22.00	$23.10	$24.34	$22.00
Expenses (fixed)	($19.00)	($19.00)	($19.00)	($19.00)
Operating profit	$3.00	$4.10	$5.34	$3.00
Other income or expenses	$0.30	$0.30	$0.30	$0.33
Net income	$3.30	$4.40	$5.64	$3.33

or two, whereas the increase in investment offered by the Big Beverage Company lifts the starting point from which all future negotiations with Shopmart will be based.

Option A is also the most difficult to achieve. This is that reason why only select manufacturers in certain categories are engaged in growth creation strategies by retailers.

Manufacturer Segmentation

Manufacturers will often be prioritized into three groups by retailers as per Table 1.3. The expectations from the retailer will change relative to the manufacturer's classification.

The value for a supplier in being classified as a strategic supplier is that it provides a broader set of areas in which to engage the retailer on initiatives to grow value for both businesses. This is important when you consider that retailer payments and rebates are often the highest expense, after the cost of the goods, on a manufacturer's profit and loss statement.

To this end, manufactures will often manage their financial and resource investments with customers by prioritizing them.

As a result of these segmenting efforts by retailers and manufacturers, each approaches the business relationship with a set of expectations that they proceed to negotiate toward achieving. As with any negotiation, there are trade-offs and concessions offered by both parties as they endeavor to

Table 1.3 Manufacturer segmentation by retailers

Priority	Description	Retailer expectations
A	**Strategic** suppliers who are able to deliver category-related growth strategies in addition to improved profit and efficiency	In addition to the expectations for tactical suppliers: • Category growth strategies • Shopper insight • Input into ranging decisions
B	**Tactical** suppliers, who offer some efficiency focus but their main benefit is brand-led growth in revenue	In addition to the expectations for transactional suppliers: • High level category trends • Promotional execution • Input into planogram decisions
C	**Transactional** suppliers who provide a source of profit	• Improved supply chain efficiency • Lower costs to increase margins

obtain their goals. As both parties move through this process, it is vital that they maintain a focus on the shopper, as this is the individual that they share a common interest in winning.

In the model that follows, popularized by Kantar Retail, the shopper interface is the one area that all three stakeholders have in common. It is here where consumers become shoppers and revenue is generated from the activities undertaken at the retail interface. It is also the point where costs incurred through the consumer interface are recouped through orders generated at the business interface. In this way, the shopper is the key profit center for both retailers and manufacturers; therefore, executing well here is critical to achieve revenue objectives.

Shoppers, therefore, are at the front of everything manufacturers should focus on with their retail partners. In turn, retailers need to ensure that their value creation strategies help improve their shopper offer.

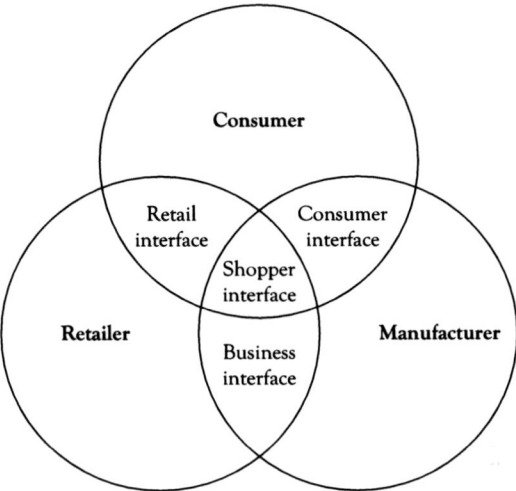

Figure 1.1 Common focus on the shopper (Kantar Retail)

Top Tips

- It is important for suppliers to understand the value creation strategies retail customers are using. They can become the focus of the benefits for any activity suppliers propose.
- Ensure that your resources are evenly deployed across the business, retail and consumer interfaces.
- Suppliers should segment their customer base and actively pursue shopper-led value-creating projects with priority retailers.

CHAPTER 2

The Key Points in This Chapter

- Retailers will often be more interested in what suppliers know about shoppers rather than consumers.
- Dependent on the shopper mission and consumption occasion, more than 30 percent of final purchase decisions are made while standing in the retail environment.
- Shopper marketing is the act of improving revenue or equity through insight-led strategies and executions that convert the shoppers along their paths to purchase.
- If executed well, shopper marketing has the potential to influence the profit and loss statement in three specific areas.

Part A: Managing Joint Projects with Customers

"So," said Reg, the managing director, "Shopmart want to know how to grow?"

In the room was a cross-functional group that included people from marketing, insights, finance, and trade marketing. Ben had called them together to help prepare the response to Shopmart's request.

"They do, they are thinking about expanding the space for certain categories and cutting back on others. Given the success Starbucks appear to be having, and all they had to go on was the number of their stores that are popping up everywhere, they wanted to know what we saw as the potential for coffee and how we could help them capture more of it" replied Jamie.

"Excellent! Great opportunity for us to talk to them about the consumer and what we can do to delight them!" And he looked across the team for emphasis, the majority of whom mumbled their agreement.

"As you read in the e-mail, Shopmart have asked for some assistance in understanding the coffee market, with the potential for working with us on a project to grow their sales. What we would like to do is share how we intend to respond and ask for your assistance in some key areas," Jamie continued.

"Ok," said Reg, "What are we going to do?"

At this point, the baton passed to Simon, "Shopmart want to know how they can unlock growth by bringing a greater focus to the shopper. The shopper is often the consumer, this is of course true; but when shopping people have unique needs and behaviors and this is what we have to understand before we can offer them a solution."

"But if the shopper is the consumer, can't a focus on the consumer achieve the same thing?" asked the marketing director Julie with a confused look. "We're a brands company; we win consumers with our brands. Shopmart is a retailer; shoppers are their domain. Don't we complement what they know?" she continued.

"Same question I had a while back," said Ben moving to the white board. "This is how I saw a research guy from Ipsos answer it at a conference recently. If I asked you to describe the things that are important when you are consuming coffee, what would you say?"

There was a moment's silence while everyone moved focus to his rather strange question.

"I'd want to know how much I should put on the spoon if it was instant coffee." Someone called out and Ben wrote *spoon amount* on the board.

Simon offered, "the temperature of the water and the quality of the milk."

"Extrinsics too, things like how it made me feel both before and afterward."

"Ok, how the jar looks, particularly if it's going to be on show ..." and this comment from Julie encouraged a reaction from Reg who thought that their cost reductions in packaging had been too severe and left them looking commoditized.

For the next two minutes they added to the list that ran along the right hand side of the whiteboard.

"Ok, great list." Ben said turning to the group, "Now the other side of the coin; what things are important to people when they are shopping for coffee?"

"I'll start us off," said Simon. "Packaging; people want to know that it will look good in their homes; just as Reg said and this is important when they're browsing the shelves."

"Price," said Jamie.

"Yep, and that's both shelf price and promotional price."

"Quantity," chipped in Julie.

"The brand and sub brand," from the marketers.

"The occasion that is suitable for the product," offered someone from insights.

"And, color and shape," said Simon, "this is how people sift through the options on shelf. After all, it's impossible to evaluate every single product on the shelf. Do you know how many roast and ground products they have in their assortment now? 72!"

They kept going until they had a list that was in equal length to the consumer attributes.

"Neat trick that Ben," surmised Reg, "so there are things that are important to people when they shop for coffee; but don't we already talk about these things anyway? Everything on that list there is something we plan for already?" But he posed it as a question, not a comment.

"We do indeed," replied Julie. "But Ben I'm betting we don't use any of this knowledge in our commercial discussions, do we?"

Ben nodded, not sure how Reg would react to this omission. "The consumer is at the heart of everything we do; that shouldn't change, but the shopper should be at the front of everything we do with the retailer."

Ben continued, "I know it's a third stakeholder to think about, but I think it's the right thing to do."

Reg leaned back in his chair and looked at the list again.

"What I do know is this; if we're not talking to retailers about consumers or as you have shown us here shoppers, and ways to win and delight them, then we're going to be talking to them about promotions and margins and that isn't a profitable conversation very often."

"What keeps me up at night is the fact that over half of our consumers can't tell our coffees from the competition's in blind taste tests." He continued looking at Julie, "I know you'll tell me that this isn't unusual, and that this is the case for many brands. But not all products are like coffee and cost the equivalent of an average 30 minutes of work per jar. We're expensive, maybe not on a per cup basis, but definitely as a pick-up price—and all this," he waved to indicate the broader company, "could disappear if the retailer gets private labels right."

"So, if this opportunity helps us become valuable beyond the owner-ship of our brands," and he smiled to lighten the mood, "then perhaps it is actually a better opportunity than we might realize. So, what are you proposing we do?"

"Well, two things;" said Simon, "the first is the way we suggest coor-dinating to address this opportunity, and that's using some steps called RACER! And the second is establishing a category vision; the sentence we'll open with when we go in to see Shopmart to explain the evolution and financial potential we see for coffee."

"It's just a simple sentence, Reg, that describes the way we believe value can be created in the future through delivering what the shopper and then the consumer will desire."

"Let's hear more," said Julie.

The meeting finished on time, Ben, Simon, and Jamie stayed behind to discuss how the session had gone and what they would do next. They were all in general agreement that things had gone well; they had met the objective of getting a broader group engaged and bridged the topic of the shopper as a stakeholder with Julie and Reg, the two stakeholders they needed to win over. There was still a lot to do, but the journey had started.

The most pressing concern was now the meeting with Shopmart. The retailer was expecting a view on market performance and a position from them on where growth would come from; it was the latter that they did not have yet. The solution they had proposed to the group was the con-struction of a category vision, and it would be difficult to produce this and align on it internally before the meeting with Shopmart.

"I think we should postpone for one week," offered Ben. "Use that time to get to an aligned position on the vision for the category and then lead with that in the meeting with Amy and her boss."

"The question though," he continued, "is whether a week is enough time?"

Part B: Using Shopper Marketing to Unlock Growth

The team at the Big Beverage Company wants to improve their shopper marketing with Shopmart in order to grow both the category and their brands.

Shopper marketing is the act of improving revenue or equity through insight-led strategies and executions that convert the shopper along their path to purchase.

The way to do shopper marketing in a simple, pragmatic way is as follows:

In my experience, the Newton's Cradle mnemonic in Figure 2.1 is one of the easiest way of illustrating the key activities that constitute shopper marketing and how they transfer energy to each other in order to deliver execution and learning.

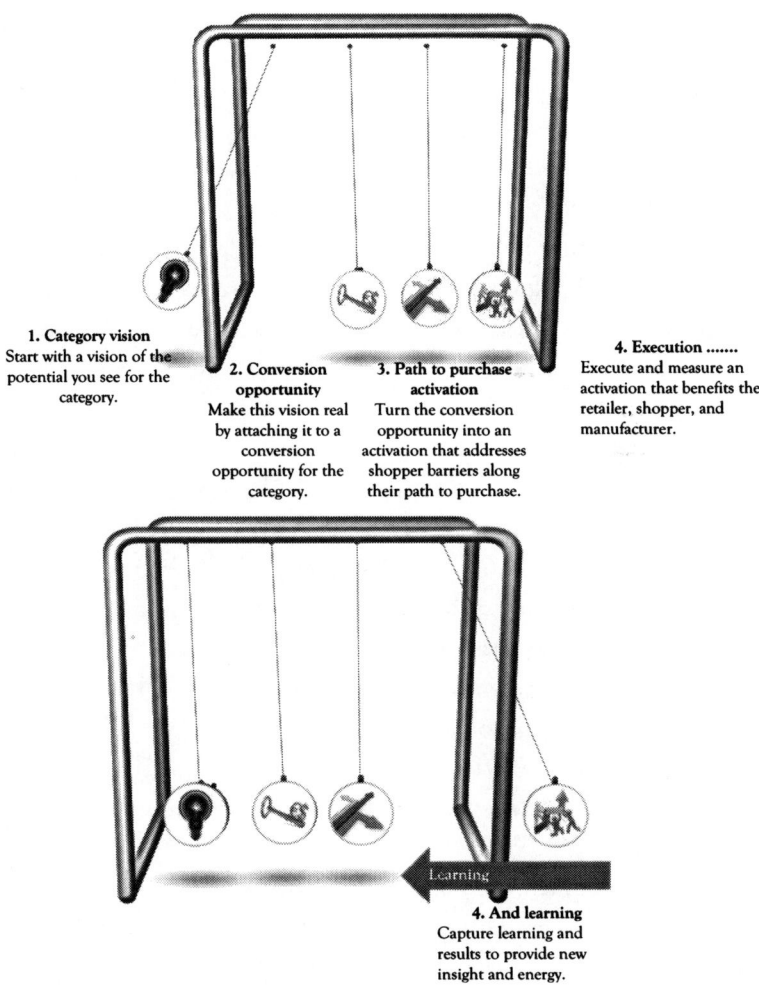

1. Category vision
Start with a vision of the potential you see for the category.

2. Conversion opportunity
Make this vision real by attaching it to a conversion opportunity for the category.

3. Path to purchase activation
Turn the conversion opportunity into an activation that addresses shopper barriers along their path to purchase.

4. Execution ....
Execute and measure an activation that benefits the retailer, shopper, and manufacturer.

4. And learning
Capture learning and results to provide new insight and energy.

Figure 2.1 Shopper marketing model

Table 2.1 Shopper marketing impact on brand P&L

Gross Sales Income	$100	1. Improving the effectiveness of invest-ments in price discounts and display space.
On Invoice Discounts	$10	
Revenue	$90	
Off Invoice Discounts	$10	2. Improved conversion from the moment a shopper identifies a need through to their exit from the store.
Net Revenue	$80	
Variable Costs	$40	
Gross Margin	$40	3. Increase in effectiveness of below-the-line marketing spend by understanding how merchandising influences product choice.
Marketing Costs	$12	
Net Margin	$28	

If executed well, it has the potential to influence the profit and loss statement in three specific areas as per Table 2.1.

The operative words here are, of course, *if executed well*.

Shopper marketing is not a remedy to all of commercial issues; however, goal alignment from both retailers and manufactures on what is best deployed to win the shopper is a starting point that can, at a minimum, allow both parties to focus their commercial interactions. When adopted by a key commercial function, it brings routine and focus on working effectively with retail partners.

The mind-set change needed to bring a common focus onto the shopper requires not only alignment with the retailer but within the functions of a supplier as well. This does not happen automatically in many companies. There is a long history of focusing on the consumer as the source of profit; this dates back to the birth of modern advertising in the early 1950s. However, when we accept that upwards of 30 percent of final purchase decisions are made while standing in the retail environment, dependent on the shopper mission and occasion a fluid environment emerges; this is where memory wrestles with attention on the immediate stimuli to influence purchase behaviors at—as P&G have famously branded—the first moment of truth.

In this environment, the distinction between the consumer and the shopper allows for a greater depth of understanding into the behaviors a brand must influence in order to be salient.

Consumers versus Shoppers

A simple way of understanding the differences between shoppers and consumers is that consumers are those who consume either directly or indirectly, while shoppers are those who source products to supply either themselves or others. What is common to understanding both is consumption; however, for the shopper we narrow this focus to understanding the occasions for which they are shopping. In this way, the occasion is central to understanding shopper's beliefs (Jones 2012).

There is a temptation to fold the understanding of both consumers and shoppers into single studies to maximize cost efficiencies and to produce segmentation algorithms that can be more broadly applied. However, the ability to derive shopper understanding away from their in-situ environment, the retail store to the home or agency office where consumer studies are often undertaken is problematic, given the disconnect between what shoppers actually do and what they report they intend to do.

The simplest example of this can be found in our own behavior; how many of us have gone into a shop for a quick top-up purchase, perhaps for bread, milk, or nappies, and emerged with a basket of goods that contains many other items? The reality is that we are prompted to buy beyond our conscious needs when we are placed in an environment that provides visual prompts to latent needs or wants.

Retailers understand this intuitively and to extract the most value they can from each shopper, they will always look to maximize the relevance of their offer to the daily needs of their shoppers.

RACER!

At the Big Beverage Company, Simon recommended the use of RACER! to coordinate the project with Shopmart. When it comes to running projects with retailers I have found the RACER! tool to be one of the easier ways to align objectives and expectations. RACER! is a tool designed to complement existing joint business plans or scorecards as a means of bringing alignment and commitment to a joint project with a retailer. It is summarized as follows:

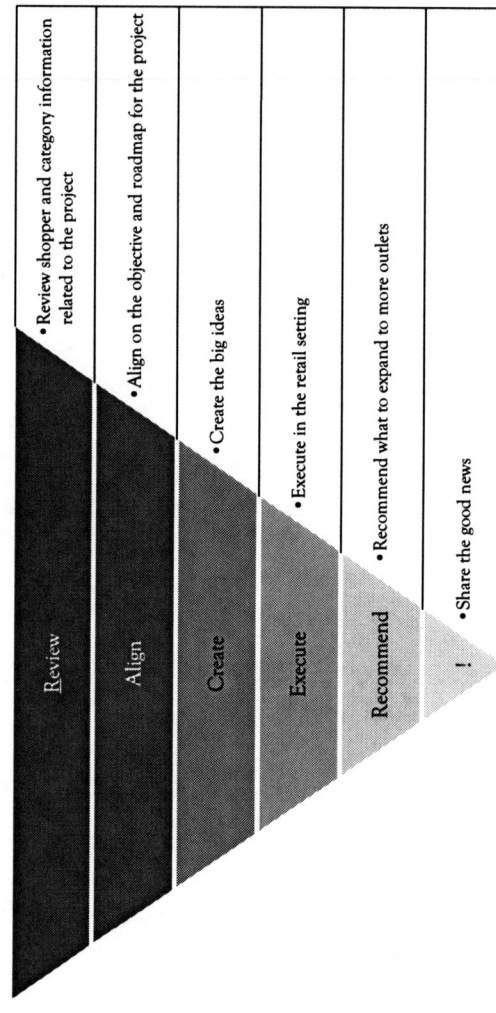

Figure 2.2 The RACER! model

Table 2.2 The RACER! model in more detail

Step	Key tasks	Tips
Review	• Category review • Shopper insight review • High level trends	• Keep it brief and show the insights, not pages of graphs and observations • Use real videos of the shopper in the retail environment • Have a view of what you see as the potential for the category and the drivers that will support this
Align	• What is the objective? • What questions do we have to answer to meet our objectives? • What is the scorecard we will use? • What are the stages or timeline of this project? • Who will be involved from both companies at each stage?	• Start with understanding the overall objectives of both teams, then align on one shared set of objectives • Make sure the scorecard has a balance of qualitative and quantitative measures • Set out a responsibility plan, make it high level, and assume the retailer will want the supplier to do a lot of the early work
Create	• Create the research or tests to answer our questions • Create time for both companies to see the research or test first hand • Create ideas from the knowledge and insight gathered from the research • Prioritize the ideas developed and create the action plan	• If you are using a research agency, make them a partner in the project; they will have broader experience that can help • Make sure there is someone at the retailer who can help with approvals to test or research in-store. When you are testing or researching in-store, you should have a signed letter from the retailer giving approval and a contact number for the store if they have questions • Create ideas away from the office using an ideation tool like a Hot house • Make sure you create a one page selling story the retailer can use to get alignment within their business

(Continued)

Table 2.2 The RACER! model in more detail (Continued)

Step	Key tasks	Tips
Execute	• Execute the ideas using operations people from both companies • Gather feedback from the shopper about the execution	• Video or photograph the execution in-store • Ensure that the scorecard you setup can be populated with the right data before the execution begins • Set up control stores that will allow you to understand the impact
Recommend	• Review the results and synthesize them into insights • Agree on what you learnt along the way and what you will do differently next time • Agree on a recommendation for next steps	• Don't rush toward a full execution across all stores; if the learnings are ambiguous test again
!	• Announce the learning and the journey you have undertaken together to senior management of both companies so that everyone knows progress is being made • Return to the align step	• Manage stake holders throughout the process so that everyone is aware of the time and commitment of both companies

Top Tips

- Implement a shopper marketing model that is pragmatic enough to work within your current structure and resource base.
- Separate your thinking on people into consumers and shoppers; this will improve the chance of your executions winning in the retail environment.
- To coordinate projects between retailers and suppliers use the RACER! Model. Ensure both parties understand the steps before work starts.

CHAPTER 3

The Key Points in This Chapter

- The first step in shopper marketing is to create a category vision.
- A category vision starts with a sentence that explains your vision for the evolution of the category to both external retailers and internal functions. It should describe the way you believe value can be created in the future through delivering what the shopper and ultimately consumer will desire.
- The category vision should be supported with a set of growth opportunities.
- Growth opportunities need to convince both the internal functions and external customers that there is enough financial potential in the category to warrant additional resource and time investment. They should set the stage for a more focused conversation on what needs to happen in order to unlock growth.

Part A: The Category Vision

The team met at an old bank that had been refurbished into a creative thinking space called *the Vault* at 7:30 a.m. It was fitted out with bean bags, smart boards, large north-facing windows, and no wifi; it was the ideal place for a team meeting where you wanted people to use a little imagination.

Simon and his team had worked late through the backend of the week prior to prepare for the workshop. He would have preferred much longer but the request from Shopmart had expedited things. As part of the preparation the team secretary had conducted ten interviews with a cross section of people that included sales representatives in the Far East of the country, junior brand managers through to the managing director. She asked them three questions and then transcribed their answers without interruption or clarification.

The questions were:

1. If a retailer asked you how they could grow their coffee category sales, what would you say?
2. What areas could the coffee category expand into to grow faster?
3. Why should a retailer support the coffee category?

As people helped themselves to a light breakfast, Simon stuck up large sheets of paper that summarized the themes discovered from the responses to their survey.

"What's this?" asked Jamie.

"A snapshot of our offer to the market place," he replied.

"Our objective is to grow ahead of the category; our company vision is to change the way people think about and consume coffee, and our mission is to make coffee the hot drink of choice. That's how everything fits together!" They had finished the information review, and the task of writing the category vision had started. Julie was summarizing her view on how everything fitted together.

"You might be right," replied Ben. "But that doesn't come through on the words you see written on the walls. People aren't clear on what we have to do to grow coffee."

Simon was facilitating the Category Vision workshop. In his previous role this had been something he had helped with on several occasions. But this was the first he had led, and so he was anxious to keep things focused and moving forward.

"Let's try something a little different then," Simon followed after a small pause.

"Working in pairs, please spend the next 20 minutes trying to create a category vision by answering these questions," and he wrote them on a flip chart as he talked through them.

WHAT does the category need to do to grow beyond its present organic rate in the channels we play in?

HOW can this be done?

As he turned back around, Ben nodded his approval.

Later, after they had eaten lunch and voted on each other's work, Simon read the winning category vision to the group.

To create an obsessive passion for coffee culture.
By extending the functional and emotional benefits that coffee has to offer.
So that people pay more for experiences in familiar occasions.

He looked up to find people nodding.

"That's our working vision then. We'll circle back and check it again at the end of the day. But now we have to move on. If I have done my sums correctly, in the next four hours over 200,000 cups of coffee will be consumed from the category our vision serves. The next part of our meeting is to try and figure out where the growth to extend this will come from."

"And to do that, we are going to review a set of growth opportunities that the insights team prepared earlier; they are value pools that can be addressed by the coffee category to increase its total size. We found them by assessing the volume open to coffee in all beverage consumption occasions and combined this with an understanding of the trends influencing consumer need states, and shopping behaviors and attitudes."

He unveiled the poster that summarized the growth opportunities.

"We found five main ones which you can see here. We've given them succinct, memorable names that we hope can act as a rallying force both internally and with the retailer."

The insights director handed out booklets with the detail behind each opportunity.

"These growth opportunities will be used in two main ways, the first is with the retailer, where in the future everything we agree to focus on with them will tie back to one of these opportunities. While internally, the hope is that any one of the 28 innovation projects we are working on as a business today link back to at least one of these opportunities. If they don't, we have to question whether they are worthwhile."

People started to flick through the booklets.

"So here's the task. Take 20 minutes to read through these; then, working in pairs, we are going to allocate you two growth opportunities to interrogate. Make changes, write questions; challenge the data. Then you get to present your growth opportunity to the group with the objective of either aligning behind it or discarding it."

"For this, I need an extra strong coffee!" said Reg.

The booklets had been the focus of much of last week's work. The process of piecing them together had been like a forensic geometry; *how did a trend in consumption habits of 18- to 24-year-olds tie with the shopping habits of their mothers? What did the rise of flavored, geographic-focused coffees mean for afternoon consumption occasions?* And on it went until they had five buckets of growth opportunities tangible enough for any of them to relate to. It had been an exercise in art more than science, and he wondered now if it was as obvious to them as it was to him.

His phone vibrated with an incoming call.

It was his wife, "How's it going?"

He looked out again across the room at the people who were scratching red and blue ink across his work, "Ok, I think."

"It's not that I disagree with any of this," said Julie the marketing director. "It's just a lot to take in all at once."

"I realize that, but we have a meeting with the commercial director and buyer at Shopmart on Friday, and we have to go in with a position on the growth potential for the category, not just charts showing trends," replied Ben.

They had reached the end of the day, and after reviewing the vision and growth opportunities they had developed were discussing whether or not they were ready to share it with a retailer.

"You can't take it back once you say it though Ben; you go in with something like this and they shoot holes in it and we back down, then what does that say about our understanding of the market?" Reg was challenging Ben to test his resolve.

"I feel more confident with the framework we have put together today than in any of the other retailer presentations I have seen in the last few years! We always go with opportunities around trade up or usage expansion and they're just too generic."

"What's your concern Julie?" asked Reg.

"Despite everything we do, we still have a divide between sales and marketing; that will probably always be the case given the tension between the time horizons they manage. But something like this could just push us further apart unless we can align on it before we put it out there."

"Well, why can't we?" asked Ben. "Let's pressure test this with a group from marketing and sales tomorrow."

"But even before we test it, are we sure this is a big idea? Is this just a shiny new toy or something that's going to stick? The marketing gang will want to know what this means for their brands, and I or we," looking at Reg, "need to have that ready for them."

What was pleasing to Simon was not that there was deep resistance to what they had pulled together throughout the day, but rather the discussion around alignment.

"Julie" asked Reg, "If we got 10 to 12 of our high potential people in a room tomorrow afternoon, could you facilitate a discussion on this? I think we should take this to Shopmart this week; if it develops into a project, it's a good opportunity for us at a time when we are struggling for growth. But I am sensitive to what you are saying and so I want to test this for simplicity and meaningfulness with our internal team."

Reg spoke with an energy that was not typical for him; it was easy to tell that he was excited.

"We could align behind this as a business, and I'd like to do that by launching the idea at our end of quarter town hall meeting. Julie, I think you should own this; a category vision coming from marketing will sound revolutionary to the sales team!" and everyone laughed.

Part B: Category Visions and Growth Opportunities

The category vision provides the initial energy for the shopper marketing model.

A category vision starts with a single sentence that explains your vision for the evolution of the category to both external retailers and internal functions. It should describe the way you believe value can be created in the future through delivering what the shopper and ultimately consumer will desire.

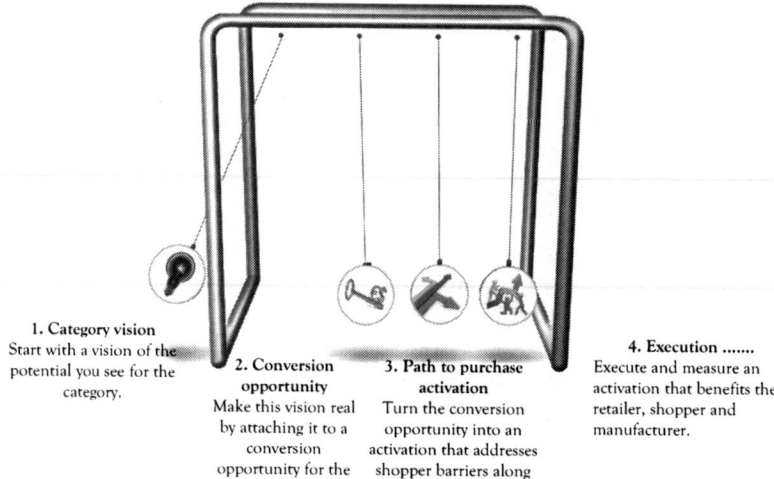

1. Category vision
Start with a vision of the
potential you see for the
category.

**2. Conversion
opportunity**
Make this vision real
by attaching it to a
conversion
opportunity for the
category.

**3. Path to purchase
activation**
Turn the conversion
opportunity into an
activation that addresses
shopper barriers along
their path to purchase.

4. Execution ....
Execute and measure an
activation that benefits the
retailer, shopper and
manufacturer.

Figure 3.1 Shopper marketing model

For example:

"Changing the way people think about bread ... "

Then the addition of a supporting sentence that describes the vision
in more detail; for example:

*"... by extending the functional and emotional benefits of everything bread
can be, so that people will pay more for familiar consumption, more often."*

Here are some examples of category visions:

- From Kellogg's: To make cereal the breakfast of choice, everyday (IGD 2011a)
- From Danone UK: Inspiring Hydration for Life: A bottle for
  every need (Medford 2014)
- From Twinings Tea UK: The contemporary drink of choice,
  creating a new generation of tea lovers (Taphouse 2014)

To write a category vision, it is always necessary to understand the
broader trends that are influencing the consumption, purchase, and sale
of the products within the category and, based on these, the implications
for the category.

In some instances it may be necessary to start by defining the actual category and the segments within it. This provides the initial frame to start the analysis, and it can assist in breaking paradigms about how far the category can stretch into new segments and types of products. For example, when looking at the Pet Care category, it can be defined as follows:

Dry food	Moist food	Wet food	Litter	Treats	Health	Grooming	Toys	Bedding	Clothing	Control	Housing	Travel	Education	Literature

Narrow ---→ Broad

After reviewing this material, it is beneficial to distill the observations into a simple SWOT analysis from the category's perspective. In doing this, you firstly ask; what **strengths** and **weaknesses** does the category have in consumption usage and attitudes, shopping behavior and attitudes and customer support? From these two areas, it is then possible to form a view on what the category *could* do in order to develop.

Then, secondly ask what **threats** and **opportunities** does the category face in consumption usage and attitudes, shopping behavior and attitudes and customer support? From these two areas we can then discern what the category *must* do in order to develop.

When you have a category vision, you can test it for effectiveness using these four questions:

1. Does it call out the prospect of growth for the retailer and supplier?
2. Is it consistent with the longer term strategic priorities of the supplier?
3. Is it a vision that the supplier can execute against?
4. Does it bring clarity and alignment to the internal functions at the supplier?

When you have a vision you can then begin to look for the growth opportunities that will empower it. (Although in some instances, it may be easier to start with the growth opportunities and then write your category vision afterward.)

If you are lucky enough to have a broad segmentation database, then you may be able to identify the value that is open to your category across consumption occasions. This will provide you with a long list of growth opportunities that might look something like this:

- Switch consumer segment X into coffee from soft drinks on pre-night out occasions to access 100 tons/US$13 million.

However, the reality is that studies that provide this kind of detail are very expensive and, for the most part, are not available. So, instead a more pragmatic way is needed to find opportunities across the market you participate in. One way of achieving this is to review all existing information and look for an opportunity in any one of these six areas:

1. Is there an opportunity to increase purchase frequency, amount, or value in a given channel relative to the rest of your market?
   For example: Basket penetration for shoppers in hard discounters is well below the average for supermarkets.
2. Is there an opportunity to satisfy any presently unmet consumption needs?
   For example: Coffee under indexes in the summer months, where it fails to meet the need for something refreshing.
3. Is there an opportunity to establish usage in any new occasions?
   For example: Coffee is rarely consumed by younger consumers before they head out for either formal or informal social occasions.
4. Is there any functional or emotional benefit that the category can extend into?
   For example: Coffee is not seen as being as healthy for you as other beverages like tea, while the emotional benefits like the energize area are owned by soft drinks and alcohol.
5. Is there a consumer segment that represents a new source of volume?
   For example: Coffee at home under trades in the 16 to 25 age cohort.
6. Is there a geographic region that represents an underdeveloped source of volume?
   For example: Coffee under trades in the far north where the climate is much more tropical.

Once you have found a growth opportunity in any one of these six areas above it becomes the anchor point that you try and build from.

For example:

Focus areas	Opportunity
Channel	Supermarkets
Consumption need	To energize
Occasion	With friends or by oneself
Benefits	Caffeine loading to energize
Consumer segment	16 to 21 year olds (**Anchor**)
Geography	National

This category growth opportunity might be known as "Wynd Up" and be described as: Making coffee a key part of the pre-night out preparation ritual for 16- to 21-year-olds.

It then needs to be valued. The easiest way I have found to do this is to use a four-way model as per Figure 3.2.

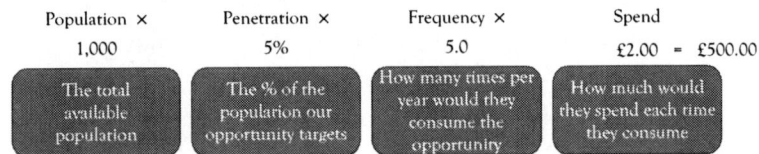

Figure 3.2 Four-way model

For the above Wynd-Up opportunity, a four-way model might look like this:

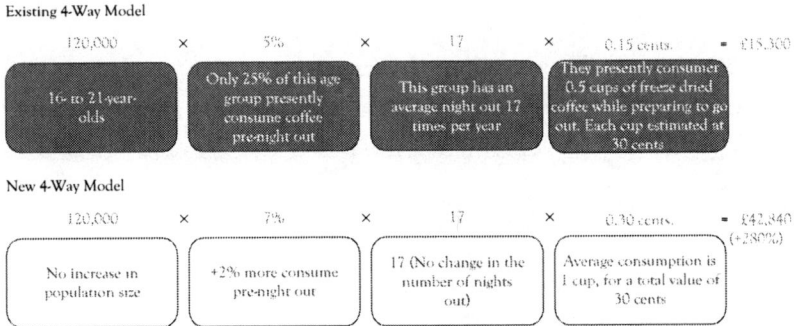

The benefits of using a four-way model are that it provides a concise set of estimates that can be measured to gauge the present understanding and progress toward realizing the opportunity. However, there will be challenges in finding precise data on which to build the four-way model, regardless of the sophistication of the market you are working in.

The need for precision has to be balanced against the practicalities of the research investment required to find the existing four-way data, and the time needed to mine this data. In the coming chapters, we will discuss how to make the category growth opportunities real for the retailer by attaching them to a conversion opportunity in their store. Investing available time and money against this task will lead to greater commitment from the retailer as it uses data that is more directly linked to its store and shopper. Therefore, given a choice, I would recommend focusing here instead. That said, you do need to value your opportunities and as long as you do this in a way that is defendable then it is better than having no value at all.

Category growth opportunities need to convince both the internal functions and employees and external customers that there is enough financial potential in the category to warrant additional resource and time investment. They should set the stage for a more focused conversation on what needs to happen in order to unlock growth.

Here is an example:

Kellogg's: To make cereal the breakfast of choice everyday (IGD 2011a)

- Portable breakfast: adapting to breakfast behaviors
- Building a firm foundation: Pleasure seeking at breakfast
- Changing behaviors: The favorite breakfast for kids

There is no definitive number of category growth opportunities you should try to find; whether it is three or eight, the most important thing is that you have alignment internally that they represent the best sources of opportunity.

The Consumer and Shopper Insight

After you have constructed the list of the key growth opportunities it is important to articulate a relevant consumer and shopper insight to illustrate both. This insight will help provide direction and context when creating the point of purchase activation. An example of the consumer insight for Wynd-Up might be:

On a night out with friends, anything can happen. And preparing for this is where the fun starts. A caffeine hit gets the anticipation going and gets you in the mood so you're ready for any adventure.

And the corresponding shopper insight for the target consumer might be:

I shop for my own personal care products and keep them in my own space. I have different needs now from the rest of the household. This also applies to my taste in coffee.

However, an alternative shopper insight might focus on the mother, who is still buying the products for the family:

I buy coffee for the household now. The kids use it as fuel and focus on strength over taste and so just heap it in. So I buy one that is cheaper per serving for the family and something separate for me.

As multiple shoppers can serve a single consumer, it is important to choose a shopper insight that reflects the intent of your growth opportunity. In Chapter 4 we will cover how to write shopper insights.

The Consumer, Shopper, and Customer Change Needed

The final step in articulating a growth opportunity is to describe the key change needed from our three stakeholders in order to realize the financial potential.

The strategies and actions needed to realize these changes can then be allocated to either a brand or particular channel or customer team to develop further in their business plan. This step is critical to ensure that the strategic intent from your category growth opportunities is operationalized by the brand and customer teams.

To this end in 2010, The Institute of Grocery Distribution in the UK released the results of their study into the use of category visions in a report entitled: Category Management Shopper Marketing 2011 (retailcustomerexperience.com, 2010). They surveyed 181 companies (where 84 percent were manufacturers and 16 percent retailers) and found that

Table 3.1 The stakeholder change needed

	Consumer	**Shopper**	**Customer**
Behavior change required	Begin drinking coffee as they prepare for a night out with friends	Target consumer begins buying their own coffee on a personal care replenishment mission	Coffee is displayed in health and beauty as many of the target shoppers do not enter the coffee aisle
Barrier to change	Habituated preference for other beverages like energy drinks	No existing products considered as suited to their specific needs	Coffee is not a product that appears often in the health and beauty basket

85 percent of respondents claimed to have a category vision or strategy, while 40 percent claimed that their category vision was completed before their brand or customer plans and helped drive the overarching business strategy.

It is therefore easy to understand why Julie was concerned about taking their category growth opportunities to Shopmart before they had aligned their broader business to them. Without the connection back to a particular brand or channel manager, they can be de-prioritized and not allocated sufficient resources, while for growth opportunities that require new product development the link may often have to include a cross functional team. Reg's solution of launching them at the company's next town hall meeting (an informal gathering to share the latest news and results) is a good way of signaling their arrival and the organization's intent on using them, but the connection with this and the annual business planning process is more critical.

Here is an example of what a finished growth opportunity should look like; this example comes from the body wash category:

	My Home Spa
Define opportunity	Appealing to mothers with a young family who don't have the time to indulge in a spa experience but still crave the time to withdraw into their own space for a few minutes of pampering
Consumer insight	A shower is a few minutes of peace in an otherwise chaotic day. It is little pleasures like this that help me re-charge and accomplish everything I need to.
Shopper insight	Shopping for body wash is pleasurable; there are always new varieties, scents, and packaging. When I have finished shopping for the family, I take a little time to find a product that is for me alone.
Change required • Consumer • Shopper • Customer	**Consumer change:** Use their own shower products not the family's, reserve them in the bathroom and be able to identify the scents and aesthetics as feminine and relevant for her. **Shopper change:** Make incremental body wash purchases for products that resonate with them and help them meet their emotional (de-stress, relax) and functional (hydrate, moisturize, scrub) needs. **Customer change:** Create a lifestyle based layout with areas for products for the family, female, and male usage. Support with range architecture that emphasizes benefits in female and male and value for the family segments.
Value	Penetration among women with children at home is 23%, target is 35%. Annual weight of purchase is 3.1 bottles, target is 3.9 bottles. Average unit price is $4.79, target is $5.49. Total value of opportunity is $23 mil.
Who is the key consumer target?	Status Stacy, Experiential Emma, Browsing Belinda (42% of the total market).
Key shopping missions	Replenishment—added on while shopping for the family or while replenishing skincare or cosmetics in a personal care store.
Priority channels	Hypermarkets, personal care stores.

Top Tips

- Take the time to create a category vision for key categories. This might mean that you have to start by defining which products should be included within the category.
- Ensure that any retail executions or projects link to one of the growth opportunities that has been identified.
- Internal alignment on the category vision and growth opportunities at manufacturers will help prioritize the actions of sales and marketing teams.

CHAPTER 4

The Key Points in This Chapter

- If shopper marketing is about building brands and revenue at retail, then point-of-sale material (POSM) execution is one of the fundamental ways of achieving this.
- The shopper is usually in motion, and so POSM must capture attention within narrow time and attention spans.
- The six key POSM design elements are: color, shape, key visual, text, price, and brand logo.
- The places where POSM is positioned in known as a touch point. Shoppers use multiple outlets and shopping missions to meet their needs. This provides multiple touch points where we can communicate with them.

Part A: The Category Review

"I worked part-time in a supermarket from 15 all the way to the end of college." Simon and Jamie were walking in to the large Shopmart that sat between their office and the Shopmart headquarters. Their meeting with Amy was later that afternoon and they wanted to visit a store to prime themselves in the retail reality they were trying to influence.

"It was a great experience. In fact, when I went for my interview with Unilever they were more interested in the fact that I could implement a planogram or build an end cap, than my academic results!"

They turned left and walked along the front of the store, surveying the end cap displays and the POSM that decorated them. Shopmart was beginning to limit the amount of POSM they allowed in-store; they felt it added to the clutter and wanted anything displayed to have, at a minimum, some kind of educational message.

They stopped at the end cap display of their coffee. It was positioned at the top of the hot beverages aisle and displayed on a portable pallet that was designed to take the product from the truck directly into the store. The pallet itself was hidden with a wraparound plastic banner that said the brand name over and over again should you not be able to already notice it printed on the cartons that displayed the jars. The outer cartons were stacked eight high, to what was elbow height for the average female, and were open fronted so that you could see the jars inside. On the sides and top of the cartons, the brand name was written in high contrast against a backdrop of coffee beans and a single red mug of steaming coffee. The display had been further merchandised with cardboard coffee jars that were approximately 15 inches long and had been stapled to the sides of the cartons.

Above the pallet were three, difficult to reach shelves that had been stacked with 5 oz glass jars. The shelf edge below them held a merchandising strip that, like the pallet wraparound, repeated the brand name. Price flags in Shopmart's yellow and red hung from the shelf edge as well, announcing the price per jar in large black numbers, and in the lower right corner, there was the original price with a cross through it. Above the shelves was a header board that announced the price in much larger numbers.

"Nice display," said Jamie watching people walk past it. "Good stock weight and well merchandised."

A lady with a small child sitting in her cart stopped at the display; she looked up to the header board and then back down to the display, deciding it represented value and was indeed something she needed, she placed it in her cart and carried on.

"Gone in three seconds!" was Jamie's enthusiastic summary of her purchase and therefore indirectly, contribution to his sales performance for the month.

"We'll sell 200,000 cartons this week; now we just need that to happen a few more times."

The store was quiet, and with no store manager to be seen; Jamie snapped a surreptitious photo of the display.

"Number of facings on display, and the total amount of stock held, are the two things I always ask the team to focus on when working on their promotional program. I like Coke's mentality where they aim to have two times the average week's sale in the store at any time. What do you look for in a display?" asked Jamie.

"At my last company they taught us to look for four things. The first is what is the insight and occasion the display is built around; the second is does it get attention, the third thing is relevance against the overall brand look, and the fourth is does it help get the sale by overcoming a purchase barrier."

"I use the word *TarGet* to help me remember," said Simon. "Do you know how we much we spend on POSM relative to total marketing spend on above the line executions?" he continued.

Jamie shrugged.

"For every dollar we spend above-the-line, we spend 60 cents on below-the-line material. But if you take out all the agency fees and other indirect costs that marketing pays and look just at what we spend to fight above-the-line media, either on TV, in the press or online, then the ratio is one for one!"

"Yeah? That's surprising given how little we can actually do in some of these stores."

"And that's without even thinking about the cost to put the stuff up."

"So what do you think of this display then? I'm curious, particularly as it was your team that produced the material for it." probed Jamie.

"Well, let's look at it together. Does it link with an insight we have about the shopper?"

They both stared at the display again.

"People buy from end caps, and they like to know the price before they commit to putting it in their basket." But Jamie replied more as a question, than as a firm belief.

"I'm interested to see what you think before I tell you what I think; this can be a shop-along for me with one of my stakeholders!"

"What about this; is there a link with an occasion that we know the shopper is thinking about?"

The marketing team often talked about occasions, but they were something not connected to what he mostly talked to customers about—things like discounts, stock levels, and delivery performance—that he hadn't engaged with the concept much at all.

"Occasions are more than just a hot cup of coffee at home, right?" and he said it with a smile in a way that indicated he should know but it didn't because he hadn't considered it important before.

"Well, that is indeed an occasion, but if we connected a key consumption need with it, we'd have a richer description. For instance, the new TV commercial we're about to air is around *that moment when we pause and re-group before charging back into the day.* Remember, Reg got up at the company forum in February and said it was revolutionary because it was all about the idea of a '*coffee break*', and everyone laughed?"

Jamie smiled at the memory.

"So when you look at this display, do you see any evidence of an occasion?"

"All I see is the red cup of steaming coffee that is on the packaging."

"Fair enough; that's all I see too." replied Simon. "What about the insight? Does this display connect with something we know about the shopper?"

"Like what?"

"Well, for example, at a basic level we know that front gondola ends are the best display space in store because they are visible to more shoppers than back of store displays. We also know that coffee is kept in reserve in the pantry and that households don't often run out. We also know they are stockpiling different types of coffee too—instant, roast and ground, freeze dried, flavored—so they can create a coffee house experience at home. So, when they approach a display like this, they are thinking about what they need to top off their coffee bar at home."

Jamie gave Simon a skeptical look.

"Well if that is a little too academic for you, how about this: this display is at the end of the hot beverages aisle; if you assume that most people go through the official entry like we did, the shopper we just saw is back tracking. So if you look down the coffee aisle you'll see that most people are approaching us, not going away; so this display is something they will come across after they have browsed the coffee section!"

"Oh yeah!" Jamie experienced a slight epiphany.

"Let's keep going through. What about attention? Does this display get it?"

This time, he paused before replying. "I think it does, because I know it will help sell over 200,000 cases this week; OK some of that, maybe half will come from the main shelf. But the mere fact that it is here, right in the main thoroughfare means that it must get attention!"

"To a large degree that is true. But I guess it depends a little on your definition of attention. Without looking, can you tell me what the gondola ends behind you are?" asked Simon.

"Well, I know that there are laundry, pet food, and toilet paper displays; but that's because they are always there."

"True, but do you know the brand that is on them? Or whether or not any of them had any point-of-sale material?"

"I could guess," replied Jamie, "but I won't" and he turned around to see what he had missed.

"For people, these types of supermarkets are all about taking short cuts, using what they call heuristics, little rules of thumb to help you get through this mass of stimuli. So even though we just walked past these other displays, they weren't important for us given our purpose today, so we tuned them out; we showed *selective inattention* to them. And this is how most people shop."

They were in the Shopmart lobby waiting to be collected for their meeting.

Megan, Amy's assistant, met them and took them through to the meeting room where Amy and Murray were waiting for them.

"Hi Jamie; Simon."

"Afternoon Amy; Murray," replied Jamie.

Pleasantries were exchanged; queries on the performance of each other's businesses were made and then orders for coffee were taken.

"We're looking forward to this," said Amy. "We've been looking at this as well and think it represents an opportunity worth pursuing." Jamie probed further to try and understand who they may have been talking to, but Amy gave little away.

"I was talking to Reg last week," intoned Murray, "and he said you have been busy preparing for today; he said you even dragged him away from his beloved monthly review with the regional team to get involved." Reg had not shared this with Jamie or Simon but that was not unusual; he had good relationships with many of the industry's senior people.

"You know Reg, always looking for any excuse to get back into the day-to-day cut and thrust," replied Jamie.

"What we have done is prepare a very short presentation, just 15 slides that talk about the opportunity we believe exists in coffee. We've kept it short, but at the end have some thoughts on what we can do to try and unlock growth." Jamie handed a copy of the presentation to Murray and Amy.

"We have looked across the domestic coffee market and compared its performance and development with other countries to arrive at a projected growth rate of 8.7 percent for each of the next three years; this equates to the amount you see in large font on page one." Simon took over from Jamie.

"If you do nothing, you can expect 2 to 3 percent of this; which is what we estimate your present share is. However, we have identified six category growth opportunities that, if executed, can increase this figure substantially." Murray was flicking ahead to try and find the answer.

"If I can get you to turn the page, I'd like to firstly take you through the vision we have for the category, as it is this that has helped shape the six category growth opportunities that we will explain to you shortly."

"Our vision for the coffee category, across all channels and geographies in this country is: *To create an obsessive passion for coffee culture. By extending the functional and emotional benefits that coffee has to offer, so that people pay more for experiences in familiar occasions.*" He paused for a moment to let the words resonate. Amy and Murray were re-reading them.

"What do you think?" asked Jamie.

Part B: Shopper Insights

In order to bring the shopper into both your interactions with retailers and internal stakeholders, it is necessary to have insight into both their attitudes and behaviors. Shopper insights can be described as: statements of hidden truth, which provoke a positive response from the target audience and imply an action.

1. *Statements of hidden truth*

   What is hidden from one person may not be hidden for the next. Social context and the types of information available mean that the definition of what is hidden can change from one market to another. A good way to determine if something is hidden is to ask whether it is available in a summary report through a data provider like IRI or Nielsen, or in an open source document like an article or omnibus report. If it is, then it is not hidden enough for the purposes of our definition.

Finding a hidden truth requires linking different pieces of information together to help answer the question *why*. The best way to do this is to start by listing all the information you can find that relates to a topic you want to write an insight about.

In this example, I am trying to find an insight about the way men shop in the health and beauty area. The information can come from a variety of sources like consumer usage and attitudes studies from marketing, a piece of shopper research that the trade marketing team ran, a standard Nielsen scan sales report, an article in the press about male shopping habits and so on. As I read through these sources, I copy in pieces of information I think are connected to the insight I am trying to write.

Information	Insight	Action
• Shopping is not a preferred leisure activity for men in the way that it is for women. • Men shop for their own toiletries until moving in with someone at which point they hand across purchasing to their partner. • Men represent around 20% of all basket transactions in a standard supermarket. • Men are worried about the potential embarrassment of having to browse for their toiletries next to feminine products like tampons. • Men *are buyers and not browsers*; they want to get their toiletry shopping done quickly. • 15% of men purchased facial skincare products with wrinkle-reducing properties in 2010, compared with 10% in 2009. • Men prefer mild, unscented products with multiple benefits. • Male attitudes toward toiletries are changing, particularly for younger men who see fewer stigmas attached to caring for their appearance. • Men have high levels of brand loyalty and will quote brand names to those shopping for them.		

We now have to start linking this information together to help find the hidden truth. To start, find the piece of information that you consider to be the most basic or foundational.

Men represent around 20 percent of all basket transactions in a standard supermarket.

Now we have to start peeling the onion below this statement. We peel away each layer to get to the hidden truth by asking why; and hopefully the answer to the why question is within the list of Information we have above. If it isn't, then we have to broaden our search to try and find an answer.

Why do men only represent 20 percent of all basket transactions? Men have traditionally left shopping to their partners; as a result, they are less experienced than women in navigating grocery stores and deciding between what can be expensive multiple product alternatives.

Why is this important? When men do shop, they tend to be *buyers and not browsers in supermarkets*; they want to get their toiletry shopping done quickly and don't notice new products.

Why is this important? First, because this isn't the way they behave in other outlets like hardware or electronic shops; given the time and space, they will browse for longer, looking at technical information about products and secondly because this makes it hard to grow their usage of broader male toiletries.

Why do they behave differently? Men are worried about the potential embarrassment of having to browse for their toiletries next to feminine products like tampons.

We could continue asking why questions around the area of embarrassment, but as a general rule if you can peel away at least two layers of the onion, you should be able to distill what you have found into a hidden truth.

There will be times when you do not have an answer as to why something is important or why it is happening when this is the case, resist making it up. Instead, go back to your internal colleagues and ask them why, or better still go on an accompanied shopping trip with a shopper and ask them yourself.

Here is my interpretation of the hidden truth from this information.

Hidden Truth

The potential embarrassment of finding themselves next to women who are shopping for intimate products, or making an incorrect product choice on what can be expensive products, leaves men both reluctant to even enter the health and beauty area, let alone browse for new, regime expanding products.

Once you have a hidden truth, it needs to be tested against the second part of our definition.

2. *That provoke a positive response from the target audience*

Ask yourself, "Will the person you are delivering the insight to want to know more?"

Examples of positive responses include: What drove this result? Is there anything we can learn from this? Is there something we should be doing differently?

Negative responses are usually very brief. Examples include: Who cares! So what! Why!

What we want to do with our statements of hidden truth is stand out from the crowd. We want the distillation of our analysis to be so compelling that the buyer, trading director, or store manager—or if our target is an internal one like the marketing director or brand manager—pauses for the briefest of moments and looks our way wanting to know more.

If you are then certain that your hidden truth can provoke a positive response from your target audience, move to the third part of our definition.

3. *Imply an action*

This implication is the last sentence of your insight and should direct the target audience toward the actions you want to take. It shouldn't be a long list of actions, but rather a high-level how that you believe will help turn your hidden truth into something tangible than can influence the shopper.

Adding your implication to your hidden truth creates an insight.

The potential embarrassment of finding themselves next to women who are shopping for intimate products, or making an incorrect product choice on what can be expensive products, leaves men both reluctant to even enter the health and beauty area, let alone browse for new, regime expanding products.

Creating male friendly spaces, where technical information can be considered, can help win more males into stores, a shopping group that has been traditionally hard to capture in supermarkets.

And a good insight is like a fridge. Why? Because when you look at it a light should go on (Bullmore 2005) and that light should lead you to many action ideas.

Once you have your insight, you can begin writing actions that you believe can best bring the insight to life in the retail outlet.

Information	Insight	Action
• Shopping is not a preferred leisure activity for men in the way that it is for women. • Men shop for their own toiletries until moving in with someone at which point they hand across purchasing to their partner. • Men represent around 20% of all basket transactions in a standard supermarket. • Men are worried about the potential embarrassment of having to browse for their toiletries next to feminine products like tampons. • Men *are buyers and not browsers*; they want to get their toiletry shopping done quickly.	The potential embarrassment of finding themselves next to women who are shopping for intimate products, or making an incorrect product choice on what can be expensive products, leaves men both reluctant to even enter the health and beauty area, let alone browse for new, regime expanding products. Creating male friendly spaces, where technical information can be considered, can help win more males into stores, a shopping group that has been traditionally hard to capture in supermarkets.	• Create a male only aisle with products that appeal to men. • Provide technical information about products not already on the pack at the shelf edge. • Offer male discount days, 10% when you spend a certain amount. • Create ways to link regimes of products together so men understand how things complement each other.

• 15% of men purchased facial skincare products with wrinkle-reducing properties in 2010, compared with 10% in 2009. • Men prefer mild, unscented products with multiple benefits. • Male attitudes toward toiletries are changing, particularly for younger men who see fewer stigmas attached to caring for their appearance. • Men have high levels of brand loyalty and will quote brand names to those shopping for them.		• Use terms like Good or Better or Best to group products together. • Position male products away from female products. • Provide guaranteed return policies on incorrect choices. • Provide simple usage tips about categories of products.

Consumer insights are different from shopper insights in many ways, not the least of which is their actual definition.

Johnson & Johnson use this definition of a consumer insight:

A statement expressing a deep understanding of your target consumers' attitudes and beliefs relating to a specific area/subject.

Which connects at an emotional level with your consumer.

Provoking a clear response and when leveraged has the power to change consumer behavior.

At an operational level, there are also significant differences.

Who

- Consumer insights target the consumer, the person who either directly or indirectly uses the product. (Indirect usage might be a mother applying lotion to her baby.)
- Shopper insights have a dual target; either the customer, who holds access to the media (the store) that we want to access or the person who is making the actual purchase decision.

What

- Consumer insights focus primarily on the consumption occasion and the prevailing attitudes and behaviors associated with it.
- Shopper insights focus on the behaviors and attitudes of people in the act of making a purchase decision.

Where

- Consumer insights should be focused on the moments surrounding consumption, both before and immediately after.
- Shopper insights are derived from the path to purchase; this is the time from the realization of a need until a product has been purchased for consumption.

Emotions, behavior, and attitudes

- Consumer insights need to connect with their target at an emotional level, not just provoke a positive response as shopper insights must.
- When targeting shoppers, insights need to influence both emotional and functional attitudes and behaviors, the majority of which reside in the subconscious of the shopper or are difficult for them to explain. When targeting the customer, they primarily seek to influence the functional and pragmatic needs they have to create value in their business.

How

- The research methods and location used to uncover both types of insights are often quite different, with tools like eye tracking, shop-alongs, in-store intercepts, and scan and loyalty card data being popular and effective in gathering shopper insight. Focus groups and in-home observation are preferred tools in gathering consumer insight.

Here are some examples of shopper insights and the corresponding action.

Flu Vaccinations

Insight

The best thing any mother can do for her family is to stay healthy, so she can care for them.

And staying healthy in flu season means planning ahead of time.

At Walgreens there is everything to help you arm yourself (Breen 2011).

Action

"Arm yourself" by getting your flu vaccination at Walgreens campaign.

Result

- 450 percent increase in number of flu shots given
- 22 percentage point increase in unaided consumer awareness of Walgreens as a destination for flu shots "provider of health services"
- 45 percentage point increase in equity measure "provider of health services that are easy to access"

Baby Care

Insights

The arrival of a baby brings about fundamental change to the routines of the household.

New patterns of shopping behavior are created, and parents begin visiting new stores or new parts of presently used retail outlets. At the same time their basket sizes grow, their household income may drop and the time available to shop also reduces.

Learning about so many new products at once, many of which are quite expensive, adds to both the joy and the stress of the arrival of a new child.

Stores that make baby shopping easy and enjoyable are best placed to win this valuable and changing shopper (Bordier 2011).

Action

Baby World implemented where all baby products are located in one place.

Result

+11.6 percent

Feminine Hygiene

Insight

The Feminine Hygiene category carries with it the stigma of embarrassment, and an associated feeling of low health; it is therefore not somewhere the shopper wants to browse for a long time.

This is why it is one of the most quickly shopped categories in the health and beauty department.

The main shopping behavior is to "grab and go" with women using pack shape and color as the key means of navigation.

Incorporating brand and color cues into the planogram design is the single most important thing to do to lift shopper satisfaction.

Action

Planogram laid out by pack color

Results

+11 percent value increase

The Shoppers' Attention and Point-of-Sale Material

If shopper marketing is about building brands and revenue at retail, then POSM execution is one of the fundamental ways of achieving this. Shopper insight is fundamental in the design and execution of any POSM that you intend to place in a retail space.

The job of all shopper marketers is to create POSM that leverages conscious and subconscious shopper behavior to improve revenue and build equity. POSM is able to do this by making the brand and category temporarily more accessible in your memory so that it can be associated with a need (Nedungadi 1990; Shapiro, MacInnis, and Heckler 1997).

It is important to note that activation of one brand will spread to other related brands in the category; therefore, if you don't get your design right, you may well be spending money on POSM that simply cues the category and not your specific brand! (McKoon and Ratcliff 1986).

It is also crucial to remember that the shopper is usually in motion, and so our POSM must capture attention within narrow time and attention spans in much the same way that outdoor advertising does.

To this end the shopper's attention is captured in two different ways: The first is called "top-down" attention. This is where we look for things that are on our list, either written or in the memory. The second is called "bottom-up" attention, where the contrast of the stimulus associated with the product attracts our attention (Wedel and Pieters 2008; Wolfe 2005).

The factors that influence bottom-up attention, like the contrast of the package or POSM, are twice as important in determining the speed with which a shopper can undertake a successful brand search when compared with top-down factors that are often influenced by out-of-store communication (Chandon et al. 2009; Lans, Pieters, and Wedel 2008).

Given that a large percentage of shoppers will not go down the aisle where your products are found, because it is not something they are allocating top-down attention to in that shopping trip, activating their latent need for the product through bottom-up attention is critical.

Fluency

The ease with which we process information like POSM is known as processing fluency.

Processing fluency is influenced by the familiarity of the stimulus, so for example an advertising visual or message, which has been exposed to the shopper repeatedly through an integrated campaign, will be processed by them more easily and quickly (Alter and Oppenheimer 2009).

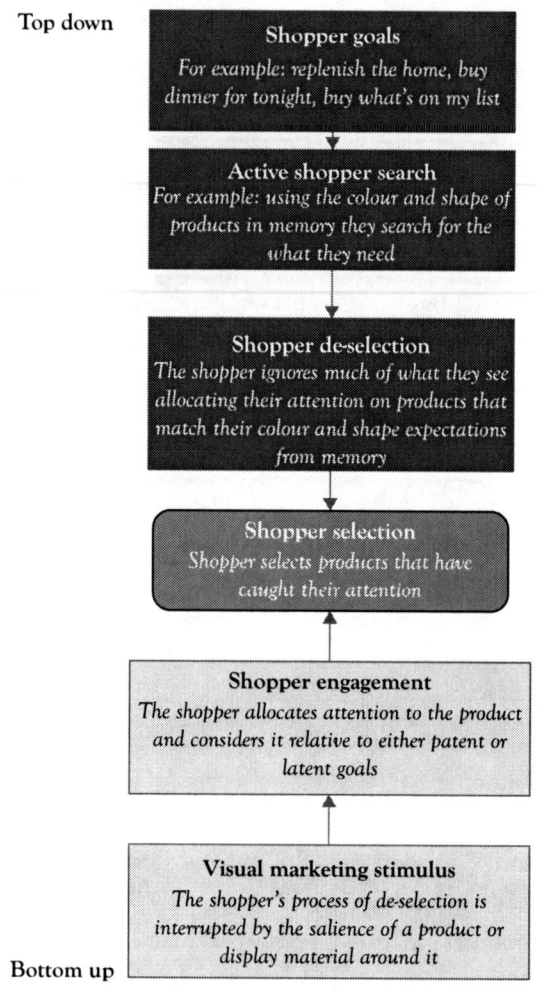

Figure 4.1 Top-down and bottom-up attention

Because of this, try to make the POSM easy to process for the shopper by:

- *linking it with visuals that are part of an integrated campaign*
- *and using design that is able to be simply processed*

But, don't just take images from other media and plaster it all over the POSM; think about where, when, and how the shopper will be coming in contact with it and what their barriers and drivers will be at that time.

Designing POSM

When designing POSM to achieve processing fluency, consider these six key design elements:

1. Color
2. Shape
3. Key visual
4. Text
5. Price
6. Brand logo

(Deherder and Blatt 2011; Meurs and Aristoff 2009; Pieters and Wedel 2007; Wolfe 2005)

Color

Color helps create contrast from the surroundings and thereby attract visual attention from the shopper (Pieters and Wedel 2007; Scamell-Katz 2012; Wolfe 2005), and we are able to recognize color much faster than the physical environment around us (Vul and MacLeod 2006).

Shoppers use color as one of the means to help them first de-select what is not relevant in their surroundings. To this end, over two-thirds of all fixations in a supermarket are on color (Itti 2005; Scamell-Katz 2012). In this way, it helps speed brand or product recognition. This can sometimes be difficult, especially where the brand owns a color that is common across the category, for example, with red, green, or blue in beer. In this instance, color needs to be used in conjunction with other design variables to create a brand identity that can capture attention in an environment where competing POSM can be displayed side by side.

Colors also have the ability to evoke images, ideas, and feelings and these associations can change by country or culture. But too many colors can create clutter, which leads to confusion (Meurs and Aristoff 2009).

Because of this use a base color to either connect with the brand's existing footprint, or choose a high contrast color from the existing category code to draw attention by standing out.

Also, focus on fewer colors and understand the image and feeling you expect it to evoke.

Shape

While color can be processed and recognized quickly, the same is not always true for shapes (Spring and Jennings 1993; Treisman 1986). However, when the shape is unique, or at least in contrast to those around it, there is the possibility of improving the speed with which it is recognized (Hawley, Johnston, and Farnham 1994; Treisman 1986). For example, a needle in a haystack is indeed hard to find because it is similar in shape to the hay around it. However a red tennis ball in a haystack would be much easier to find! (Treisman 1986).

Because of this, use the combination of shape and color to create an identity that is unique and therefore easier to be recognized quickly by the shopper.

Figure 4.2 Color and shape owned by Haribo

Source: Photo from author.

Images

Pictures are more memorable than words; they are, therefore, a key link to building fluency with the shopper in-store (Lutz and Lutz 1978).

Images are simple to process and are more likely to be viewed before text (MacInnis and Price 1987; Meurs and Aristoff 2009; Pieters and Wedel 2007). When they are used instead of words on in-store signage, they have been shown to increase shopper conversion to purchase (Quinn 2012). They are also easier to remember, so easier to associate with prior learning (Itti 2005).

When the image is a person and they appear to be making eye contact, the shopper will feel more directly addressed by the POSM (Meurs and Aristoff 2009).

To this end, the use of human faces in POSM can be important. In fact, when it comes to TV advertising, 76 percent of all visual gaze activity is on faces. Faces attract strong visual attention because they

Figure 4.3 The ubiquitous use of faces in skincare

Source: Photo from author.

provide valuable information about mood and intent. They lift the emotional engagement of any advertising (Ahern 2010) while also providing an access point for what can often be quite an abstract advertising message (Cody 2011). Faces can also increase the perception of trustworthiness (Riegelsberger, Sasse, and McCarthy 2004).

Because of this, prioritize images of people to attract attention over text.

However, as the number of visual elements goes up, recall and recognition goes down (Meurs and Aristoff 2009). And so while a person may attract attention, the product visual may only receive secondary attention.

Because of this minimize the number of visual elements in the POSM.

But realize that the image of the people may detract from visual recognition of the product.

People will look at the eyes first; good design finds a way to link the eye gaze of the person in the POSM with the product.

Celebrities versus Products

At the 2012 Shopper Insight to Action conference in Amsterdam, Pepsi presented an interesting case where they tested the effectiveness of their POSM, which featured one of the most popular people in India, their cricket captain, MS Dhoni.

What it found was that people had strong recall and like for the image of Dhoni, but when asked afterward what product he was holding, only half could identify it as Pepsi!

A product shot speeds up recognition and recall and therefore assists in building fluency (Meurs and Aristoff 2009).

Because of this, where your POSM is used away from the actual product, then use a product shot to generate recall or recognition.

But where your POSM is used with a product display, this is not necessary.

Merchandising imagery that reflects the prior knowledge or experiences of the shopper elicits a deeper recognition response (Pieters and Wedel 2007). This may be because shoppers constantly have to project themselves into the future, where the product they are considering will be consumed, in order to make a final purchase decision about its utility (Thaler 1980). In some instances, imagery may even provide a surrogate experience (Macinnis and Price 1987). To this end, merchandising in

Figure 4.4 Great combination of eyes and product (Vivid brand)

Figure 4.5 Coke is clearly available in this Russian kiosk

Source: Photo from author.

Figure 4.6 One of my main dislikes is the use of product shots next to the real product!

Source: Photo from author.

support of key consumer rituals, such as home-based eating, is reported as delivering strong and noteworthy sales lift in the United States in 2012 (SymphonyIRI Group 2012).

Because of this, use imagery that reflects everyday occasions.

Our visual system is sensitive to motion given the possible threat that predators once played in our daily lives.

Because of this, the use of inferred motion can often attract attention over still objects.

Text

Fact: Verbal suggestive selling to shoppers increases sales.

Whether it is McDonald's asking if we would like fries with that, children being asked if they would like fruit, or associated selling in a café, prompting people with questions increases sales (Hoffman 2011; Schwartz 2007).

Because of this, find ways to call to action in your messaging.

If it gets their attention, shoppers will look at POSM for just a few seconds, and given their reading speed, are only likely to take in up to five words (Meurs and Aristoff 2009; Yang 2012).

Chances are that they won't read the whole word either, instead fixating between the beginning and middle of the word when reading it (Hoffman 1998).

Too much text, or if it is difficult to read, will affect attention, recognition, recall, and the appeal of the POSM (Itti 2005).

Because of this make sure the message uses a large, everyday font, preferably in black, that anchors the meaning of the pictorial (Pieters and Wedel 2007).

Using words with an image anchors the meaning of the message and can lead to more consistent interpretation of the ad (Lutz and Lutz 1978).

Benefit messaging appeals to users, social messaging appeals to nonusers (Path to Purchase Institute 2012).

Figure 4.7 Coke are very good at incorporating occasion imagery into their POSM

Source: Photo from author.

Because of this, identify who is the target of your POSM and design the message accordingly.

Also consider their mission and the buying mode.

When words follow the image, they help the shopper recognize the product or brand (Rossiter 1982). To this end, words that are below the image receive more attention than words above the picture (Garcia, Ponsoda, and Aranz 2000).

Because of this, place your main text below the visual.

Here are examples of some of the key types of messaging you can use:

- Competitive comparisons
- Functional benefits
- Product demonstration
- Convenience benefits
- Endorsement
- Guarantees
- Promotional offers
- Prize offers
- Loyalty bonuses
- Price

While fluency is important, my preference is to use similar images to above-the-line media, but couple them with more practical, benefit-led messages using the list above (Dhar 2012).

Price

Shoppers engage in very little price comparison in-store (Dickson and Sawyer 1990; Hoyer 1984; Sorensen 2009; Underhill 1999). However, shoppers are sensitive to relative prices not absolute prices. Anchoring shoppers in a base price and then showing them the discount, allows them to understand the relative value of the offer (Tversky and Kahneman 1974).

When comparing promotional offers, shoppers often neglect base prices when processing percentage change information. For example, a price discount may be presented as a 33 percent price reduction on a $10 item, and a bonus pack may be presented as a 50 percent quantity increment on a 350-mL can. This results in an advantage for promotions that offer a percentage free over an equivalent price discount (Chen et al. 2012).

Because of this, use the word Free over Discount.

Because of this, show the base price and promoted price together.

We will look at price in more detail in Chapter 12.

Figure 4.8 Always make sure the nonpromoted price is prominent; in this example, it's not

Source: Photo from author.

Brand Logo

Mentioning the brand in the headline speeds up the recognition of the POSM (Franzen 1994; Meurs and Aristoff 2009). The branding will also receive the most eye fixations per unit of surface area (Wedel and Pieters 2000).

Because of this, provide branding prominently in the headline.

Design Layout

Bringing these elements into harmony is critical so that the message can be understood in a single gaze and thereby achieve a faster impact on the shopper.

Figure 4.9 Brand logo in the headline

Source: Photo from author.

Because of this, the design of the layout must be structured for the fastest recognition possible, while addressing the main purchase driver or barrier of the targeted shopper.

When we look more closely at what drives or prevents our purchasing behavior, it is very different by category.

Drivers are factors that motivate people to do what we want them to; we want to re-enforce and strengthen these with our POSM. In the alcohol category, a recent UK study found that the reasons shoppers make unplanned or impulse decisions in-store is: *to treat myself or others* (IGD Shopper Vista 2011).

Barriers are factors that prevent people to do what we want them to; we need to overcome or work around these. Barriers come from either analyzing research or direct observation of the shopper in-store.

When you assess your final design, ask yourself if it overcomes a purchase barrier you have identified for the brand. A list of generic purchase barriers to consider is shown in the following table.

Table 4.1 Generic barriers

Barrier	How would this be expressed by the shopper?
The brand has weak equity with consumers.	It's not a brand I ever think of or look for.
The brand identity is not clear to the shopper.	It's not a brand for me.
The brand lacks emotional closeness.	It's not a brand that means anything.
The brand communication lacks visibility in-store.	It's never something I think of when I browse.
The taste perception is poor.	I tried it before and didn't like it.
There is low loyalty for the brand.	I buy it sometimes but not very often.
The brand only appeals to a limited number of occasions or needs.	It's a little niche, I wouldn't consume it often.

(Continued)

Table 4.1 Generic barriers (Continued)

Barrier	How would this be expressed by the shopper?
There is a pricing problem that works against the brand.	The value isn't good.
The packaging lacks visibility at retail.	I never notice it.
There are lot of consumers who have tried and rejected the brand.	It doesn't do what it says it will.
There is an issue with shoppers forgetting what brand or variant they bought last time.	It's so long between purchases that I can't remember what I bought last time.
The brand is not visible enough at retail.	I have to search so hard to find it.
The brand availability is not sufficient.	It's only available in random places.
There is confusion about or among brand variants.	They look so similar on the shelf.
The brand is just one of a large repertoire.	I like to experiment across brands.
The brand is not associated with the need state behind the occasion.	It's not the right product for the occasion.
The product benefit is not clear in-store.	The packaging doesn't say what it does.
The shopper does not understand how the products differ and defaults to the cheapest item.	I don't understand how they are all different.
The category has an image problem.	I would never shop products from there!
The category is uninviting and is quickly browsed.	I just grab and go.
The category is not shopped regularly.	I only shop these products occasionally.
The category is viewed as a commodity and the shopper acts accordingly.	I look for what's cheapest.
The category is not easy to shop and so most browsing time is spent orientating rather than looking for something new.	It's like a puzzle at the shelf!
There is a lack of relevant occasions for use of this category or brand.	When would I ever use it?
There is a problem around lack of perceived difference between brands in the category.	They all do the same thing.
Selection at the bar or shelf is heavily ingrained.	I buy the same thing most of the time.

Touch Points

Information obtained through the hands is known as haptic information and when shopping, the use of hands to evaluate the product is very important (Peck and Childers 2003). When combined with visual attributes, touch helps inform judgments relating to the social, psychological, and sensorial benefits of the product (Rahman 2012).

The use of hands while shopping increases the person's involvement; and the more involved a shopper is, the more motivated they are to deploy their attention (Celsi and Olson 1988).

POSM is often the bridge between attention and purchase; in order for it to achieve this, it must first convert attention to touch. Therefore, displays or packaging that prevents this should be avoided.

The places where we position our POSM is known as a touch point. Shoppers use multiple outlets and shopping missions to meet their needs. This provides multiple touch points where we can communicate with them.

Because of this and what we know about shopper behavior, we have to be targeted and choiceful about what we spend time and energy placing in front of them.

In general, the following guidelines about POSM location are something I frequently use when putting together an execution plan.

Outside outlet

- Minimize the POSM used outside the retail outlet; use only items that can help the shopper understand what is inside the retailer.
- In windows, feature new products, using nonabstract messaging and visuals.

The outlet's entrance

- The area around the door handle receives the most visual attention.

- The area around waiting baskets and carts also receives visual attention.
- The landing zone after the entrance is where the shoppers will stop and orientate themselves; high-level signage that can be seen from here can help them.

Navigating around outlet

- POSM should be faced in the direction of the shopper traffic flow.
- The racetrack around the store is often more visited than the individual aisles and a good place to locate material.
- POSM in natural intersections where the shopper changes direction is more effective.
- The area near stairs, corners, or doors will be ineffective as the shopper is busy navigating.
- Products will get a halo effect from the areas they are placed in; for example, displaying your product in the fresh fruit and vegetable area will cue freshness.

Browsing at selection point

- Shelf wobblers direct attention to the area immediately around them, not necessarily at them.
- A shelf barker (a small billboard fixed to the edge of the shelf) will receive the most visual attention of all POSM.
- The area behind service staff receives some visual attention.

All of the above suggestions can be summarized in the Target score-card that I use when designing and evaluating a piece of POSM.

Target Scorecard

The Insight and Occasion

- Does it link with an insight we have about the shopper? If so, what is that insight about?

- Is there a link with an occasion that we know the shopper is thinking about?

Attention

- Is the brand highly visible in the headline?
- Would it get the shoppers' attention, in a crowded retail space, given the mission they are on?
- Is every visual element readable from 1m distance?
- Is the font in high enough contrast to be read from a distance?
- Is the shape used to create contrast from other POSM that will be displayed near it?
- Is there a texture that conveys meaning?
- Are words to the right and images to the left?
- Is there a single key visual element?
- Is the POSM visible on the background of the installment spot?
- Does the POSM communicate one simple thing?

Relevance

- Is it consistent with the rest of the brand look?
- Is the color linked with the brand?
- Does it connect with images from the integrated campaign?
- Do the words associate with the brand?

Get the Purchase

- Does this message overcome a purchase barrier?
- Is the main claim made of no more than five simple words at the maximum?
- Is the price font type very clear?
- Is the price font color in high contrast to the background?

Based on the answers to the above questions I then decide if the POSM should be thrown away, re-designed or kept.

Top Tips

- The word insight can be used incorrectly. Align on a definition of what a shopper insight is and then make sure the insights you create meet this standard.
- Gather all existing POSM in a large room. Review all of it using the TarGet tool. Don't be surprised if you decide to throw a lot of it away as a result.
- Make sure that all future POSM is designed for shopper-impact, not brand salience.
- Remove POSM from all touch points that are not maximized for shopper impact.

CHAPTER 5

The Key Points in This Chapter

- The second step in shopper marketing is to identify a shopper conversion opportunity.
- An increase in shopper conversion will lead to increased profit and shopper loyalty.
- There are five key ways of finding a conversion opportunity, ranging from simple (e.g., outlet or scan data) to advanced (e.g., shopper funnel data).
- It is not necessary to have a conversion opportunity to execute shopper marketing but without it, it is difficult to show the retail impact of your activations when evaluating them.

Part A: Finding a Shopper Conversion Opportunity

"Think of it like a marketing funnel" Simon was trying to explain to the project team how they would turn their category vision into something more tangible for Shopmart.

"The funnel we use to track Grande Blend is something like: awareness, consideration, trialed, preferred, and most often right?" and he looked at the insight director for affirmation. He nodded so he continued writing on the whiteboard, "from memory our Grande Blend funnel is something like 90 percent awareness, 80 percent consideration, 65 percent trialed, 20 percent preferred and 20 percent most often used. So 20/90 means that we convert about 18 percent of all people who know about Grande Blend into most often consumption."

"We have to do the same for coffee as a category in Shopmart; we have to determine how many of their shoppers they convert into coffee and at what frequency they are able to do this. Then we have to use this as our base for improvement."

"Think of it as the *Shoppertunity*," he continued, "It's how we take the growth opportunities we have and turn it into a more manageable target for the retailer, one they realize through changing the behaviors of their shoppers."

"Surely it would be easier to try and grow their share of the category, simpler and easier to understand and track" replied the marketing manager.

"The problem with share is that it's a relative number and not an absolute number; and Shopmart want absolute growth" countered Jamie.

"I'm pretty sure that any business school in the world will tell you that the quickest way to grow sales is to grow share," Julie was trying to keep the conversation grounded, "so I'm not sure I buy your relative/absolute argument. But what I do know is that share in total coffee, not just the channels we play in, is impossible to track accurately and keep updated and so I'm not sure we could use that as an indicator of growth anyway."

"What I want to be able to do," said Ben, "is tell Shopmart something like this: of all your shoppers you get only x percent to actually buy any coffee. This compares to a benchmark of y percent. The reasons they don't buy is … and we can help overcome this by …."

"We buy so much data, don't we already know this?" asked Julie.

The conversation turned to the types of data they already bought and the merits of each source.

Ben was a fan of numbers, he liked them over words. They were somehow truer and less prone to misinterpretation. He liked his team to present numbers in simple tables that showed comparisons across prior periods. He liked to see the numbers before they were presented in graph form too, because the scales used on a graph can be misleading when you view them one after the other.

Retailers liked numbers too he knew; in fact they were obsessed by them. It started with prices and their fixation with being lower than their competitors, there was profit per facing on the shelf and inventory ROI they got from everything they carried in their range, and from there it extended to their margin percent and on again into the bar codes, that allowed products to enter their internal systems for shipment and sale to the shopper. In his mind, retail was a numbers game in the way that marketing was a pictures game.

Shopper Marketing was a blend of numbers and pictures, not pictures and then numbers like consumer marketing was. The tension was that it didn't feel like the consumer was at the heart of what it was about, and this is why the marketing team would always be a little combative when it came to discussing it.

"Retailers like numbers; we have to find them some that make the juice from this project worth the squeeze."

"Well there is your answer then, Ben will pay for you to find the data you need!" and with a flourish Julie closed her notebook to illustrate that the discussion was finished.

"I have to go, but I'll leave you here to work through the details." She concluded.

"I have to go too," said Ben checking his watch. "We'll work out the funding; just get a plan in place that gets this done with the minimum of fuss. When are we due back to Shopmart on this?"

"Next Monday, that's when we have to agree exactly how and what we are going to do." And he pointed to a flip chart with the relevant bullets:

- What is the objective?
- What questions do we have to answer to meet our objectives?
- What is the scorecard we will use?
- What are the stages or timeline of this project?
- Who will be involved from both companies at each stage?

"The objective is going to be the conversion opportunity we identify together through creating a shopper funnel in a selection of their stores."

"But for now," said Simon, "we'll try and create the data for that little wish paragraph of yours from earlier."

"Excellent!"

Part B: Valuing the Shopper Conversion Opportunity

The main topic in this chapter has been finding a conversion opportunity to make the category vision more tangible for the retailer; this is the second step in shopper marketing. A focus on conversion is important,

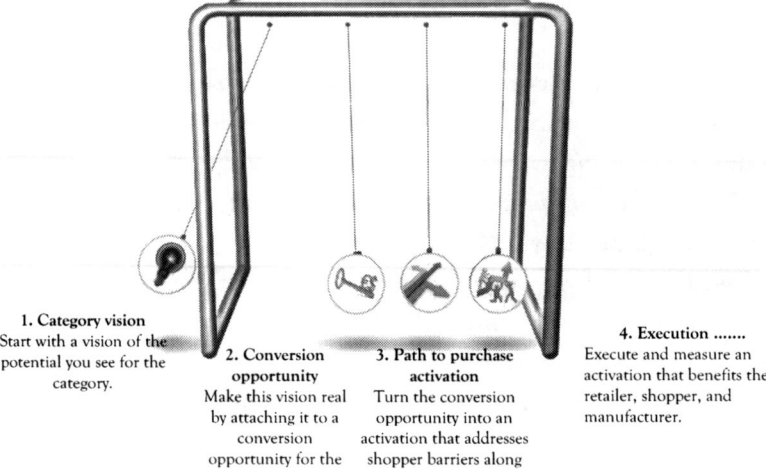

1. Category vision
Start with a vision of the
potential you see for the
category.

**2. Conversion
opportunity**
Make this vision real
by attaching it to a
conversion
opportunity for the
category.

**3. Path to purchase
activation**
Turn the conversion
opportunity into an
activation that addresses
shopper barriers along
their path to purchase.

4. Execution ....
Execute and measure an
activation that benefits the
retailer, shopper, and
manufacturer.

Figure 5.1 Shopper marketing model

because lost conversion and reduced shopper loyalty are strongly related
(Conroy and Bearse 2006).

A conversion opportunity is a performance gap relative to an appropriate benchmark.

It is not necessary to have a conversion opportunity to do shopper
marketing, but without it, it is difficult to show the retail impact of your
activations when evaluating them. It is a much simpler step than creating
a category vision and, if done well, will provide the fulcrum for moving
many difficult discussions with retailers forward.

Shopper Conversion is a retail obsession! As it is more profitable to
help a shopper finish their purchase quickly than interrupt and slow
them down (Sorensen 2010a), branded suppliers and retailers who work
together to convert more shoppers to purchase stand a better chance at
winning over time. Why? Because a 5 percent increase can increase profits
by 125 percent (Allen et al. 2005; Reichheld 2001).

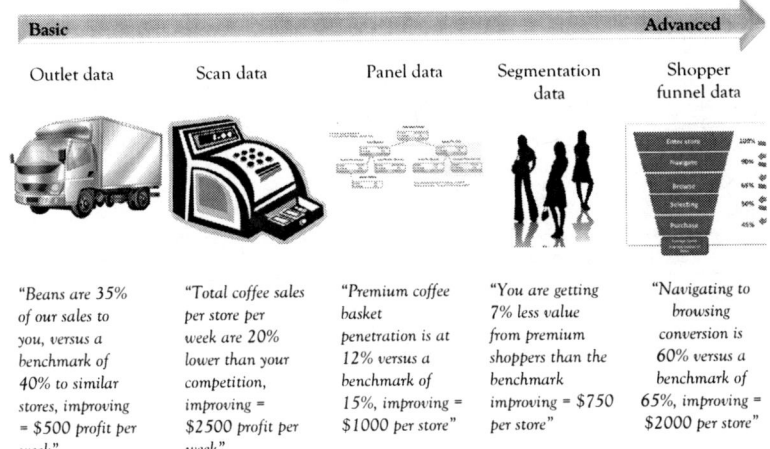

Basic   **Advanced**

| Outlet data | Scan data | Panel data | Segmentation data | Shopper funnel data |

"Beans are 35% of our sales to you, versus a benchmark of 40% to similar stores, improving = $500 profit per week"

"Total coffee sales per store per week are 20% lower than your competition, improving = $2500 profit per week"

"Premium coffee basket penetration is at 12% versus a benchmark of 15%, improving = $1000 per store"

"You are getting 7% less value from premium shoppers than the benchmark improving = $750 per store"

"Navigating to browsing conversion is 60% versus a benchmark of 65%, improving = $2000 per store"

Figure 5.2 Finding conversion opportunities

There are five key ways of finding a conversion opportunity, ranging from simple to advanced.

Using Outlet Data

The simplest form of data is often sell-in information. This is the base information that you have available from your invoice transactions. Many retailers do not release their scan data to providers like Nielsen, so you have to rely on a retail audit or panel data to gauge their sell-out performance. However, sell-in data can still provide the information needed to find a conversion opportunity, albeit one that is based on your own and not category data. Here is an example using coffee data for the *average* store:

	How is the Big Beverage company performing in Shopmart versus performance with similar/competing retailers?	Benchmark
Sell In Data		
Volume Sales (kgs) per outlet	95.0 kg	100.0 kg
Value Sales per outlet	$1,774.60	$1,924.00
Value per volume unit	$18.68	$19.24
% Growth	3.2%	5.50%
Segment Sales Mix		
Beans	8.0%	10%
Roast and Ground	9.0%	10%
Freeze Dried	19.0%	20%
Granules	32.0%	30%
Powder	20.0%	20%
Mixes	12.0%	10%

In this instance, we could calculate the conversion opportunity in numerous ways.

For example, we could say that the retailer sells five less kilograms per store versus the benchmark and that by increasing sales by this amount, they could realize an additional 5.2 percent growth.

Or we could say that their value per kilogram is 3 percent less than the benchmark, and that by selling more beans, or roast and ground they could increase this amount and lift sales.

The main downside of course is that it is only manufacturer data and not category data.

Using Scan Data

The most ubiquitous data for finding conversion opportunities is scan data. It exists through either retailer sources like Nielsen or direct from retailers in most markets.

Here is an example using coffee data:

	How is the Coffee Category performing in Shopmart versus their competitive benchmark?	Benchmark	How is the Big Beverage Company performing in Shopmart versus performance with similar/competing retailers?	Bench-mark
Scan (Sell-Out) Data				
Category Scanned Volume (kgs)	30,204,900	29,706,570	4,459,051	4,341,065
Category Scan Sales ($mils)	$1,006,830,000	$980,688,142	$153,094,095.00	$145,555,922
Volume Sales (Kgs) per outlet	405	392	122	120
Value Sales per outlet	$13,500	$12,940.90	$4,171.50	$4,023.60
Value per volume unit	$33.33	$33.01	$34.33	$33.53
Average volume of each item (Kgs)	0.375	0.400		0.350
% Growth	0.9%	2.2%	1.1%	1.8%
Segment Sales Mix				
Beans	5.0%	4%	6.0%	5%
Roast and Ground	6.0%	6%	7.0%	6%
Freeze Dried	17.0%	20%	18.0%	17%
Granules	37.0%	35%	38.0%	37%
Powder	32.0%	30%	28.0%	33%
Mixes	3.0%	5%	2.0%	2%
Market Share	19.0%	20%	30.0%	30%

In this example, we have both category data and Big Beverage Company data compared against a benchmark.

A summary for the retailer would be: if Shopmart can lift its growth rate to the market average of 2.2 percent, it will grow an additional $13.1 million.

You can also use market share comparisons using All Commodity Volume (ACV) ratios, for example:

Shopmart has 19 percent of the national coffee category but 19.5 percent of the total market ACV. Closing this 0.5 percent share gap would equate to $26.5 million in value. The segments where this growth can be unlocked are usually the ones where the retailer undertrades; in the above example, this is mixes and freeze dried.

While it is always best to lead with category-based conversion opportunities, it is also important to understand the conversion opportunity for your own brand portfolio. Retailers understand that manufacturers are in business to make a profit and that their motives for growth are not ultraistic, so you should be prepared to discuss this with the retailer. In fact, if they have started to ask you about "what's-in-this-for-you" it may be a good sign that the category conversion opportunity you have identified is motivating for them.

In the above example, the Big Beverage Company has a 30 percent share of the Shopmart coffee category and the same in the benchmark, so their conversion opportunity is to lift the growth rate to be ahead of the benchmark; given that they are already growing above the category, this might be difficult. They slightly undertrade in mixes and skew heavily against coffee powder, so this represents an opportunity.

Using Panel Data

A great data source for calculating conversion opportunities is panel data. It comes primarily from two sources: household panel data or retailer basket data. It provides data that can be used to build a model of category value; the value it delivers may differ from the reported size of the category, but do not worry about this as its true value is that it breaks this value down into levers that give much greater insight into shopper behavior.

Here are examples of the three types of models this data can help construct:

Household Penetration Model

	How is the Coffee Category performing in Shopmart versus their competitive benchmark?	Benchmark	How is the Big Beverage Company performing in Shopmart versus performance with similar/ competing retailers?	Benchmark
Household Penetration Model				
A. Total Households	11,300,000	11,300,000	11,300,000	11,300,000
B. Household Penetration	25.0%	23%	14.0%	14.1%
C. Purchase Frequency	5.50	5.7	2.3	2.2
D. Average basket spend	$12.96	13.2	$8.42	8.3
Category Value (A*B)*(C*D)	$201,366,000	$196,137,628	$30,618,819	$29,111,184

This model tells us that the coffee category in Shopmart has two immediate areas where it can improve: purchase frequency and average basket spend.

A summary for the retailer would be: If we can increase the number of purchases from the category that your shoppers already make by 0.2 percent to be the same as the benchmark, or in real terms an additional 56,500 transactions per year, we could grow the category by 3.3 percent.

When we look at the Big Beverage Company data, we can see that their main problem is household penetration. If they can increase penetration by 0.1 percent, or in real terms 11,300 households, they can grow their sales by 0.7 percent.

Four-Way Model

	How is the coffee category performing in Shopmart versus their competitive benchmark?	Bench-mark	How is the Big Beverage Company performing in Shopmart versus performance with similar/competing retailers?	Bench-mark
4-Way Model				
A. Total Baskets per week	6,215,000	5,717,800	6,215,000.0	5,717,800
B. Basket Penetration	4.8%	4.9%	1.1%	1.2%
C. Number of items purchased	1.8	1.9	1.1	1.1
D. Average price of items purchased	$7.20	$6.95	$7.65	$7.55
Category Value ((A*B)*52)* (C*D)	$201,043,814	$192,383,043	$29,915,157	$29,631,469

The four-way model uses basket data, which is becoming more common as computing power becomes more affordable.

The data shows that the coffee category in Shopmart has 0.1 percent less baskets per week with coffee in them, while within those baskets there is 0.1 less items than the benchmark. If Shopmart can increase baskets with coffee in them by 6,215 baskets in total and add an additional one item in every tenth basket, it can grow sales by an impressive 8 percent! While, for the Big Beverage Company increasing basket penetration by 0.1 percent or 248 baskets per week would translate into an 8 percent sales increase also.

P.I.T.A Model

The PITA model is a formula that focuses on the total trips per year a household makes to a particular retailer, and then within those trips, how many contain the category.

	How is the Coffee Category performing in Shopmart versus their competitive benchmark?	Bench-mark	How is the Big Beverage Company performing in Shopmart versus perfor-mance with similar/ competing retailers?	Bench-mark
PITA Model				
A. Population	2,825,000	2,599,000	2,825,000	2,599,000
B. Inter-purchase frequency	46.0	45	46.0	45
C. Transaction Frequency	12.0%	12.7%	2.8%	3.1%
D. Amount spent	$12.96	$13.21	$8.42	$8.31
Category Value (A*B)*(C*D)	$202,098,240	$196,137,628	$30,072,054	$30,209,763

The data shows that 2.8 million households shop at Shopmart in a given year. They make an average of 46 trips and 12 percent of these contain coffee; however, this is 0.7 percent less than the benchmark. Therefore, if Shopmart can lift penetration by 0.7 percent or an additional three trips over a year, they could grow sales by 6 percent.

For the Big Beverage Company, the problem is also less penetration on shopping trips. They are 0.3 percent behind the benchmark. If they could close this gap, in real terms an additional 1.3 trips per year, they could grow sales by an impressive 13 percent.

Using Shopper Segmentation Data

Shopper segmentation is becoming more popular as a means of gathering insight; however, it can also be used to generate a conversion opportunity.

Shopper segments are often used by retailers as a foundation to ground their marketing campaigns and assortment decisions. For example, when I was working with Watsons in Thailand they used these shopper segments to represent their retailer universe.

- Cosmetic lovers
- Sophisticated big spenders
- Occasional shoppers
- Sensitive skin
- All rounders
- Skincare starters
- Fun PC lovers
- Juggling mums

When they were then evaluating new products, for example, they would ask: Is this a product our Cosmetic Lovers would want to buy from us? Other retailers have similar shopper segments, here is another example (Hoyt 2007):

Wal-Mart

- Brand aspirationals
- Price value shoppers
- Trendy quality seekers
- Price sensitive affluents
- One stop hoppers
- Conscientious objectors
- Social shoppers

Manufacturers are also using shopper segments, as a means of understanding more about the behavioral and attitudinal insights around why people buy their products. Shopper segments are found using algorithms that distinguish observed behaviors and/or answers to surveys. Here is an example of the questions you could use to classify a shopper in the skincare category.

- Good skincare only requires a few basic products like a cleanser and moisturizer
- I choose skincare products that reduce lines and wrinkles on my skin
- I know a lot about skincare
- I would only go to a dermatologist if I had a serious skin problem
- Over the counter products are better than those available on the shelf
- When choosing products I place a lot of importance on anti-aging benefits.

I have used shopper segmentation to calculate a conversion opportunity where no other form of accurate data has been available, or when competitors were already using panel data and we wanted to differentiate ourselves with the retailer. Here is an example:

	How is the Coffee Category performing in Shopmart versus their competitive benchmark?	Benchmark	How is the Big Beverage Company performing in Shopmart versus performance with similar/competing retailers?	Benchmark
Shopper Segmentation Data				
Category Volume (kgs)	$30,204,900	29,706,570	4,459,051	4,341,065
Category Sales ($mils)	$1,006,830,000	$980,688,142	$153,094,095	$145,555,922
Premium Shopper				
% Volume	27%	25%	32.0%	33%
% Value	35%	35%	37.0%	36%
	$13,051,500	$14,095,620	$11,641,472	$10,983,600
Promotional Shopper				
% Volume	37%	35%	35.0%	34%
% Value	37%	34%	34.0%	33%
	$10,068,300	$9,780,634	$9,780,634	$5,772,174

Economy Shopper				
% Volume	28%	30%	23.0%	27%
% Value	22%	21%	22.0%	25%
	$7,910,807	$7,047,810	$9,630,548	$9,322,500
Occasional Shopper				
% Volume	8%	10%	10.0%	6%
% Value	6%	10%	7.0%	6%
	$7,551,225	$10,068,300	$7,047,810	$10,068,300

In this example, Shopmart are getting 7 percent less value from their premium shoppers than the benchmark ($13 051 500/$14 095 620). If they are able to increase the value they get from these shoppers to the same as the benchmark, they would realize an additional $36.5 million or 3.6 percent ($14 095 620 – $13 051 500) * (35% * 100).

Using Shopper Funnel Data

A shopper funnel is made up of distinct steps that represent the shoppers' path to purchase from the moment of entry through to the purchase. These steps represent points in the shoppers' journey, when they have the opportunity to engage with the category or brand under investigation.

Here is an example for the coffee category:

	How is the Coffee Category performing in Shopmart versus their competitive benchmark?	Bench-mark	How is the Big Beverage company performing in Shopmart versus performance with similar/ competing retailers?	Bench-mark
Shopper Entering the store	100%	100%	100%	100%
A. Shopper Navigating into the category aisle	19.0%	21%	19.0%	21%
B. Shoppers Browsing the category	12.0%	13%	12.0%	13%
C. Shoppers touching a sku	8.0%	9%	1.6%	2%
D. Shopper Purchasing	7.0%	8%	1.4%	2%
(Entry to Navigating Conversion)	19%	21%	19%	21%

(Navigating to Browsing Conversion)	63%	62%	63%	62%
(Browsing to Selecting Conversion)	67%	69%	13%	14%
(Selecting to Purchasing Conversion)	88%	89%	87%	89%

When shopper funnels were first used, it was necessary to physically count the number of shoppers moving through each step; however, in recent times, technology has evolved to the point where this data can be gleaned through video recordings.

The real advantage in the use of shopper funnels is that they can be combined with in-store intercept interviews to gather associated behavioral and attitudinal insight. The most beneficial is often an understanding of the barriers that prevented shoppers from moving from one step to the next along the path to purchase.

Shopper funnels are difficult to do on a large scale; however, used pre- and post-in-store, combined with actual sales data they can be a good way of understanding how behavior changed because of your test.

Top Tips

- Make sure you have a Shopper Conversion opportunity for your priority Retailer customers.
- Find your conversion opportunity by starting with the data you have in the most basic area of outlet data, then work through all the other methods until you find one you can use.
- Consider having shopper funnel data for your most profitable Retailers; this will give you understanding that they may not have, and therefore add value beyond just the ownership of your brands.

CHAPTER 6

The Key Points in This Chapter

- Understanding the path to purchase your shoppers take can help you define the barriers you face in converting them to purchase as they move along.
- Along the path the shopper will mentally travel back to their homes, work, and other important places in their life in a bid to remember the needs they have or will have in the future.
- The path to purchase forms the frame from which to define the standards of perfect retail execution.

Part A: The Perfect Store

In the afternoon, Simon met with the national operations manager, Ian. He had a called a meeting with Simon in the field to discuss the National Conference that was scheduled for early the following year. It was one of Simon's main responsibility areas to ensure it was delivered with a balance of fun, inspiration, and enough perspiration to justify the cost. Last year the feedback had been somewhat underwhelming.

"Short on a bit of razz!" was how Ben had described it when he joined the company shortly afterward. "The main objective of these events is to get the company excited about our plans for the coming year, but you have to do that in a way that goes beyond PowerPoint and product sampling."

They greeted each other and then moved inside the store. Ian then described a recent small experiment he had done where he had asked 10 random people across field sales, key accounts, and trade marketing to describe to him what the perfect store should look like and why they believed their answers to be right; what he got back surprised him.

"For years I've been talking about *Block, Eye, Tray* and *No Missing Products* as the foundation for every store, and most people played that back, but otherwise, the answers we're fairly generic; they mentioned things like displays around the store, prices right on shelf, POSM up." Simon nodded, not surprised by the responses.

"My view is that we have to get better at selling from the stores, not just to the stores." Ian looked at him with half a smile, "So my question for you is, how would you describe the perfect store?"

Simon paused for a minute; it was a good question and not one he had given enough thought to. There were cycle priorities where they laid out what was expected to be displayed off location, there were planogram guidelines, the infamous block-eye-tray rule that Ian mentioned being the main one, but there wasn't an overarching frame that pulled everything together.

"I'd probably set out the expectations along the path to purchase."

The path to purchase, Simon explained, is the stepping stones that link a shopper from the moment they recognize a need until they hand over their money to make a purchase. They are interruption points when you can talk to a shopper in a way that is related to the mission they are on. He explained by starting with the consumption occasion the shopper will have either planned for pre-store or recognized a need for as they browsed.

"But once in the store is when it counts from the field execution perspective. The shopper will start by entering the store, this area is important for people on a quick trip who don't want to run up and down the aisles. Coke do a good job here you see" and he pointed to their impulse fridges and the meal deal they were part of at the start of the chilled aisle.

"Most shoppers will then head into the fresh area and then through to the power aisle that crosses the store. As they navigate through these areas off location displays that link with the consumption occasion can work well." Ian nodded.

"But what's interesting is that not all displays payback when you add in all the costs associated with them. That's the data from industry studies though; it's not something we have."

"I had Reg out with me last week and he was asking questions about payback on displays too; I didn't like the fact that I didn't have an answer," continued Ian. "It's something we do because we know getting the stock onto that display has to be better than not doing it. We need to challenge that."

"It's not just displays though, it's all the Point-of-sale Material we make; my fear is that well over 50 percent just isn't impacting the shopper."

They stopped at the top of the power aisle and looked across the store at the POSM that was spread out in front of them; multi-colored and cluttered, it was noisy just to look at it.

"I'm going to figure out how much time we spend sorting, building, and placing this stuff; and then we need to compare that with what it does for sales. We might be wasting a lot of effort."

Simon moved into the coffee aisle and watched a middle-aged woman push her cart to the center of the category, pause for just the briefest of moments and then reach forward and pick up a jar of their competition in the freeze dried segment. She was gone in less than 10 seconds. Not for the first time, he questioned the relevance of his role, all the discussion, debate, and effort for such a brief reflex-moment by an otherwise harried shopper. He knew that the top of the marketing funnel was still where the foundations for brand preference were born; this is where at least half of the battle was won. The other half was in the execution, that ranged from the investment package you negotiated with the retailer, through to the facings on shelf and the quality of your promotions; and the difference here that shopper marketing could make would at best be a third. And if you took away the cost of winning this third would it payback?

Watching shoppers amble along in a fog of distraction always had this effect on him. It was such an instinctive, mindless activity and yet it was central to many of the discussions in his work life. If you believed in the 80/20 rule of effort, the reality was that shopper marketing was firmly in the 20. It was about that second glance you got from the shopper in the aisle, or the briefest of recognition for the display that was placed in their path. And yet it was the small difference of these actions that was often the difference between growing and declining.

When he had worked at Shopperscan, one of the owners was a gnarled old FMCG survivor called Mike. He was in his early seventies and apart from being a font of selling-to-retailers knowledge, he was also a keen golfer. Shopper marketing, he liked to say, was just like golf.

The difference between number 1 ranked player and number 120 was often less than just two strokes per round. And two strokes against par is around 3 percent. Improve half of that 3 percent and your performance and earnings sky rocket; let it drift south and before you know it, you are a club professional teaching lessons to overweight trade marketing managers.

That 3 percent is what good shopper marketing delivers; it's the difference between winning and losing in retail stores of all sizes. And that 3 percent is the hardest of all percentages to get right.

"Ian we have project Java going now with Shopmart, Ben has just agreed to give us some money to research in-store, I think we should use some of the findings from that to build a picture of what we want our perfect store to be."

"Sounds like a good place to start."

Part B: The Path to Purchase

My mother tells me that "People don't start shopping when they go to the shops anymore; they shop all the time wherever they are!" Her view seems to be shared by industry leaders too; branded integration with links to purchase options into much of our digital consumption means that we are all constant shoppers now (The Hartman Group 2012).

This fragmentation of media away from the traditional sources has brought a renewed focus on understanding the journey a person moves through from the moment they recognize a need to the point where they feel compelled enough by consumption to advocate the product to another person. Understanding the path to purchase your shoppers take can help you define the barriers you face in converting the shopper to purchase as they move along. It is the backbone of your shopper marketing efforts, and the steps that you choose to populate it will represent the points in the shopper's journey where you can focus your efforts to influence their decision making.

In this chapter, it is reflected as a linear journey with five key steps, starting from the time a person enters the store through to their purchase. Having only five steps inside the store to partition the shopping process can be too many or even too few depending on how pure your view is; my experience though is that five steps is the point, where shopper behavior can be explained quickly and easily.

However, it is often helpful to have two steps in your path to purchase that start outside the store to provide context; they are:

1. What **needs** does this shopper have?
2. What **mission** are they using to meet their needs in this store?

The Path to Purchase Model

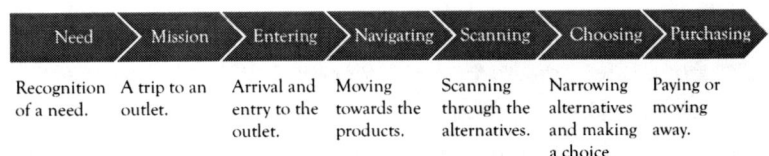

Need	Mission	Entering	Navigating	Scanning	Choosing	Purchasing
Recognition of a need.	A trip to an outlet.	Arrival and entry to the outlet.	Moving towards the products.	Scanning through the alternatives.	Narrowing alternatives and making a choice	Paying or moving away.

Along the path, the shopper will mentally travel back to their homes, work, and other important places in their life in a bid to remember the needs they have or will have in the future. As they time travel, the sources of product information that come to them through traditional push sources like TV and print and pull sources like social media recommendations and product reviews will slip in and out of their consciousness. In some instances, shoppers may even stop along the path and access digital information to guide their purchase decisions.

In Chapter 7, there is a description of each step on the path to purchase, what the shopper is likely thinking and doing, and what types of understanding you should be looking to find out in order to improve your conversion.

The objective of this section is to discuss how it can first be used as a framework to align on what the perfect in-store execution is.

Here is an example of what one for the coffee category could look like. It is important to note that each of these standards is built from a shopper insight.

Entering

- Is the coffee gondola end visible from the store entry?

Navigating

- Is coffee merchandised together with other hot drinks?
- Is granulated coffee (the signpost) visible from the top of the aisle?
- Is coffee in the same aisle as cookies and snacks?
- Is there a coffee display visible in a high traffic area near snacking products?

Scanning

- Are the key coffee segments (for example, instant or roast and ground) separated from each other on shelf?
- Are brand blocks visible within the coffee segments?
- Are brand logos and category colors used to highlight the category?

Choosing

- Are ranges grouped together within the segments?
- Are new products highlighted on the shelf?
- Are single promotional offers available within a brand to make it clear where the best offer can be found?
- Are mainstream, economy, and premium offers grouped so that the shopper can compare easily?
- Is shelf edge signage visible for priority brands to help overcome purchase barriers?

Purchasing

- Are all products within their sell-by date?

A shopper's path through the store should not feel like a treasure hunt (unless this is a specific, hedonic mission you are targeting). It should feel like a sequential flow through the products that meet your life needs (Sorensen 2010a).

The path to purchase is essential to your shopper marketing efforts and if you haven't yet chosen one for you company, simply Google the term and you will be provided with many different models from which to choose. In the next chapter, we will explain how the understanding you derive from your path to purchase can be incorporated into your category management efforts.

Observing Shoppers

When you start using a path to purchase to analyze shopper behavior in-store, you may very well be flooded with a sense of despair! Doubting your ability to change shopper behavior is an unavoidable part of working in shopper marketing; if you haven't experienced it yet, you haven't spent enough time watching shoppers browse your products. A good brand marketer will regularly (that means more than once per year) visit consumers in their homes or other places where their product is consumed. A shopper marketer should be just as active.

The teams I have managed have had to spend time either observing shoppers or completing shop-alongs with them. This provides them with anecdotes to make their presentations more authentic as well as a source of feedback on how well their activations are impacting the shopper. As we discussed in Chapter 4, shopper insights are also the foundation for good strategy, and immersing yourself in their behaviors in-store on a regular basis is a cheap and effective way of making sure your insights stay grounded in execution truths.

The paradox is of course that the more time you spend watching them, the more you see how rote and uninvolved the process of shopping for utilitarian products like household staples is. Even if shopping for hedonic products, items like skincare, shampoo, smart phones, or new clothing, you will see browsing behavior that ignores the majority of products in the category.

In my experience though, the benefits of immersing yourselves in your shopper should outweigh the downside of any doubt that the process incurs.

When observing shoppers, I always try and camouflage myself by being one of them! I push a cart or carry a basket and try to not stare at them as they go about their mission. I have the following list noted in my phone and will refer to it as I watch the shopper.

Entering

- What mission are they on?
- Who are they buying for?
- What high level signage (if any) are they using?

Navigating

- What helped them navigate to the category?
- Did they start browsing at the signpost brand or somewhere else?

Scanning

- How frequently do they shop this category?
- What are they not seeing as they browse?
- Are they looking for a preferred brand or exploring across a repertoire?
- How difficult is it to locate what they are looking for?

Choosing

- How many products did they touch?
- How active was their price comparison?
- What product attributes were they comparing?
- What, if anything, is delaying them from making a quick purchase?

Purchasing

- After they chose a product did they continue looking at the category?

- Did they shop the adjacent category after they chose their product?
- How many products did they buy from the category?
- Did any POSM influence them?
- How long did it take from browsing to purchase?

I try and jot down a few notes on my phone after each has left the category. If it's possible, I try and snap a quick picture as a reference for later.

Shop-Alongs with Shoppers

Sometimes it is also beneficial to accompany shoppers as they move around and ask them questions directly. This is often a cheap and effective way to build your insight base. It is always best to recruit the shoppers beforehand, as interrupting shoppers outside the store and asking them, if you can accompany them can be time consuming and not always provide a good demographic or psychographic cross section.

As you interview them, try to use plain language that the shopper will understand. They may not understand words like categories or segmentation.

I don't always tell them which company I am from, but I do ask them to buy at least one product from the category we are interested in studying. Sometimes I ask questions as we move around the store; other times I ask all of the questions after the trip has finished.

If it is possible, I also take photographs and videos, as a matter of precaution I get the shopper to sign a standard release document which can be downloaded easily from many sites.

Top Tips

- If you don't already have one, create a Path to Purchase for your organization. Then help the different functions understand what it is and how it can be used.
- Retail execution standards should then be grouped by each step on the Path to Purchase. Each standard that you choose should exist to help shoppers meet their needs or alternatively be linked to one of the organization's strategic goals.
- All commercial staff at either Retailers or Suppliers should spend time regularly in-store interacting with shoppers. This provides them with anecdotes to make their presentations more authentic as well as a source of feedback on how well their activations are impacting the shopper.

CHAPTER 7

The Key Points in This Chapter

- When retailers and suppliers can understand the thought process and behaviors of shoppers from the realization of a product need through to purchase, they can create products, in-store assortments, shelf layouts, and promotions to meet expectations better.
- Shoppers enter the retail store on a specific mission. The mission describes the motivations for the trip to the outlet.
- Shoppers identify categories using signpost brands.
- Shoppers use color and shape of products to shortlist those that form part of their purchase repertoire.

Part A: Being Valuable to Retailers Beyond the Ownership of Your Brands

Amy had a choice to make; her assistant had double-booked her for the next hour. In reception was the team from giant K&K, here to talk about their plans for the next tea category review, and a smaller supplier of locally grown tea, here to discuss their promotional program. This had not happened to her before and she wasn't sure what to do next. The simplest thing to do would be to explain the mix up to one of them and offer to buy them a drink while they waited. The smaller supplier would probably understand this but she doubted K&K would, and their CEO was close with her boss Murray, so any mishap like this might get reported up the line.

However, the K&K team was always so definitive in their explanations and recommendations; there was little room for interpretation. They arrived in packs with presentations that were long and crammed with high-level trends and learnings from overseas; content she found esoteric and removed from the local reality. The small company, by contrast, worked a little harder when they met; they asked more questions, were more flexible in their offers, and were generally more relaxed.

She had told the K&K team after their last category review that they needed to be more objective when it came to recommending ranging and planogram solutions.

"I like the fact that you show the consumer and shopper benefit of your recommendations," she had said in response to their surprising request for feedback, "but benefit statements aren't a strategy, and that's what we need." This led to a well-intentioned attempt at writing a category strategy together using the eight-step process that had been popular way back when she had started as a buying assistant. After a few months of workshops they had come to the conclusion that tea was a "routine" category and that flavored teas were "profit drivers" and world teas "excitement generators."

"So let's try and do something a little different at shelf then?" she had urged at the time. "Let's expand the range in flavored and world teas, and maybe even look at opening up the health space?" At the time these segments were underdeveloped relative to the overseas data they had presented. The K&K key account manager had matched her enthusiasm, even suggesting that they might be able to do something exclusive with Shopmart. There was a flurry of activity, forecasts were built and tentative timing discussed; but it never progressed and now here they were two years later and still no action.

That hadn't stopped her from asking others for ranging in these segments though, and thanks to the smaller tea company and the team at Twining's, she was starting to grow the nonblack range quicker than the market. This result had still not spurred K&K into action; their main excuse was that without media support, these new ranges would not progress beyond novelty value and with brand profitability so low they couldn't afford to support a full range expansion.

"Megan!" she called out to her assistant who was the person responsible for the clash of appointment.

"Take the K&K team into the meeting room and set them up with drinks, explain that a small issue has popped up and I will be 20 minutes late. Please apologize and explain that it was unavoidable. After they are settled, take the people from N&N into one of the small meeting rooms on the second floor. I'll see them first."

Simon and Jamie arrived an hour later for their meeting, as they signed in at reception and took off their coats, they saw the K&K team being led out by Amy.

"Thanks!" they heard her say, "Some progress at last!" And she smiled in the frustrated way retailers often do when they have had to caution an errant supplier. Jamie knew the top K&K guy and he saw him return a smile in the pained way you often had to when chided by a customer.

What's in store for us he thought, and looked at Simon who he could see was thinking the same thing.

Amy spotted them and came across; I need five minutes she mouthed, before heading back through the security doors into the buying department.

At 4:05 p.m. they were seated and exchanging small talk about the upcoming long weekend. Jamie could tell that Amy was still a little wound up from her last meeting and was trying unsuccessfully to lighten the mood.

"Sorry guys," Amy's patience had worn thin. "It's been a long day."

"Ok," Jamie said, switching back to all business, "the objective today is for us to present what we think the conversion opportunity for coffee is in Shopmart. Once we can agree on that, we will start work on building some solutions with you to pilot."

"OK, let's go."

Simon slid across the presentation they had been working on.

"We went through all the scan and basket data we had, compared it to a benchmark and found a couple of interesting things."

He took her through the numbers, outlining the differences they had found versus the benchmark and referencing the same data for their other categories with Shopmart, things like milk mixes and powdered milk, to give her added context.

"Interesting," was her first remark after they had outlined the conversion opportunity.

"Who is the benchmark you have used?"

They had anticipated this and Jamie took the lead in answering. "Amy, it's one of your competitors, we don't want to say which one; just as we would never share your data with others, we don't want to share theirs with you."

After the slightest pause, she frowned and said, "fair enough."

"But what if, just as you say, we have a slightly different shopper base, and those people consume coffee from specialty outlets in a higher amount?"

"What we want to do Amy, to get even closer to why this difference exists is to undertake a path to purchase analysis in a selection of your stores."

"What's that?"

"We want to measure how many of your shoppers enter the hot beverages aisle, what percentage stop to browse, touch a product, and then ultimately purchase. At the same time, we want to talk to shoppers in-store to find out what prevents them from purchasing."

"What will this help us with?"

"It give us a benchmark to fix when we put our solution in-store."

Do I believe this? thought Amy, *Is this another project that never goes anywhere?* She often wondered why it was that these big corporations didn't have ready-to-go solutions for stores like Shopmart. What did they do all day if it wasn't focusing on growing sales?

"I'm OK with this, but I don't want to drag it out over months and months; once we get this *conversion opportunity*," and she emphasized it in a way that indicated she believed in its benefit. "I want to move quickly to piloting ideas. Surely you have some success models from overseas we could use?"

Jamie saw Simon's slight hesitation and chose to answer for them.

"Amy, we do. And we're going to talk you through those when we move to the create phase of this project. I'm sorry if you think we're not going quickly enough; we took you through the timeline at our last meeting and hoped that met your needs. Does it?"

"It did, it does, it's fine" her stance softened. "Let's do this research; send me a summary paragraph and I'll get store operations support. But let's start work too on the solution to get coffee growing to at least the market rate. We have the planogram change coming up next month; could you bring some ideas to that even though the research isn't finished? Think strategically too, not just tactically around new lines etc."

Jamie kept the lead, "we will, for sure."

Part B: Shopper Behavior Along the Path to Purchase

The mundane, brief decisions shoppers make in retail settings are the foundation for the activation ideas in the third part of the shopper marketing model.

When retailers and suppliers can understand the thought process and behaviors of shoppers from the realization of a product need through to purchase, they can create products, in-store assortments, shelf layouts, and promotions to better meet expectations.

So, the purpose of this chapter is to look at how shoppers behave along the path to purchase and then outline how this knowledge can be brought into the application of shopper marketing.

Shopper Needs: The Starting Point

As long as there are needs, people will shop!

There are four key types of needs that form the commencement of the shopper decision-making process:

1. Dependency Need: A machine or appliance that needs something to function, for example, dishwasher soap to clean crockery.
2. Occasion-Based Need: A situation that requires certain products, for example, food and drink for a family picnic.

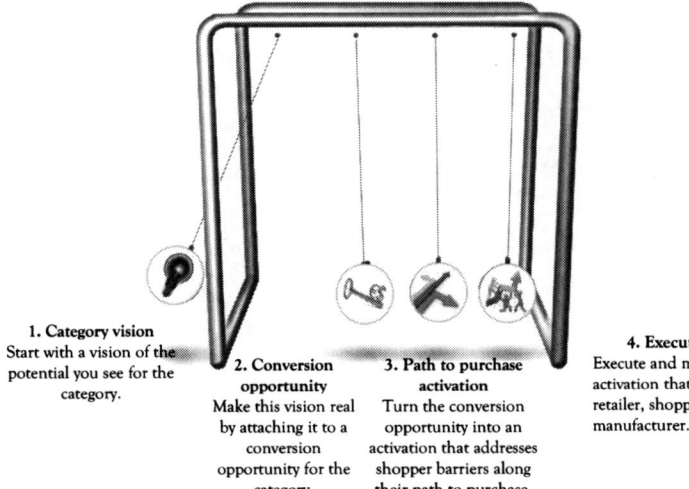

1. **Category vision**
Start with a vision of the potential you see for the category.

2. **Conversion opportunity**
Make this vision real by attaching it to a conversion opportunity for the category.

3. **Path to purchase activation**
Turn the conversion opportunity into an activation that addresses shopper barriers along their path to purchase.

4. **Execution** ....
Execute and measure an activation that benefits the retailer, shopper, and manufacturer.

Figure 7.1 Shopper marketing model

3. Consumer-Based Need: A requirement that arises from ongoing activities, for example, core household staples like bread and milk.
4. Product-Based Need: A requirement for a specific type of product, for example, low sugar or fat products for special diets.

Shoppers will have multiple needs on any single shopping trip. These needs form the basis of the daily routines that make up our lives, so an understanding of them will provide the context for interpreting the behavior you see the shoppers display in store (The Hartman Group 2012).

During the shopping trip new needs may be recognized thanks to prompts like point-of-sale material (POSM), promotions (analogue and digital), seeing the product, or staff suggestions. The recognition of these needs interrupts the shopper, if only for the briefest of moments; and in turn these interruptions can lead to improved but more likely reduced decision-making capacity as it redirects mental cognition. For this reason alone, interruption marketing must be approached with caution (Speier, Valacich, and Vessey 1999).

Shopper Missions

Shoppers enter the store on a specific mission. The mission describes the motivations for the trip to the outlet. For example: *I'm here today to replenish the house.*

This mission will influence how much of the store they visit and the degree of time they are willing to invest in shopping. When collecting mission observations from the shopper you should also be able to gain context on what needs the trip serves, why they chose the outlet and the associated in-store behavior this produces.

For example: *I have two teenage children at home and I don't work, so I am the household chief buying officer. I need to shop smart to find the best value, so I shop here every two weeks to get more value on the things we use every day.*

The same shopper will exhibit different missions over time, each having a specific set of motivations that may be influenced by consumption needs and channel format.

The four main shopping missions are:

The Main Shop Mission

What is it?	Household replenishment for the week(s) ahead.
How is it done?	Usually with a cart. The journey to the store is planned and there may be a written shopping list. In some markets it skews toward women with children.
In which store formats does it happen?	In larger stores where the possibility of one-stop shopping is possible.
What else is in the basket?	Household staples like bread, vegetables, toilet paper, and cleaning products.

The Top-Up Mission

What is it?	Is a household top up of products for the days ahead.
How is it done?	Usually with a basket. The journey to the store is planned on the way to somewhere else like home and usually involves a mental list. Can skew toward either males or females.
In which store formats does it happen?	In stores that have quick accessibility and are conveniently located.
What else is in the basket?	Products for more immediate consumption like fresh fruit and vegetables or meat or bread.

The For-Tonight Mission

What is it?	Is a purchase for that evening.
How is it done?	Usually completed quickly, sometimes with a basket. Often done on the way home.
In which store formats does it happen?	In stores that have quick accessibility and are conveniently located.
What else is in the basket?	Products for that night's meal or snacks.

The Specific Need Mission

What is it?	Could be something for lunch, a drink, or a snack for on-the-spot consumption, something for a party, or even an emergency purchase.
How is it done?	Can be from a nearby location if it is for immediate consumption or a specific venue if buying for a special event.
In which store formats does it happen?	In stores that have quick accessibility and are conveniently located through to specialist merchants that need to be traveled to.
What else is in the basket?	Accompanying products.

Understanding the missions that are used to buy your product will help you make recommendations on where in the store your category should be located. It will also help you write your shopper strategies which we will discuss further in Chapter 9.

With a mission propelling them, the shopper now enters the store.

Entering

With at least some key needs motivating their mission, the shopper enters the store. As the shopper transitions into a store, they are looking ahead to orientate themselves and for this reason will often miss most of what is placed at the entry (Underhill 1999). Any information placed at the entrance will most likely be seen only from afar as the shopper approaches and so for this reason make sure it is bold, simple to understand, and is facing the main traffic flow from which the shopper will approach (Claus Ebster 2011).

There is also evidence that displays placed outside will inform the shopper's impression of what can be found inside; for this reason, it should not simply be reserved for imperfect or sale items (Cornelius, Natter, and Faure 2009).

In studies I have been involved with in India, we found that the front of small traditional stores should allow the shopper to look into the store and see how crowded the store is and therefore how long it will likely take them to be served. In these types of stores, product cleanliness and

Figure 7.2 Guess what? Cakes can be brought here!

authenticity are a key consideration for the shopper and many retailers use the store fronts as a place to illustrate how clean and orderly their stores are (D'Andrea, Stengel, and Goebel-Krstelj 2004).

Entrances can also be used by larger food stores to try and win the smaller basket, specific need mission for immediate consumption. By placing coolers with drinks and hot and cold snacks next to magazines the store creates a convenience store within a store that can offer a quick shopping experience. This is a strategy Tesco employ quite well in many of their stores across Europe.

Shoppers will also enter the store with a degree of planned purchases already in mind; this combined with the type of mission they are on, will influence the travel path they take around the store.

Planned V's Unplanned Decisions

In the United States, the industry association POPAI reports that the in-store decision rate, which they classify as all purchases that could not be identified by brand before the shopping trip, has climbed from 70 percent in 1995 to 76 percent in 2012 (POPAI 2012).

In a similar study in the UK, though not comparative in its method-ology, the industry association IGD, surveyed shoppers to understand claimed behavior (it is important to note that this is not actual data and it is quite reasonable to assume a wide difference between claimed and actual behavior when researching shoppers) (Wells and Sciuto 1966), they find the opposite: that shopping decisions made in-store have declined from 35 percent at the beginning of 2008 to 15 percent in 2012 (IGD ShopperVista 2011).

A global study from Ogilvy Action found that 72 percent of shoppers enter the store knowing which brand they will buy and then go on to buy that brand. They claim that only 28 percent of shoppers either change from their intended choice or postpone deciding until they are in-store (WPP 2012).

Three relatively new studies spread along a continuum of planned purchasing. What can we make of this? At a top line level, it points to the degree of variability in research findings that are often produced by the world's leading authorities on shopper insight. At a more granular level, it reinforces the need to understand the specific type of purchase decision being referenced.

In summary, it seems reasonable to assume that shoppers choose among a small repertoire of brands and products, and will most of the time enter the store with a plan, either written, or in memory, to buy a particular product.

Household Repertoires

Actual household purchasing data shows that 69 percent of supermarket shoppers buy the same brand as they did last time they purchased from a category, while 45 percent buy exactly the same product (McCann 2012). While the number of actual unique products a U.S. household buys per year has dropped from 393 in 2008 to 361 in 2008 (Johnson 2009), with only half of that number being purchased regularly each month (Sorensen 2009). My only caution with these statistics is that households who participate in panels do not always track their smaller, top-up purchases. This can often be seen when you compare the average basket size of Household panel data versus Basket data from sources like Dunhumby.

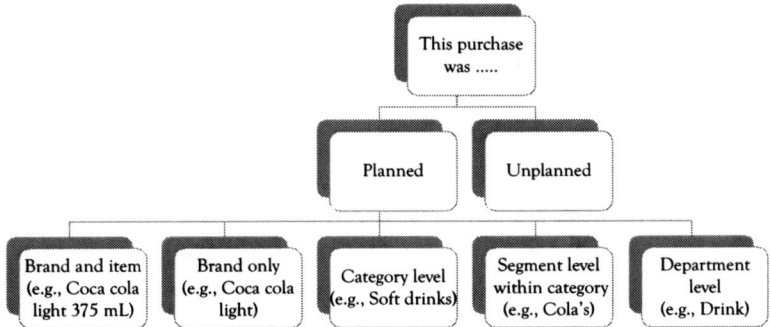

Figure 7.3 Planned and unplanned decisions
Source: Adapted from Kollat and Willett (1967).

A simple way to understand the degree of planned behavior is to classify purchases from your category into one of these buckets. The methodology behind this should be carefully constructed and done as close as possible to the point of purchase as shoppers are unlikely to remember for long if what they bought was indeed planned or not!

Lists

The global financial crisis of 2008 may eventually come to be viewed as the moment where shopping habits changed forever. The media seems to be full of analysis suggesting that the use of lists, written, memorized, or organized through the plethora of apps now available, has increased. The line goes that pre-planning has increased, with the majority of shoppers now using a list of some sort, in order to reduce unnecessary spend (although only one in three shoppers who make a list stick to it) (The Hartman Group 2013; Martin 2009; Street 2013).

Others point to the fact that the decline of hypermarkets in Europe at the same time leads to an insight about shoppers wanting to be less tempted in large stores; and with the cost of the whole trip (including travel) now a consideration, people are shopping more frequently in stores that are close to home on an as needed basis.

Only time will tell if this trend is temporary or part of a larger societal shift; however, what is known is that shopping lists have a long and well-researched history that provides us with several key observations.

- There is no link with the amount of advertising spend and the presence of a brand name on a shopping list (Ruiz n.d.; Schmidt 2012).
- Trying to make a list of what you need while in a store uses mental resources that might otherwise be used to counter impulse purchases; the net effect being that you choose more hedonic over appropriate options (Yuval, Sanjay, and Lyle 2007).
- Of the items on a written list, 25 percent are brand names; however for beer, cereals, household cleaning products, and personal care products, the brand name is written half of the time (Spiggle 1987).
- List users spend less time shopping than nonlist users (Thomas and Garland 1996).
- Nonlist users look to store displays or specials to prompt their purchasing (Bassett, Beagan, and Chapman 2008).

Navigating

In this step the shopper navigates toward the category they want to shop. This is the step where a lot of the total time for the shopping mission is wasted. The reality is that shoppers find it difficult to locate product categories (Black, Clemmensen, and Skov 2009). They will often skirt the outside of the center aisles looking inward to find the products they want. In doing this shoppers identify categories using signpost brands (Scamell-Katz 2012; Sorensen 2009).

A signpost brand is one that is so recognizable that it defines the category. Shoppers use these brands to find the boundaries between product categories (Scamell-Katz 2012; Sorensen 2009).

They tend to move toward the signpost brand and then begin browsing from there (Scott and Jonathan 2009a); as they do so, 50 percent of eye fixations for the category will be within the same brand (Chandon, Hutchinson, and Bradlow 2005).

As discussed in the chapter on POSM, shoppers never take in the details of everything that surrounds them. We selectively apportion our attention based on high-level interest, ignoring what we consider to be irrelevant.

As shoppers, this means that we de-select large parts of the store we are presented with, visually ignoring up to one-third of the categories we eventually buy from (Young 2005).

Scanning

For shoppers without a plan relating to which brand to buy, the sight zone will act as a prompt on available alternatives (Drèze, Hoch, and Purk 1994; Simonson 1999). The sight zone is the area 1 to 1.4 meters from the ground. It is the area most likely to be seen by the shopper. This is the reason why the vertical distance of a product's display will significantly impact sales (Drèze, Hoch, and Purk 1994; Kamaşak 2008; Sorensen 2009).

In a famous 1994 study it was found that by moving from the outside to inside of the sight zone, sales increased by up to 39 percent (Drèze, Hoch, and Purk 1994). In another study, a strategic re-organization of the sight zone shelf space led to a 12 percent sales increase in a Belgian grocer (Bultez and Naert 1988).

It seems that being seen first by the shopper has a high correlation with being eventually purchased (Scott and Jonathan 2009a), particularly for shoppers who may not be familiar with the store, or are experiencing a degree of time pressure (Park, Iyer, and Smith 1989).

The best horizontal position on the shelf would appear to be closer to the left edge of the display in larger supermarket categories (Porcheddu and Venturi 2011; Sorensen Associates Inc 2004). However, in smaller convenience stores, in the center might be better (Chung et al. 2007; Concordia University 2012).

There is also evidence to suggest that brands placed in the horizontal center of either a shelf assortment or fridge receive more visual attention and in turn are more likely to be chosen (Atalay, Bodur, and Rasolofoar-ison 2012; Chandon et al. 2009; Tobii n.d.). While products placed on the top shelf and the right-hand side of shelves tend to be considered of higher price and quality (Valenzuela and Raghubir 2009).

Figure 7.4 Center is best in convenience stores
Source: Photo from author.

Shopper Decision Trees Part 1

To present the view on how shoppers select what to buy while in store, we use a "Shopper Decision Tree" which refers to the conscious or subconscious process that a shopper goes through when evaluating the physical attributes of products in order to make a purchase decision.

For example, as per Figure 7.5, we know that toothbrush shoppers arrive at the category with decisions predominantly made about the user (adults or children) and brush type (manual or power). Therefore these are the major sections that should form the foundations for the category.

Structuring the category into these blocks allows the shopper to more quickly and efficiently, that is with less cognitive strain, begin the process of de-selecting the products that are irrelevant to their need (Park, Iyer, and Smith 1989). And with upward of 80 percent of shopping time in a normal supermarket trip wasted on tasks like navigating, anything you can do to save the shopper time will be greatly appreciated. This is why shopper insight pioneer Herb Sorensen says that one of the best things you can do for the shopper and in turn your own profit line is to:

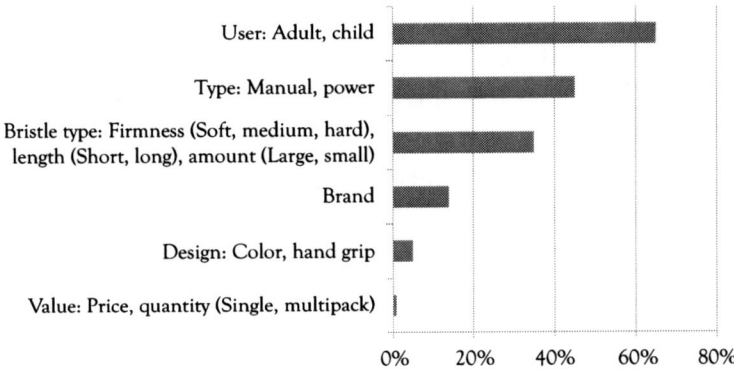

User: Adult, child

Type: Manual, power

Bristle type: Firmness (Soft, medium, hard), length (Short, long), amount (Large, small)

Brand

Design: Color, hand grip

Value: Price, quantity (Single, multipack)

0%   20%   40%   60%   80%

Figure 7.5 Shopper arrives at category with which decision already made?

1. Tell the shopper where to go!
2. And what to buy! (Sorensen, http://blogs.tnsglobal.com 2010)

To this end, your shopper decision tree will help you do this and should therefore ultimately be used to support shelf layout and ranging recommendations. We will discuss how to do this in Chapter 8.

Choosing

After a period of scanning, the shopper uses the color and shape of products to zoom in on those that form part of their purchase repertoire (Scamell-Katz 2012; Young 2008). (This practice has been coined selective inattention by some behavioral economists; if you Google the Levin and Simons Monkey Illusion you can see an illustration of it.)

As you watch the shopper do this, they will often exhibit a relatively low level of activity and engagement, regardless of whether the product is more or less frequently purchased. For example, they will complete their purchase in the category usually within a minute, touch only a few products, and engage in very little price comparison (Chung and Szymanski, 1997; Hoyer 1984; Underhill 1999).

If the shopper has planned for a specific brand or product, they may not even compare alternatives across their repertoire, instead just simply locate their desired product and walk away with it (Kim and Meyers-Levy 2008).

If, however, they do not have a specific brand or product planned, or they cannot find their desired product because it is not patently visible to them, the majority will choose from the available alternatives, while a smaller percentage will postpone their purchase until another time (Borin and Farris 1995; Drèze, Hoch, and Purk 1994; Simonson 1999; Wang and Chi 2009).

The first step in evaluating the alternatives is to create a consideration set (Payne 1976). This helps narrow down the available alternatives into a manageable subset that can be evaluated (Hauser and Wernerfelt 1990).

This set will represent the repertoire of products the shopper is either aware of or uses frequently, as such it is open to change and, through this fluidity presents an opportunity for market share growth for all product suppliers.

However, the sheer number of the available alternatives and their location and visibility on shelf will have a significant impact on the construction of the consideration set and the eventual choice. In this way, the context in which the products are presented will influence choice (Simonson and Tversky 1992).

As a shopper compares attributes across alternatives, for example, pack size, sugar content, or active ingredients, the more alienable these attributes are on the shelf, the easier the process of comparison will be (Broniarczyk 2006; Gourville and Soman 2005; Kahn and Wansink 2004; Luce, Bettman, and Payne 1997).

While the better the match between the way the shopper perceives the most important category attributes and the way they are actually displayed, the more likely they are to be satisfied with their eventual choice and positively perceive the range on offer (Gourville and Soman 2005; Morales 2005).

One reason for this is that shoppers evaluate the options the way they are organized on the shelf, rather than reorganizing them in their mind (Simonson 1999).

As they begin to compare, they are more likely to do so for products that are side by side on the shelf (Scott and Jonathan 2009a). While the longer they actually look at a product through this process the more likely they are to actually choose it (Armel, Beaumel, and Rangel 2008; Krajbich, Armel, and Rangel 2010).

When presenting products with similar attributes on shelf, it can also help to categorize them into groups and use signage to flag their presence to the shopper. This can help the shopper:

- see the differences between products
- refine their options
- positively influence their perception of the variety on offer

In turn, this categorization can increase sales (Areni, Duhan, and Kiecker 1999) and purchase satisfaction (Mogilne, Rudnick, and Iyengar 2008).

Categorization on the shelf is able to deliver these benefits because it minimizes the number of items needed to be stored in the shoppers' memory as they compare (Soars 2003). This in turn allows them to more quickly move toward the decision on whether or not to purchase.

Sometimes though, retailers use a categorization where nonphysical attributes are used, like the usage occasion or end benefit, to segment the category.

When this is done, the goal is often to reinvent the category by presenting the products in a way that forces the shopper to re-evaluate why they need the product rather than simply what they need. This type of shelf organization can encourage more abstract reasoning and heighten the differences between the products; unfortunately though it can also lead to shoppers choosing a lower priced item (Lamberton and Diehl 2013).

In this instance, decision trees are initially overlooked as we create groups of products that we hope will prompt the shopper to consider other ranges of products for needs they have.

Some examples of reinventing the category with nonphysical attributes are:

- a baby care section where products are segmented by child age rather than type (wash, wipes, powder etc.);
- a chocolate category defined by occasion: gifting, sharing, and so on;

- and a bread category defined by consumption occasion: lunch, BBQ, snacking.

Price is also a variable the shopper uses to evaluate alternatives. Retail prices, however, are not something we generally store in our long-term memory. We use them to make comparative judgments while evaluating different products at the shelf and then quickly forget them after the decision has been made (Dickson and Sawyer 1990).

The price of the alternatives we consider when standing in front of the shelf is a relative comparison, not necessarily an absolute comparison (Kahneman 2011). This is why less than 50 percent of shoppers can recall the price of a product when interviewed only moments after placing it in their basket (Dickson and Sawyer 1990). Ask them if the product was more or less expensive than the alternative they were considering though, and the accuracy goes up significantly.

There are some products though for which this is not true; these are the big traffic building brands whose prices are embedded in our long term memories (Wakefield and Inman 1993). These are the types of products that will get us to switch from our primary store (if we have one) to secondary or tertiary outlets. In my career, products like Nescafe, Gambrinus beer, and Huggies diapers have been able to do this on a regular basis.

Shopper Decision Trees Part 2

An understanding of the decisions the shopper makes in-store while standing by the shelf will help influence the way the products are displayed within the segments.

In this example in Figure 7.6, it would make most sense to have segments formed at pack quantity level, then by brand and within brand by bristle strength.

As the shopper moves through this decision-making process, they may encounter a point where their core need cannot be met by the assortment. For example, if they are looking for a soft bristle strength toothbrush and there are none in the range, the shopper has to decide to switch to another product or to walk away.

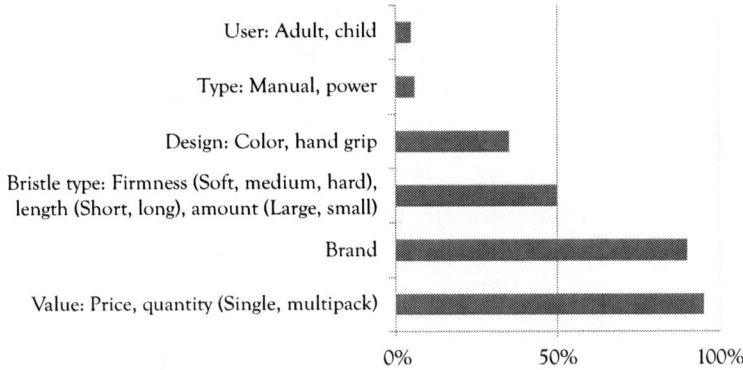

Figure 7.6 Which decisions does the shopper make in-store?

Assortments

A retailer's product assortment is the fundamental reason shoppers visit their store irrespective of the type of outlet, for example, hypermarket, discount, or convenience and is therefore the main focus of their decision making (Carpenter and Moore 2006). Retailers construct this assortment with the goal of maximizing their sales or gross profit within their specific constraints, such as space and available cash to invest in inventory (Kök, Fisher, and Vaidyanathan 2009). For this reason, they are often focused on both understanding how their assortment compares with their competition's and how effective it is at winning the shopper both into their store and the specific category.

The key assortment decisions retailers must make are:

1. the degree of attribute width (known as "entropy" in some literature) (e.g., how many red, blue, or white shoes);
2. the number of actual products offered (e.g., 100, 125, or 175), and
3. the number of products with similar attributes (depth) (e.g., how many different sizes and styles of white shoes) (Broniarczyk 2006)

When product attributes are evenly distributed across a range, it is referred to as having high width. Shoppers rate high width ranges as having more variety but also being more complex (Kahn and Wansink 2004).

And choosing from large assortments will be difficult for shoppers who do not have defined repertoires (Chernev 2003). In this environment, numerous studies have shown that shoppers may switch from searching for desirable products to simply those that they are able to justify to themselves (Hoyer 1984; Young 2004). While in other studies, the larger the assortment the shopper was exposed to, the lower their loyalty was to any specific brand (Bawa, Landwehr, and Krishna 1989).

Purchasing

In this path to purchase model, the purchasing decision occurs when the shopper places the product in the basket and walks away. At this point the shopper stops shopping the category and will need a subsequent trigger like an off-location display to capture their attention.

As the shopper moves away from the category, you may notice that some continue to scan the products. I have seen this behavioral trait in my time working in skincare and beer, categories that are difficult to merchandise on the shelf because of their size (beer) and number of attributes (skincare). This behavior may point to an underlying belief from the shopper that they didn't do a complete scan and have an underlying concern that they may have missed something.

There is of a course a second purchase moment too, the transaction that occurs at the cash register. Shopper marketing at the cash register has a long and effective history, albeit one that is now waning! The growth of smartphones means that many waiting shoppers don't browse the magazines and chocolate, but instead check their Facebook and e-mail accounts (Edwards 2013).

If the shopper isn't playing with their smartphone though, there is a wonderful opportunity to prompt what is often an impulse purchase. And that purchase does not have to be on hedonic products like sweets. In a recent trial, fruit replaced these snack products and revenue did not significantly decrease (Just and Wansink 2009). It seems that the mere visibility of food has been found to increase desire and as a result sales (Volkow et al. 2002).

Top Tips

- The primary aim of shopper marketing activities should be to make it easier for the shopper to meet their needs, not to interrupt them.
- Understand the needs that your category helps the shopper meet. Add to this with an understanding of the main shopping missions that bring them into the retail outlet. This will help you understand the motivations and expectations they arrive with.
- Create an illustration, using either video or still pictures, of the way your shoppers move along the path to purchase on separate missions. Capture examples from your own or other categories on what is done in the outlet to make it easier for the shopper.
- Understand the shopper decision trees that the shopper uses for your category.

CHAPTER 8

The Key Points in This Chapter

- The third step in the shopper marketing model is path to purchase activation; this is where you turn the conversion opportunity identified in the second step, into an activation that addresses shopper barriers.
- Category management is a core component of this step.
- Category management is able to improve sales or profits because shopper behavior is malleable and open to influence through in-store marketing tactics like shelf display and location.

Part A: Shopper-Led Category Management

"What you put at peoples' elbows, they buy. It's one of the simplest tricks a supermarket uses." It was the third Thursday of the month and Simon was out replenishing household supplies with his dad.

In the 40 years his parents had been married, grocery shopping had been the singular domain of his mother; and now that she had passed his father was left to fend for himself amidst the bewildering choice in the soap, toilet paper, and dairy aisles.

"What the heck?" had been his first reaction when it was time to buy toothpaste from the six meters of space he was confronted with. "What's the difference?" and he looked at Simon with horrid disbelief.

"This will do," he said picking up a pack from the bottom shelf, "the bottom shelf is where the no nonsense stuff is found. That's another trick these places use; they put the cheaper stuff at the bottom and the more expensive stuff on the top shelf, just like with whiskies!" His dad just nodded.

Left to his own devices, everyone worried that he would live off frozen meals and hotdogs, so he and his brother alternated turns going to the local Shopmart with their dad, followed by dinner afterward.

"So what's going on at work?" asked his father when they swung into the coffee aisle.

"Things are tough; more and more people are buying this kind of stuff," he said pointing to the private label brands. "Or this stuff," pointing to instant coffee powder. "The more premium stuff is getting left behind too as people trade up into coffee machines."

"Well, times are tough for some."

"I know."

"So what are you doing about it?"

"That's what we are trying to figure out."

Over the next few days he built the planogram and range recommendations with his category team from the hypothesis that growth would need to come from segments other than mainstream and economy granulated coffee, and that to unlock this opportunity, space would need to be reapportioned and the range architecture altered to expand what would initially be slower selling lines. He had tried to link the proposed solutions to the growth opportunities they had articulated at the start of the project too; however, without a firm Shopmart conversion opportunity, the proposal felt too loose and as if it was not preceded by a relevant insight.

When he shared the final plan with Jamie, he was supportive but cautious.

"The objective of growing the higher value segments feels right, but I wish we had tighter numbers to back it up."

"We will, when the research is finished; but till then we just have panel data to work with."

The category management strategy was to increase space in roast and ground and freeze dried, move them plus beans into the sight zone and reduce space and sight zone presence for powder and granules. There would be no extra space for mixes, but part of it would move into the sight zone. The hot spot would now be dominated with roast and ground and freeze dried. The category flow would also change; milk modifiers would move to the top of the aisle, followed by coffee, tea would be next and adjacent to these categories would be an aisle of cookies.

It would require significant change in terms of product movement and the subsequent man hours to execute it, but when they calculated the net margin impact for Shopmart, it was significant.

"This could move your margin by 1.2 percentage points," had been Simon's headline when he presented it to Amy. "But of course it will take a conversion change to realize it." Amy had been cautiously supportive.

"Let's pilot this first in our hypermarkets," had been Amy's summation, "it's a big change we should understand more before we go further."

This applied to the changes in the aisle flow too. "This kind of change has to be part of larger commitment from you and us to get the category growing again to justify the cost of moving all these products and categories around."

Part B: A Shopper-Led Category Management Model

Category management is a core component of path to purchase activation. The third step in the shopper marketing model.

A working definition of category management is: *the strategic management of product groups through trade partnerships, which aims to maximize sales and profit by satisfying consumer and shopper needs* (Institute of Grocery Distribution n.d.).

There is no single way of *doing* category management though; while it was popularized by the eight-step process proposed by Dr. Brian Harris of the Partnering Group in the 1980s, it is predominately a tactical exercise (IGD 2013) implemented differently across companies and markets.

What is accepted though is that the application of category management principles can increase sales and profits for the retailer and supplier. To this end, category management represents the view the retailer and supplier have on the source of future profits.

In my time working with Nestle, Johnson & Johnson, and SABMiller, I have been fortunate enough to work on many projects that have (and have not!) succeeded in growing revenue and profit. These projects have been in large, modern stores and small neighborhood stores alike.

There are also notable academic and industry studies showing that category management can improve shopper satisfaction and lift retailer and supplier profit:

- A 4 to 6 percent increase in total sales and profits across eight diverse categories (Drèze, Hoch, and Purk 1994)
- A 6 to 10 percent increase in milk sales (Chung et al. 2007)
- A 6.9 to 33.8 percent increase across coffee, biscuits, canned fruit, and pet foods (Bultez and Naert 1988)
- A 37 percent increase in shampoos (Hugh Phillips 2009)
- A 5 to 7 percent increase in private label teas, in contrast an 11 percent reduction in branded teas (Kamaşak 2008)

Category management is able to produce these results because shopper behavior, like we discussed in earlier chapters, is malleable and therefore open to influence through in-store marketing tactics like shelf display and location.

To this end, I use the following steps to bring shopper insight into the category management process. It places the shopper in the center of the process and uses knowledge of their behaviors and attitudes to inform strategy. It has six key parts. I have used a fictional example from the coffee category to illustrate its usage.

Part 1: The Objective

Discuss the merchandising objectives with the sales and channel teams to ensure there is alignment on three key principles:

I. Revenue objectives

What is it we are trying to achieve with this planogram?

II. Shopper objectives

What is it we would like to make more visible to the shopper and why?

III. Customer objectives

What are the customers' objectives for the new planogram?

Part 2: The Segments

Choose segments for the category. These can be based on the decisions a shopper has already made before they arrive at the category, (The Shopper Decision Tree Part 1) or the existing segmentation that the customer uses. Establishing segmentation will provide you with the building blocks to allocate space and range depth and width.

Then review both the insights and higher-level understanding you have on shopper attitudes, behaviors, consumption occasions, and need states. From this, allocate one of the six possible strategies for each segment. Allocating a strategy to each segment will set the expectations on how it will be executed at the shelf.

Then list your shopper-based reasons for recommending the strategy. Having shopper insight-led reasons will help convince the retailer that your recommendations are not biased.

Coffee category example:

Segments	Shelf strategy	Shopper-led rationale
Freeze dried	Profit generating	Freeze-dried coffee is purchased by the shopper as a premium pack for shared consumption occasions. They claim that they taste and smell better and that their packaging looks more premium when displayed in the kitchen. Powder and Granulated shoppers will trade into Freeze Dried once or twice per year.

Shelf Strategies

There are six generic shelf strategies to choose from as per Table 8.1. These strategies were originally proposed by Dr. Brian Harris and are still valid today. Here is a high level description of each.

Part 3: Space and Profit

The next part involves allocating space for each of your segments and estimating the impact to retailer profit of your recommended planogram. You achieve this by showing how space, margin, and sales are shared at present and then how you believe this will change given your recommendation.

Table 8.1 Shelf strategies

Strategy	Description	Segment Share of Category	Frequency of Purchase	Margin relative to rest of Category	Price Elasticity	Shelf Execution
Traffic Builder	Traffic Building segments aim to draw shoppers into the store and/or aisle and/or category	High	High	Low	High	Shelf space in line or below % sales share, positioned partly in sight zone but priority given to profit and transaction building products
Transaction Building	Transaction Building segments aim to increase the size of the average category purchase through expanding consumption	Medium	Medium	Medium	High	Shelf space higher than % sales share and at hot spot on shelf to encourage purchase
Profit Generating	Profit Generation segments aim to increased either % or $ profit for the category	Low to Medium	Medium	Very High	Medium to High	Shelf space higher than % sales share and at hotspot on shelf to encourage purchase

Image Building	Image Building segments focus on communicating the retailer's equity position to the shopper	Low	Low	High	Low	Shelf space in line or below % sales share but position within sight zone
Turf Protecting	Turf Protecting segments aim to maintain the shopper's ongoing loyalty for essential products	High	Very High	Low	High	Shelf space in line or above % sales share and position at least partly within sight zone
Excitement Creating	Excitement Creating segments aim to distract the shopper from their routine behavior by surprising them with an unexpected product or promotion	Low	Very Low	Very High	Low	Shelf space higher than % sales share to encourage purchase, positioned outside sight zone but near traffic builder

This step is important because to have the greatest chance of acceptance by the customer, shelf merchandizing plans must show how they can increase profit. Illustrating this proactively can also show your commitment to meeting the retailers' needs while pursuing your own objectives.

In the Table 8.2, the percentage of average margin is an estimate of the front margin (shelf price—invoice price/shelf price) for the key segments. To find this number, I often found it easiest to just ask a selection of your retailers and then take the average of their answers. The goal of this step is to show directionally how your solution can grow profit and so it does not need to be 100 percent accurate. Unless you work in the United States, and are a designated category captain by a retailer, it is also unlikely that you will have access to profit data at the segment or product level, and therefore you will need to work with estimates. In my experience the mere fact that you are taking a retailer view on profit and how to grow it will be appreciated over the fact of accuracy.

What is interesting in this exercise is how difficult you will find it to grow category profit! If your margin growth isn't enough to meet the customer's objective, you can go back and look at the strategies you recommended and try different iterations until you find one that gets closer to the objective. In doing this you may be surprised by the scope of change necessary to meet the retailer's needs.

To this end, one strategy you may want to try is to present successive changes that cover multiple years to illustrate how the strategy can evolve over time to meet the retailer's needs.

Part 4: The Look

The next part of the model is to illustrate how your strategy is reflected on the shelf by allocating product segments and the corresponding strategy across the available space. In doing this, you have to place the segments strategically through the sight zone as per the shelf execution that matches your proposed strategy. You also need to ensure your segments can be distinguished by the shopper by creating defined blocks where possible. In this step it is also necessary to allocate where you would place

Table 8.2 Example for coffee category

Category value	$100,000

Shelf strategy today

Segment	% Average margin	% of Category sales	$ Sales	% Category space
Roast and Ground	15%	10%	$ 10,000	10%
Beans	15%	10%	$ 10,000	10%
Granulated	12%	35%	$ 35,000	35%
Instant Powder	8%	25%	$ 25,000	25%
Freeze Dried	14%	15%	$ 15,000	10%
Mixes	20%	5%	$ 5,000	10%
Total	12.3%	100%	$ 100,000	100%

New shelf strategy

Strategy	Target % sales increase / decrease	Target $ sales	Recommended % category space	$ Category margin
Image Building	5%	$ 10,500	12%	$ 1,575
Transaction Building	5%	$ 10,500	12%	$ 1,575
Traffic Builder	1%	$ 35,350	30%	$ 4,242
Turf Protecting	0%	$ 25,000	20%	$ 2,000
Profit Generating	5%	$ 15,750	15%	$ 2,205
Excitement Creating	10%	$ 5,500	11%	$ 1,100
		$ 102,600	100%	$ 12,697

Projected $ Sales % change	2.6%
Projected Category Margin	**12.4%**
% Change	3.2%

the signpost brand. If the signpost brand is not one of yours, ensure your key brand is placed as close to it as possible to maximize the exposure it will receive.

To complete this step, I start with a blank sheet of paper and create a high-level sketch. I start with a set of boxes to illustrate the number of shelves the category has in the average store.

Then I allocate the segments, while ensuring the sight zone and hotspot objectives are met.

Part 5: The Range

A retailer's product range is the fundamental reason shoppers visit their store.

The purpose of a manufacturer-led range review is to help the retailer make decisions on what products to offer the shopper in order to improve the performance of the category.

Retailers construct this range with the goal of maximizing their sales or gross profit within their specific constraints, such as space and available cash to invest in inventory.

For this reason, they are focused on understanding how their range is performing and compares with their competition. To achieve this they will look at a mix of performance indicators such as:

- Hurdle rate performance
- Margin performance
- Sales
- Or mix of sales

Often they ask for help in completing their reviews, or require suppliers to provide range recommendations when presenting new lines. It is important that you do this in an objective way that builds credibility as a category partner.

The ranging strategy a retailer adopts will ultimately come from the corporate mission and goals they follow. Here is an example from a Tesco annual report. "With such a strong variety of ranges to appeal to the needs of different customers, we will also be applying more personalization and localization in stores to help them tailor their ranges much more for their local area."

It's important to understand this as it will help give clarity on what this means for the category ranging plan. While ranging decisions influence just about all retailer operations.

For example:

- Warehousing needs to accommodate the total size of the range
- Inventory levels need to be set at a minimum to meet shopper demand
- Retail labor has to be assigned to stock, present, and sell the range

Therefore, a retailer's ranging strategy has to balance the cost that comes from holding products with the needs of the shoppers they are targeting. This balance between range and costs is something that they are always focused on.

The key range decisions retailers must make are:

1. The degree of attribute *width*, for example, how many red, blue, or green running shoes.
2. The number of products with similar attributes (depth); for example, how many different sizes and styles of red running shoes.
3. *Size* in number of actual products offered, for example, 17 pairs of runners.

There are four key steps to go through to complete a range review:

Step 1: Ranging Objective

The first step is to set a ranging objective. Here are some examples of objectives you might discuss with your retailer.

- **Wide range:** a large number of products, offer unique and different products.
- **Limited range:** keep only the best sellers, remove niche products.

- **Large size strategy**: focus on large packs and remove smaller sizes.

After reviewing the category data and discussing the retailer's needs, an example for a raging objective might be something like this:

Ranging Objective: Requires efficient use of space to ensure maximum profitability and promotional impact while eliminating/minimizing slow moving products.

If the retailer doesn't have a ranging strategy, then you can propose one that is consistent with the category management objectives you are proposing.

Step 2: Category Coverage

The next step is determining the category coverage point. This is the point from which we will start looking for suggested deletions, upgrades, or downgrades within the range.

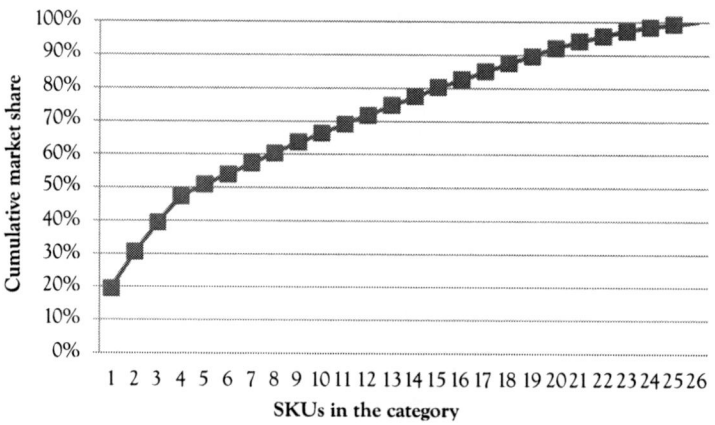

For example, this chart shows the number of products across the bottom and their percent share of the category on the left axis. We can see that product number one has around 20 percent share of the total category. We can also see that from product five onward, the products are smaller sellers contributing to what looks like a very long tail. Products

1 to 10 contribute about 60 percent of the sales and all the other products about 40 percent.

Step 3: Assess Performance

This is the step where we answer questions like:

- Should we remove all of the slowest selling products?
- Should we retain all of the borderline products in our line up?
- Should we add all of the top selling products we do not stock?

In order to answer this, it's important to have an understanding of what criteria the customer uses to help them make ranging decisions.

For example:

- Does this product deliver higher than average sales per store?
- Does the product have higher than average profit margin?
- Is it a product whose sales cannot be easily switched to another product?
- Does the product belong to a brand with the type of image that matches the retailers' shopper proposition?
- Is the product growing faster than the category?

There are many kinds of criteria a retailer might use and the reality is that the criteria can change given shifts in corporate strategy they may be facing. It is always best to have an aligned view on the criteria you will use to complete the range review as you can often produce extensive data based reviews that use expensive demand-substitutability models only to find that the retailer is using a mix of qualitative and quantitative criteria to decide on which of the many products in their long tail they want to range.

Even if your retailer won't commit to giving you the criteria they use, or they simply don't have any, you can choose criteria that you think are best for the category and model the results. Through a process of iteration you will be able to find the criteria that meet the needs of both your retailer and yourself.

It's also important to weight the criteria you use as per the example above.

In Table 8.3 is an example of a range assessment.

Product's that score above the average are classified as "contributing to the category."

Step 4: Create a New Range

Now that we have our market coverage and a list of products that are contributing to the category, we need to answer three key questions.

1. Should we retain the products within the category coverage point?
   - If it's "contributing to the category" and within the category coverage point, retain it.
   - If it's *not* "contributing to the category," then recommend it for downgraded distribution.
2. Should we recommend to delete or upgrade products (either ours or the competitors') below our category coverage point (i.e., those in the range tail)?
   - If it's "contributing to the category" an argument can be made for retaining the product and possibly upgrading its distribution.
   - However, if it's *not* "contributing to the category." AND in the range tail it is a candidate for potential deletion.

Recommending deletions of competitors' products is a delicate issue, so please ensure that there are objectively justifiable reason that are directed at maximizing the legitimate commercial interests of the customer, for recommending the retention or deletion of any product. Recommendations must not be motivated by an intention to disadvantage competitors' products or to unfairly favor those of your company!

3. Which products should we add into the range?
   The final step involves asking if there are new products which could be recommended to be added to the range.
   When presenting new lines for addition to the range, try to answer these fundamental questions:

Table 8.3 *Example of a range assessment*

| Product | Qtr performance against hurdle rate | Unique/Niche product | High loyalty and low switching | Brand performance-high | Margin performance | Score | Contributing to the category |
| | | | Criteria | | | | |
	Weight = 25	Weight = 10	Weight = 15	Weight = 20	Weight = 30		
Product 1	25			20		45	Yes
Product 2	25			20		45	Yes
Product 3	25			20	30	75	Yes
Product 4	25		15	20		60	Yes
Product 5		10				10	No
Average						29	

- What does the product offer that others don't?
- Why should this product be added?
- What benefit does it offer the retailer?
- Why will the shopper buy it?
- How has it performed in tests or other markets?
- What is the sales forecast?

The retailer will have to ultimately decide what their range looks like. And to do that, they will be thinking about the trade-off they have to make between costs and shopper needs.

From this analysis you should then be able to make a recommendation on a final range for the retailer.

Part 6: Check the Look

The next part of the model is to illustrate how your planogram and recommended range will look in the planogram. Color and product shape are important considerations and should now be allocated within the strategy groups you have identified. Here is a simple checklist you can use to evaluate your final solution.

Final Checklist

- Are priority products in the hot spots?
- Have you avoided shopper blind spots, like first in flow and behind poles?
- Have you arranged brand blocks defined by color within segments?
- Are the segments within the category clearly defined?
- Are priority segments of products on both sides of the sign post brand?
- Are there logical price groups across the shelf?
- Are the priority products or segments within the sight zone?

Top Tips

- Start the preparation for a category management proposal with revenue, shopper and retailer objectives.
- The segmentation for the category should be based on the decisions a shopper has already made before they arrive at the category.
- Allocate space for each segment and estimate how profit margin and sales are shared at present and then how this will change given the new category management proposal.
- Illustrate how your planogram and recommended range will look; use the checklist in this chapter to make sure it is appropriate given shopper behavior.

CHAPTER 9

The Key Points in This Chapter

- Collate your shopper insights on each step of your path to purchase.
- Shopper insights should then be used as the basis of your strategies.
- The first step in writing shopper-led strategies is to identify what you want the shopper to do more of, for example, *more shoppers entering the coffee aisle on main trip missions.*
- The second step in writing shopper strategies is to identify a high-level action that will overcome purchase barriers, for example, *more shoppers entering the coffee aisle on main trip missions by expanding products for refuel occasions.*

Part A: Inspiration

Simon and his wife were out to dinner at one of the chic, new eateries; while they waited for their table, they had decided to enjoy a pre-meal cocktail in the bar. It had been a long week, so it was time to relax.

Marie worked in the spirits industry as a marketing manager for a French conglomerate. As per her usual habit, she scanned the back bar and drinks menu to make sure her brand, Absolut, was well positioned. It was on the middle shelf in the center, as per the guidelines but not referenced in the menu as a separate ingredient in the cocktails that contained vodka.

"Not good enough!" she said spinning the menu round, so Simon could see it. "We pay good money to get ranged in places like this and we are supposed to get naming rights in the menu."

"At least you're placed well on the bar though," he replied motioning to the shelves.

"Menus are to us, like the shelf is to you. This is our silent salesperson in a place like this. There is very little else you can do to activate, at least in a way that gets any notice."

Marie had worked on Absolut for over a year now, and in that time had traveled to the top bars in New York and Los Angeles. She liked working on such a powerful "love-mark" as her agency called it, and in particular enjoyed the execution of the brand given that her main marketing messages were delivered in bars.

Simon flicked through the menu again, this time looking for any obvious signs of shopper, or rather diner-led marketing. Surely, there must be similarities, he thought? The rules that apply to point-of-sale material construction must apply? And he looked for font changes, color, images, or use of price symbols to divert attention.

"So what do you talk about at work when you discuss menus?"

"We have a little best practice guide that our reps are supposed to carry to give places like this tips on creating a menu that helps build their revenue. It's a nice little booklet actually; it came from our global marketing team."

"What kind of stuff does it contain?"

"Things like how people scan a menu, where the hot and cold spots are, and what you can do to highlight the most profitable items. Here, like this …" and she pointed to a Rum Daiquiri drink description that was accompanied by a small hand-drawn picture and asterix highlighting that it was a bar specialty.

"Fascinating," realizing that he had just learned a new trick. "Can you bring home a copy?"

"Sure."

The barman delivered their drinks and Simon gave Marie an update on his week and the first run of the in-store research they had completed. He described the cameras they had set up around the aisle and how this allowed them to count the number of people walking into the aisle and then continuing through to purchase. When he explained the intercept to cajole shoppers into explaining their purchase barriers he noticed her eyes glaze over the way they did whenever he got too deep into the details of his job.

"Sounds pretty boring compared to your consumer excursions into bars right!" and they both laughed.

"So, what do you feel like doing this weekend?" he asked. And they spent off the evening planning what to do for the next couple of days.

On Monday, Simon was standing at the top of the beverages aisle trying not to look like he was loitering while a man in his mid-30s was scanning the shelves in the roast and ground coffee section. He had no shopping list and was carrying a small basket with assorted top-up items like bread and fruit. *What's he looking for?* he thought. The man stepped forward to the shelf so he could narrow the area he was focusing on, he reached up and touched a blue pack with yellow font. He leaned in so that he could look more closely at the front of the package but did not commit to lifting it from the shelf. He was unsure, he leaned back and lowered his hand to his side and stepped back into the contemplation zone, a meter or so back from the shelf. He now stepped to the right, closer to the coffee beans' section and started scanning left to right again.

I wonder if he is one of our connoisseurs he thought and decided to walk past him to get a closer look.

When it came to classifying their coffee shoppers, they had five distinct segments they had started to speak about inside the trade marketing team.

There was Powder Polly, Tasty Terri, Savvy Sally, the Mixologists, and then there was the Connoisseur, a male or female shopper who brought coffee in small baskets from multiple segments. They ground their own beans but also used roast and ground in their stove top or coffee machine. They tended to not drink instant coffee, and also considered shops like Starbucks to be the antithesis of coffee culture.

As Simon walked past, he saw that there was also a fresh pack of what looked like sun-dried tomatoes from the deli and an artisanal pack of cheese in the man's basket. The bananas in his basket had red tips to indicate that they were organically grown and beside them was an assortment of toiletries that he couldn't see clearly. He was indeed a connoisseur, one of the 15 percent of coffee shoppers that made up almost 30 percent of the category's revenue.

How do we get more of you to shop the category? Just 1 percent of shoppers like you and the category would grow upward of 4 percent.

He didn't have long to finish this thought though, because Amy and Jamie appeared at the top of the aisle. They had come along to watch some of the shopper intercepts happen first hand, and then later to join the agency on one of its accompanied shopping trips. Jamie wanted to make sure that Amy stayed involved along the way so that she would have a greater sense of ownership when they presented the final results.

"Hi Simon, how's it going?" Amy pressed her hand forward.

"Well, the lady doing the intercepts is just having a small break but will be back in a minute; she's been here for the last four hours and has completed 20 interviews."

"Anything interesting?" asked Jamie.

"Plenty!"

"Like what?" He could tell from the look on both of their faces that they were expecting an answer. And not just a throw-away comment; they wanted the elevator speech that illuminated the panacea to their growth problem. This would be the line Amy repeated to her boss when she updated him on her work plan, while Jamie would reference it in his commercial conversations with her for the next few weeks.

"We don't have enough shoppers coming into the hot beverages aisle," *headline one he thought*; "the conversion rate from the shoppers in the aisle is similar to the benchmark; but the share of the connoisseur segment in Shopmart is behind the benchmark," *second headline.*

There was a moment of silence while they took this in.

And then Amy asked just what he had hoped for; "Why?"

"That's what we are trying to find out now."

A week later, Simon was reviewing the preliminary findings from Project Java in one of the breakout rooms. They had paid for the research and findings to be expedited, and he was hoping to use them to support the category management recommendations he had made to Amy and her merchandising team two weeks ago.

Simon thought about this as he stared at the opening page of the report: An investigation into shopper behavior and attitudes toward caffeine-based hot beverages. Was there anything in here that would be remotely enlightening? Or, would it be a costly addendum to the commercial discussions they would have when it came to discuss the next annual plan?

The only way to know would be to start; to pull it apart and then try and stitch the findings together with other research they already had. He turned the page to the first section; "Shopper Needs" and started reading. When he found a chart or observation that was interesting he copied it and pasted it into the relevant section of a Word document that he divided into each section on the Path to Purchase. He flicked back and forth, taking care to reference each observation with a page number from the PowerPoint document, and to make sure it was copied into the right path to purchase step. The hours passed and a mosaic gradually emerged: needs, missions, quantitative summaries, and qualitative inferences; consumers were passionate about their coffee and this came through in the way they talked about browsing and selecting it.

"Away from the big brands, it's a puzzle," one shopper verbatim read; "but it's a puzzle that I enjoy solving."

Part B: Strategies and Actions

Perhaps the easiest place to start any shopper marketing effort is with the existing research, shopper, or consumer that you have in your business. Gather it all up and start sifting.

Sift by reading each paragraph, chart, and table; if you find something you think might be relevant then copy it and put it in an appropriate place on the path to purchase using the insight writing process from Chapter 4. It can seem like a slow, laborious process but as you look at these observations through the lens of the path to purchase, you will start to see connections that were not patently evident before. For example, an observation you read in an omnibus study about health and wellness consumption trends, might connect with a study you have on the need states of these same shoppers, which in turn can build on a finding about pack cues used in-store to differentiate products. When you have reviewed everything you can you will have created a valuable database that you can keep adding to when further research comes to hand.

When I start the process of sifting, I use the following table to help me allocate information in a meaningful place. I start with a description of the shopper behavior and what they might ask themselves at each step in the channel and category. The example below is for a generic category in a grocery store. There is then a list of observations that I look for that connect with each step. I have found these observations to be a good starting point in all channels (e.g., drug stores, liquor shops, hypermarkets) and all categories.

It might feel like you are sifting through a haystack trying to find matching straws, but this is good. If writing shopper insights was easy, everyone would be doing it! And the reality is that they are not. All too often we take the surface observations and use them as foundations for our strategies and activations. When time is short, this can feel like a necessary thing to do, but in the long term it doesn't help differentiate you or the company you represent from the many suppliers waiting in reception to see the customer.

Once you have sifted through all your research and collated it into the steps on your path to purchase, it's time to start writing your shopper insights as per the method described in Chapter 4.

Need

Behavior:	Shopper identifies a need through either a passive (as presented in the media they are already using) or active process (Internet search or manual list).
Asks themselves:	• Where will I find the products to meet this need? • What types of products are out there?

Helpful Observations:	• The types of needs the shopper has
	• The key types of consumption occasions they shop for
	• Types of media used
	• List making methods used by the shoppers
	• Self versus purchase by others
	• Macro country trends like birth rates, income levels, or other demographics
	• The role of key opinion leaders influence
	• Search engine research by trying this search:
	  ○ The "brand"
	  ○ The "brand" review
	  ○ Best (insert your category) in "market"
	• Use the Google Keyword Search tool to see how your brand is being searched
	• Also try the Google Insights for search tool

Example of a needs-based shopper insights:

Art Supplies (Karolefski 2007)

Insight

Mothers and children do not enter the stationery aisle looking for art supplies; they enter looking for products to aid self-expression and creativity.

Creating a destination that provides one-stop "imagination building" and the products to support it will grow the appeal and potential of the category.

Action

Category redefined as "children's creative expressions," range expanded to satisfy mom's aspirations for her child.

Aisle redesigned with new segmentation and signage.

Results

30 to 40 percent sales uplift.

Mission

Behavior:	The shopper sets out on a mission to a chosen outlet. During this process they may research the best options available. The journey can be by physical or through a digital platform.
Asks themselves:	• What types of products are out there? • Where will I find the products to meet this need? Can I get there? • What do I know about this place?
Helpful observations:	• The different types of missions to acquire the product • Channel usage and preference • Distance and time spent acquiring the product • Limitations incurred by the journey choice • Sources of influence once on route

Example of mission-based shopper insights:

Beauty (Bordier 2011)

Insight

Taking a few moments out, from a standard household replenishment shopping trip, to spend some time browsing products that make her look and feel better, adds some excitement into what is an otherwise mundane chore.

Stores that have a captivating beauty area that offers just that little better experience have the ability to win the large basket purchase of women who are buying for their families.

Action

Redesign of beauty department in Carrefour hypermarkets to be more feminine.

Results

+19.9 percent in sales

Entering

Behavior:	Shopper arrives at the store and orientates their way to the entrance, enters the store then starts to consider what to shop for.
Asks themselves:	• What do I need • How much time do I have?
Helpful observations:	• The shopper preferred location of the department or area • The shopper-based definition of the department or area and the products they expect to find together • Imagery and signage that signpost category • External signage that helps the shopper profile the outlet • The elements of the shopper decision tree the shopper has already made at arrival

Example of an entering-based shopper insights:

McDonalds Restaurants (TNS 2010)
Insight

The majority of visual attention when shoppers enter a fast food outlet is on orientation around the counter and then ordering from the overhead menu.

POSM receives very little visual attention unless it helps with one of these tasks.

Action

POSM investment stopped for underperforming material and locations and invested in areas where it is working.

Results

• Promotional sales increased by 21 percent.
• Spend on POS reduced by 19 percent.

Navigating

Behavior:	The shopper moves toward and ultimately arrives at the category
Asks themselves:	• How do I move through this place? • Am I heading in the right direction? • Can I see the categories I need?
Helpful observations:	• What signals the categories to the shopper as they look ahead? • What types of categories does the shopper expect to be in the department surrounding beer? • The shopper's expectations around category location • The imagery and signage that helps the shopper navigate to the category • The way shoppers define the category they want to shop • The importance of off-location displays away from the category • Types of off-location displays and their role

Example of a navigating-based shopper insight:

Lottery Tickets (Frade 2009)
Insight

Lottery ticket shoppers are preoccupied by the process of buying their ticket, and so the majority of their visual attention is on the queue, the staff serving, and the counter top immediately in front of staff.

Even when they are eventually served, the complex visual background presented by cigarettes, which are normally directly behind the sales assistant, mean that getting the shoppers' attention is difficult.

So, winning visibility to queuing customers is of greatest importance when communicating key messages.

Action

• Moved POSM for nonvisually active areas like the front of store, to be visible from counter queue
• Redesigned sales counter unit for greater impact

Results
+10 to 30 percent

Scanning

Behavior:	The shopper stands back from the shelves so that their field of vision is broad. They scan across the ranges or segments that are available looking for the ones that they are interested in. The shopper zooms in on the brands they normally choose from and step toward the shelf so that they can focus on narrower group of products. If they do not immediately select a product to buy, they will choose alternatives and stand back from the shelf to evaluate them where there is more light.
Asks themselves:	• Can I find the types of products I want? • Are my brands here? • Is this the right product? • Will it do what I want it to? • What else do I need?
Helpful observations:	• The degree of searching versus grab-and-go behavior • How does the shopper define the category and segments (ranges) within it? • The shopper decision tree used to evaluate the category and its segments • The elements that frustrate or help their orientation of the category • What is cued in the shopper's mind as they browse? • The role that brands play in signposting the category • The reasons for brand switching • The types of information around the variants the shopper needs • The role of testers or other trial mechanisms at the shelf

Example of a browsing-based shopper insight:

Over-the-counter Medicines
Insight

People often visit pharmacies when they are suffering an ailment, since they are feeling unwell and looking to complete their trip as quickly as possible.

When they arrive at the medicine shelves, they are confronted with a wall of products that often claim to treat multiple symptoms and look very similar.

With staff not always available, the shopper then has to read packs in what can often be low lighting, something they obviously do not enjoy while feeling unwell.

Figure 9.1 Ailment-based signage in Japan

Helping them find the right product to match their ailment quickly is something they, therefore, greatly appreciate.

Action

- Ailment segmentation, for example, colds and flu, back pain, children
- Improved usage instructions on pack

Results

+10 percent sales value

Choosing

Behavior:	The shopper narrows their selection down. They may look back to the shelf and evaluate whether or not to buy based on value. This value question is made relative to other pack sizes within the variant or platform and could even extend to going back over other brands in their repertoire to see if they offer better value. If they decide it doesn't represent good value they begin the buying process again from browsing. The shopper chooses a particular product
Asks themselves:	• Will this do what I need? • Is it value for money? • Is there something new I didn't notice?

Helpful observations:	<ul><li>How influential is the in-store activity to the final decision?</li><li>Did the shopper's original purchase plan alter?</li><li>Did they buy what they came in for?</li><li>How long did the shopper dwell making their decision?</li><li>How do shoppers differentiate between products?</li><li>What is the role of packaging?</li><li>What is the role of point-of-sale cues in assisting shoppers to overcome any purchase inhibitors?</li><li>The role of different variants within the brand</li><li>What purchase inhibitors are there?</li><li>What information is required?</li><li>How do they gain more information in-store?</li><li>How do they compare?</li><li>The degree of impulse versus planned purchasing</li><li>Impact of price and promotions in assisting shoppers to overcome any purchase inhibitors</li><li>The role of price</li><li>The role or different promotional mechanisms</li><li>What role does "new" play?</li></ul>

Example of a selecting-based shopper insight:

Canned Soup (Heller 2006)
Insight

The shopper tells us that soup is the second most difficult category to shop for in the store.

Similarities in packaging and relatively few facings on the shelf mean that the majority of the time spent shopping the section is spent finding the products you want rather than scanning for anything else that might be new or interesting.

At the same, the soup is classified by the shopper as a "simple meal" and one they are willing to pantry stock for quick and convenient consumption occasions. To this extent, the average soup consumer has 9.5 products in their home at any one time!

Allowing them to find the desired product earlier and thereby freeing up more time for searching for new products will help build the repertoire of the shopper and their annual spend on the category.

Action

The Soup IQ shelf system was launched, that has gravity-feed units organized by soup by flavors, which are clearly marked with mini-billboards at the front of the shelf.

Results

Four percent sales increase in year one of its introduction and maintaining a 3 percent increase the next year.

Purchasing

Behavior:	After selecting a product, the shopper moves away from the primary category toward either the register or another category. The shopper may encounter an off-location display and change their mind or purchase an additional product along this path.
Asks themselves:	• Do I want this? • Did I make the right decisions? • Am I happy with the shop?
Helpful observations:	• Value of shopper baskets including and excluding the category • When during the in-store journey they buy? • Types of shoppers that buy • Category penetration, usage frequency, and annual weight of purchase • Purchase satisfaction and dissonance

Example of a purchasing-based shopper insight:

Chewing Gum (TNS 2010)
Insight

Shoppers mentally finish choosing when they leave the aisles, and need a trigger to revert to purchasing mode at later in their mission.

Freshening is the main motivation for purchasing chewing gum and can be used to get their attention at the register.

Action

New POSM that focused on refreshment as a call to action.

Results

40 percent for total chewing gum.

Shopper Strategies

If you are using the RACER! model, you will have some high level objectives that you agreed to with the retailer in step A.

If these are in place you now need some strategies to help achieve them. These strategies will use the shopper observations and insights that you have written as their foundation.

The first step in writing shopper strategies is to identify what you want the shopper to do more of, these can be summarized as:

- More shoppers entering
- More shoppers navigating to …
- More shoppers scanning
- More shoppers choosing
- More shoppers purchasing
  - Purchasing more frequently
  - Purchasing more items
  - Spending more per item

You can also link the identified "more" with a particular mission, for example:

- More shoppers entering the coffee aisle on main trip missions
- More shoppers scanning the roast and ground segment on top-up trips
- More shoppers purchasing our coffee brand on fresh food missions

Before we can match our **More** behavior with an activity to encourage it, we have to understand what barriers are preventing the change in shopper behavior we need.

If you have a list of bespoke barriers for your category derived from in-store research, you are in luck as this will tell you the issues you have to overcome. However, if you don't have a list of research-led barriers, use the simple list in Chapter 3, and identify the ones you think are most relevant given your understanding of the shoppers.

Here are examples of relevant barriers:

- More shoppers entering the coffee aisle on main trip missions
  - Barrier: Some shoppers think that there aren't products for their consumption occasion needs ranged

- More shoppers browsing the roast and ground segment on top up trips
  - Barrier: Some shoppers believe that these products are just too complicated
- Shoppers purchasing coffee more frequently on fresh food missions
  - Barrier: Most shoppers only buy it in bulk when they run out

Now we have to think of a high-level action that will overcome these barriers. As we are writing strategies, it shouldn't be a tactical blueprint of the executions that need to happen when and where, but more a sign to point in the right direction.

If we bring all of this together, we can arrive at some final shopper strategies.

- More shoppers entering the coffee aisle on main trip missions by expanding products for refuel occasions.
- More shoppers browsing the roast and ground segment on top up trips by developing solutions around consumption regimes.
- Shoppers purchasing coffee more frequently on fresh food missions by growing bean intrinsics appreciation.

These strategies should link with the objective you have agreed with the customer and importantly be able to be connected with SMART goals, for example:

Strategies	Goals
More shoppers entering the coffee aisle on main trip missions by expanding products for refuel occasions	• 2% increase in shoppers entering the coffee aisle (target 16%) by 2018 • 5% increase in purchases for the refuel occasions (wind up, study session and afternoon pit stop) by 2017
More shoppers browsing the roast and ground segment on top up trips by developing solutions around consumption regimes	• 3% increase in browsing (and no drop in final conversion level of 2%) by 2019 • 3 annual platform regime promotions integrated with Shopmart magazines and digital by 2019
Shoppers purchasing coffee more frequently on fresh food missions by growing bean intrinsics appreciation.	10% increase of coffee in fresh food baskets by 2018

Top Tips

- Sift through your existing consumer and shopper research for observations about shoppers and then place these observations on the relevant step of the path to purchase.
- Use these observations as the ingredients for writing shopper insights that link with each step on the path to purchase.
- Create shopper strategies for your key channels and customers.

CHAPTER 10

The Key Points in This Chapter

- The process of creating activation ideas can be as simple as gathering a few people together and brainstorming; through to using a full Hothouse. Whatever method is used though, be sure to start with a solid immersion in the shoppers you need to convert.
- All activation ideas should incorporate the core principles of retail theater.
- The theater in a retail store is a "silent language" that works within and below consciousness to influence a shopper's perception of value, quality, behavior, and ultimately satisfaction.

Part A: Activation Ideas

The facilitator held up a box, and then whistled over the early morning din to get attention.

"All phones in here please," and he dropped in his to illustrate what was required.

"For the next eight hours we need your fullest attention; we'll feed you and let you out for fresh air; but not to play with your phones." The room went quiet.

"If this doesn't work for you because your partner is expecting a child or you are in the middle of an important negotiation with a customer or agency that's fine, just let us know and you can be excused."

"He's serious," said the marketing director stepping up to drop in her phone.

There was a flutter of activity as people sent off final text messages or finished their calls.

The Hothouse was Julie the marketing director's idea; she had used it successfully on other occasions. A Hothouse is a fast-paced creative thinking workshop where divergent stimulus was used to encourage new idea generation. The new ideas were tested on a panel of people in the afternoon, with the best ones to then be refined and developed further for execution. The people chosen to take part in the workshop were a cross-section of employees from functions within the Big Beverage Company. They had been nominated based on their ability to think at least a little differently from the norm. However, to ensure the ideas were extreme enough, a selection of other people had been invited to attend—a barista teacher from a local vocational college, a home decoration consultant, a packaging designer, a semi-famous chef from a reality TV show and the editor from the nation's bestselling Gourmet magazine.

The facilitator led the group through a warm-up exercise where he asked them to work in groups of three to come up with an idea for a new James Bond film. They had to write a title, identify a relevant person to play the hero, and describe their villain; then they had to outline the mission the hero sets out on, the conflicts they face and of course ultimately how it ends. The group responded well to this and when the winner had been chosen, the facilitator used this as a segue into the objective of the day.

"Coffee is the hero today; your villain is many-faced; it's all the other beverage options people choose ahead of coffee. Your mission is to help to find a way for coffee to be chosen more often by shoppers in Shopmart and the conflicts you face in doing this will be explained in detail in the next session. How our story ends will be determined by the ideas you generate today!" He then stood back and handed over to Simon to introduce the day's objective in more detail.

"We want to create an obsessive passion for coffee culture by extending the benefits that coffee has to offer. And to do that in Shopmart we need your help! We want to get an extra 248 shoppers per week to put coffee into their baskets in the average Shopmart store. Or put another way, we need your help to get the 95 percent of shoppers who don't have coffee in their basket to buy some!"

They had finalized the objectives, goals, and strategies at a session with Amy last week. They had taken her through the data from the shopper funnel, outlined the path to purchase insights they had gathered, and finished with their recommendation on the strategies and goals.

"Deliver these," Amy said when they had finished discussing them, "and we'll all get our bonuses for the next three years!"

"To give you the context of the shopper behavior and attitudes that exist today, we have created what we call a path to purchase wall over here." Simon walked to the wall covered with pictures and paper with insights written on them. Simon explained what a path to purchase was, acting out the shopper behavior as he moved along the wall.

"These steps are separated up here on the wall. So you can see exactly what we know about coffee shoppers at each step. These cartoon drawings represent what they might be doing or thinking as they move along. As a first step, I want you to come along and immerse yourself in the journey of our shopper."

The group gathered at the start of the wall and progressed through the 15 written insights and 20 cartoons with thought bubbles on the wall.

"It's a lot to take in," said the facilitator, "but take your time as these are some of the ingredients you will use today to create your ideas."

The workshop unfolded at a steady pace from there; the facilitator did an excellent job of encouraging and cajoling without interjecting himself into the process. Simon, Jamie, and Amy took his lead and rescinded into the background, observing but not bothering the five teams who were now in the process of funneling their ideas down into a smaller group to test on the Shopmart shoppers later in the afternoon.

"Is this how you generate all your ideas?" asked Amy over lunch.

"Sometimes we get a big group like this together, but usually it's smaller groups of people. We always try and start with insights though, either those we already have in the brand footprint or new ones we get from local studies."

Amy nodded, "I had this impression that everything came prepackaged from agencies or corporate HQ."

"Agencies help," said Julie who was sitting with them. "We have a few of our agency partners in the room today; but it's usually a cross functional group that works best. When you try to completely outsource your activity idea generation you often end up with things that are interesting and exciting but not always connected to what you are trying to achieve for the longer term."

"I saw the Coffee Drops idea when I was on holiday overseas last year, are you going to talk about that?"

Coffee Drops was a new product that had been launched in some parts of the world last year. It was a product that had individually wrapped coffee tablets that fizzed when you dropped them into hot water, producing a thick-tasting drink with a thin layer of crème on the top.

"We are," said Jamie, "We believe they will help us win more small baskets and at the same time increase the price per serving. The key will be to merchandise them at the express checkouts though; that's the learning."

Amy nodded.

At around 3 p.m. the teams had prepared their ideas on large-sized posters, an illustrator had been on hand to sketch their ideas to give them more context. Now they were going to discuss them with some actual Shopmart shoppers.

The ideas started with an insight, smoothed a little to make sure it had words that were free from any jargon, and then a picture of the idea followed by a sentence or two about why this idea would benefit the shopper. The teams had been warned about making sure they interacted with their shoppers politely and without too much intensity, and that a negative response from one person didn't mean the idea was dead.

"It's just feedback, and remember it's more often negative than good!"

Simon, Jamie, and Amy moved around the room, taking turns sitting at different stations and listening to the feedback from their shoppers. Shopping is such a mundane and ritualistic exercise that it was difficult to get the insight across to the people; but everyone had been warned about that earlier in the day.

"Explain the insight, but if they don't get it, don't belabor the point; get to the idea and talk them through it. If you do it well, they'll tell you how to improve it."

After 90 minutes, the shoppers were thanked for their time and an exhausted and somewhat deflated audience was given a break. When you invest so much time and energy into a process like creative thinking you get disappointed when your audience doesn't high-five you at the end of the pitch. The reality was as expected though; most ideas got a lukewarm response at best.

Jamie was upbeat, excited about the idea around fresh beans in the fruit and vegetable section that he had heard; Amy and Simon though did not share his enthusiasm.

"So what now?" asked Amy.

"Well, we are going to refine the ideas for the next hour based on the feedback we got and then choose some winning ones. From there, we'll develop them into a complete activity and present them to you."

"You reckon some of these are winning ideas?"

The facilitator replied to her "you have a few good acorns here and remember that this is where big oaks come from!"

"All right then, I'm going to leave you guys to it. Looking forward to seeing the final results next week."

The next day Simon found a quiet room to review the ideas that had come out of the Hothouse. He wanted to refine them a little, and add thoughts on the appropriate retail theater, before they went to the agency for improved graphics.

There were eight ideas in all, a good cross section that could be attached to each of the four strategies they had for category growth.

His favorite was *Coffee Carts at the Entrance*; the team's insight was "re-stocking the house is not easy; people are usually juggling children, carts and bags. It's a chore too, not something that gives you a lot of pleasure. When it's like this, making it just that little bit easier gets noticed." Their idea was to place coffee carts just inside the entrance in the landing zone and sell real coffee served by a proper barista. Their benefit for the customer was that it would prime more expensive coffee and offer differentiation as no other supermarket chain was doing this, while for the shopper it would provide the energy to complete the mission!

Then there was the *Home Café*; the team's insight was "My home is just like a café at times. It's where we stop for a moment to have the conversations that matter the most. And these little moments provide the energy to get through the day. Shopping for coffee is about preparing for these moments." Their idea was to replace the normal price tickets with chalkboard style descriptions of the products and their strength for a week or two so that they interrupt the shopper. The benefit for the customer is that it captures attention and converts more passing traffic, while for a shopper it standardizes the category code so that strength and taste indicators are quick to understand.

There was also the idea of putting a fridge in aisle within the coffee category that has chilled coffee as well as dairy products where coffee is an ingredient. Cakes and sweets that contain coffee would be added too. The idea was premised on the insight that *Coffee is more than an ingredient; it's a passion. Exploring the subtleties in taste is what makes it interesting. When shopping, people look beyond just powder or beans to explore these tastes.*

There were also ideas to add strength indicators on the shelf to compare how strong per serving each product is; to have drip filter coffee brewing in the deli and for sale at a nominal price; to run a promotional campaign around "Energy for the home CEO" in which the main grocery buyer (male or female) was encouraged to buy a small jar of something special just for themselves. Selling fresh coffee beans in the fruit and vegetable section had been a popular idea as had the idea of offering a Shopmart sponsored barista course that you purchased in the same way you brought a mobile phone re-charge card or an iTunes gift card, but advertised on the shelf.

When he added these ideas to the potential new product launch for Coffee Drops, it started to feel like a significant set of ideas. Underpinning it all was the category management strategy to increase space in roast and ground and freeze dried, move them plus beans into the sight zone and reduce space and sight zone presence for powder and granules. There would be no extra space for mixes, but part of it would move into the sight zone. The hot spot would now be dominated with roast and ground and freeze dried. The category flow would also change; milk modifiers would move to the top of the aisle, followed by coffee, tea would be next and adjacent to these categories would be an aisle of biscuits.

But there was still something missing!

Part B: Activations That Influence the Shopper

A key part of the third step in the shopper marketing model is path to purchase activation. The Big Beverage Company held a Hothouse to create ideas for Shopmart based on the research they had completed.

This is where we turn your conversion opportunity into an activation that addresses a shopper barrier along their path to purchase. It's where the marketing in shopper marketing starts to become physical.

The process of creating activation ideas can be as simple as gathering a few people together and brainstorming; it does not have to entail the full Hothouse that the Big Beverage Company used in this chapter. Whatever method is used though, be sure to start with a solid immersion in the shoppers you need to convert. This can involve shop-alongs before you

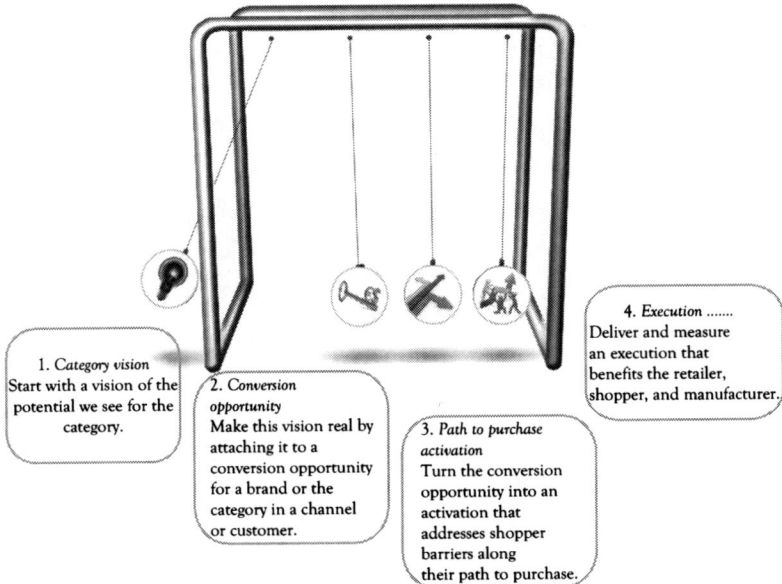

4. *Execution* ....
Deliver and measure an execution that benefits the retailer, shopper, and manufacturer.

1. *Category vision*
Start with a vision of the potential we see for the category.

2. *Conversion opportunity*
Make this vision real by attaching it to a conversion opportunity for a brand or the category in a channel or customer.

3. *Path to purchase activation*
Turn the conversion opportunity into an activation that addresses shopper barriers along their path to purchase.

Figure 10.1 Shopper marketing model

start ideating, a review of existing insights along the path to purchase or watching videos of them being interviewed using the questions outlined earlier in the book.

When you have a selection of ideas, you can then begin to refine them further, ensuring the elements of good point-of-sale material design are applied as well as the core principles of retail theater.

Retail Theater

A capsule for my Nespresso machine presently costs me 69 cents. It delivers a great cup of coffee, and over the course of a weekend I use two to three.

During the week, I will often have a cup of coffee around 3 p.m. from the small cafeteria on the ground level of my building. There a similar tasting cup of coffee costs me around $3.50.

While when I am travelling for work I will often stop in at a Starbucks or similar type café and buy a small latte; for all intents and purposes, this is similar to the coffee I have home; the cost however is usually $5 to $7.

A single experience with three very different values (and I could give similar examples for beer, sandwiches, and hamburgers!). What we see here is commodities being transformed into goods, then accompanying them with services and ultimately experiences to create economic value (Hoffman and Turley 2002). In this instance, a key driver of the transformation is the retail atmosphere that surrounded the purchase of the cup of coffee.

The atmosphere in a retail store is a "silent language" that works within and below consciousness to influence a shopper's perception of value, quality, behavior, and ultimately satisfaction with the purchase transaction (Ailawadi and Keller 2004; Bawa, Landwehr, and Krishna 1989; Kotler 1973; Mitchell, Oppewal, and Beverland 2009).

The design of this atmosphere, both its tangible (e.g., window displays, signage, and color schemes) and intangible elements (e.g., lighting, music, and scent), in order to influence the shopper is known as "retail theater" in fast moving consumer goods companies. (In academic literature they are referred to as Retail Atmospherics.)

Retail Theater works by having an emotional effect on the shopper, which in turn influences their behavior. This emotional impact on the shoppers' behavior can be explained along two key scales:

1. Pleasure—displeasure
2. Arousal—nonarousal

These emotional states cause behaviors that can be either classified as approach or avoidance. For example, approach behaviors are movement toward or exploration within an outlet; while avoidance behaviors are the opposite, for example, moving away from or out of an outlet (Donovan and Rossiter 1982).

In an FMCG context, this might mean a shopper experiencing pleasure so that they choose to browse for just a moment longer in an interesting wine aisle, or being aroused because of the smell of fresh bread in a close-by bakery and stopping to buy something.

To this end, it has been found that in stores the shopper considers pleasant dollars spent, time and enjoyment go up as arousal increases (Donovan and Rossiter 1982). And as our arousal increases, so does our tendency to make unplanned purchases (Donovan et al. 1994).

It is important though to understand what your shopper considers pleasant, as increased arousal (e.g., loud noise in a book shop), can lead to reduced sales or shopper dissatisfaction (Donovan et al. 1994).

Given the retail truth that it is easier to sell more to your existing shoppers than try and win new ones, the use of retail theater to extract more value from the existing shopper base is an important tool for all retailers and by extension the suppliers who service them.

The elements that can be altered to market to the shopper can be broadly grouped into the following variables:

1. External
2. General interior
3. Layout and design
4. Decoration
5. Human (Turley and Milliman 2000)

And they are becoming such a valuable asset that companies like Apple are now trademarking their retail theatre designs that they create to surround both their products and the shopper (Rodriguez 2013).

External Variables

External variables include things like exterior signs and walls, exterior display windows, entrances, sizes and colors of buildings, surrounding stores, lawns and gardens, addresses, and architectural style.

While eye-tracking research will often tell us that very little visual activity occurs on the approach to an outlet, the exterior does play a role in helping the shopper to profile the outlet and therefore understand whether it is relevant for them (Bitner 1992).

Exterior Display Windows

Window displays provide the shopper with a quick introduction to what they can expect to find inside and are therefore important for retailers who are less well known or focused on winning impulse purchases (Sen, Block, and Chandran 2002).

Window displays have been shown to be effective at increasing sales, particularly for new products, in a drugstore. However, it should be noted that only a small number of passing shoppers (up to 10 percent) actually glance at window displays (Edwards and Shackley 1992; Soars 2003).

Although recall is not necessarily a meaningful shopper marketing metric, window displays with the following characteristics were most likely to be recalled by the shopper:

- Featured contrasting product and background design
- Were in a large enclosure
- Contrasted with an adjacent display
- Contained products that respondents did not associate with the retailer (Edwards and Shackley 1992)

Entrances

As the shopper transitions into a store, they are looking ahead to orientate themselves and for this reason will often miss most of what is placed at the entrance (Underhill 1999). Merchandising in a graduated way from the floor upward so that the shopper is able to look out across the entire store will allow them to quickly transition and orientate themselves (Nassauer 2012).

General Interior Variables

The general interior variables include things like: the flooring and carpeting, color schemes, lighting, music, scents, movement space, wall and ceiling composition, the temperature, and merchandise for sale.

The visual component of store design, for example, the physical elements like displays, the signage and the materials the store is fitted out with come together to form a visual merchandising presentation to the shopper. Visual merchandising helps establish distinct retail brand equity by creating a joined-up physical image of the store's offer to the shopper (Bell and Ternus 2006).

Color Schemes

Interior color schemes have an impact on shopping behavior. They can physically attract shoppers toward a display and influence the perception of the store and its product range (Babin, Hardesty, and Suter 2003; Bellizzi, Crowley, and Hasty 1983).

Warm colors, like red, orange, and yellow, can produce high arousal and draw people toward them. They are therefore good to use on promotional point-of-sale material.

However, warmer colors can be too distracting when the shopper is focused on specific goals and not open to browsing (Babin, Hardesty, and Suter 2003).

While cooler colors like green and blue are considered more calming and may be more appropriate to encourage people to linger and browse longer (Bellizzi, Crowley, and Hasty 1983).

Color schemes can be powerful ways of influencing shopper arousal levels; for example, in peak times when the store is more crowded with specific mission shoppers, color could be lowered using lighting and raised at other times when crowding is lower and more stock up missions are taking place (Rompay et al. 2011).

In the retail setting, color can also be used to differentiate zones within the store or ranges of merchandise. In this way, it can help the shopper quickly categorize products and reduce the cognitive strain required to orientate themselves.

Lighting

Attention and physical movement is drawn toward areas of higher illumination (Taylor and Sucov 1974). For example, in a bar, lit beer taps receive twice as much visual attention as those that are not. While under bright versus dim conditions, more products are touched, inspected, and considered appealing (Areni and Kim 1994; Summers and Hebert 2001; Vaccaro et al. 2008). When lighting is combined with particular colors, it enhances the appeal and image of the store (Babin, Hardesty, and Suter 2003).

Lit displays are also considered to be significantly more effective at encouraging purchase (Kerfoot, Davies, and Ward 2003). This is why you will often find many beauty displays, like those for Lancome and L'oreal, illuminated in the store. This is likely because brighter lighting is the human preference for activities that require visual activity (Biner et al. 1989). It also helps achieve contrast from otherwise dim retail areas and is therefore able to capture bottom-up attention.

Lighting will also influence the service encounter in store. Shoppers talk more softly when the lights are low, the speed of the service interaction slows and the environment is perceived as more formal. By contrast, more brightly lit environments encourage louder, more frequent communication and lead to perceptions of greater informality (Hoffman and Bateson 1997).

When designing the lighting solution for the shopper (Ginthner n.d.):

A. Ensure it is adequate enough to complete the required task.

B. At an ambient level; match it with the type of emotion you are trying to elicit.

C. Most importantly, use it to spotlight areas or products where you want to direct the shopper.

Music

Shopping behavior and music have a complex interaction. It has been found to increase sales, time in store, and qualitative responses in relation the store environment (Bruner 1990; Dubé and Morin 2001; Garlin and Owen 2006). But complexity is found in the components of music that produce this impact; tempo, volume, style and whether or not it is the back or foreground all influence its ability to impact the shopper.

For example, louder music has been shown to reduce the amount of time spent in store but not sales amounts (Smith and Curnow 1966). While the music tempo can influence traffic pace in a supermarket (Milliman 1982) and in an on trade environment, it can impact the time spent at the table and the amount purchased (Milliman 1986; Oakes 2000).

The type of music has also been shown to impact shopping behaviors of males and females differently, with females preferring slower tempos and males faster tempos! (Andersson et al. 2012).

Foreground music (music designed to be actively listened to) is preferred to background music across all shopping age groups. However background music has been shown to influence the degree of attention and information processing to critical store elements like salesperson dialogue and visual merchandising (Chebat, Chebat, and Vaillant 2001).

Music can prime the purchase of certain products. When wine shoppers were studied, classical versus top 40 music resulted in increased sales as the classical music primed more sophisticated thoughts (Areni and Kim 1993). While a similar study found that when French music was played sales of French wine increased and when German music was played the next week French wine sales declined and German sales increased (North, Hargreaves, and McKendrick 1999).

Perhaps its most basic effect though is in its ability to help shape attitudes toward the store. However, the music needs to match the overall atmosphere in order to actually have an impact on behavior (Baker, Grewal, and Levy 1992; Grewal et al. 2003; Wilson 2003). For example, playing rap music in an Italian restaurant may actually annoy the diners and cause them to leave!

When music surpasses a given threshold though it will divert attention to itself and away from the main task of shopping. This reduces the amount of attention the shopper can direct to the products around them. Finding this threshold in the retail setting is vital if it is to play a role in moderating the shopper's arousal to an optimal level (Chebat, Chebat, and Vaillant 2001; Chebat and Filiatrault 1993).

Scents

Our olfactory sense has a deep and connected relationship to our brains, and it is therefore not surprising that it is a target for marketers ... and casinos! In an infamous study, a particular odor (kept secret by the author of the experiment) significantly increased the amount gambled in a Las Vegas casino (Hirsch 1995). (Although he does say that scents should remind people of their childhoods or induce feelings of safety and security) (Li 2011). Scent has similar effects in retail situations where the presence or absence of a scent affects both qualitative evaluations of variety and purchase behavior (Bone and Jantrania 1992; Deborah and Mitchell 1995; Spangenberg, Crowley, and Henderson 1996).

Scent induces arousal that increases our pleasure levels and in turn positively influences shopping behaviors like the amount of money spent shopping (Chui and Fleming 2011). For example, a 1993 study found that 84 percent of people were more likely to buy in a scented room versus an unscented room. At the same time, people reported paying more for the same product in a scented room (Vlahos 2007).

A 2005 study that paired male or female targeted scents with the relevant section in a clothing store found that both men and women spent more when the scent was present (Spangenberger, Grohmann, and Sprott 2005). A Nike store apparently lifted sales by 80 percent by adding scents, while a petrol station lifted coffee sales by 300 percent by pumping the smell out toward its customers (White 2012).

When it comes to selling real estate, scent will also apparently encourage people to pay more for the property by emotionally engaging them and removing them from their rational behavior (Vlahos 2007). Although, in the one experience I have with selling property this definitely did not work!

Scent can also improve shopper evaluation of brands that are unfamiliar with them. It therefore becomes a handy tool to consider when putting together launch plans for new products (Morrin and Ratneshwar 2000).

Where scent is a feature of the product, it is often better to find a way to give permission to the shopper to test it. A simple sign on the shelf or on the product, as P&G did recently with their "Love at First Sniff" campaign for their brand Gain, can boost sales (Buss 2011).

Temperature

The temperature is also a variable that can affect a shopper's comfort and therefore whether they continue shopping or move away (Bitner 1992).

Cleanliness or Toilets

In studies that focus on pubs I have been involved with, the cleanliness of toilets is often raised as important elements to patrons. The presence of clean and convenient amenities is also a priority for mothers shopping with small children in grocery stores.

Layout and Design Variables

This includes elements like: space design and allocation, placement of merchandise, grouping of merchandise, placement of equipment and cash registers, waiting areas, department locations, traffic flow, and display racks.

A more in-depth look at this area with specific reference to the layout of shelving, shopper paths around the store, and the arrangement of merchandise on those shelves is contained in Chapter 7.

Racks and Cases

When it comes to clothing retailing, there are four principal methods of presentation: hanging, folding, rail-based, and the use of mannequins.

Hanging allows the shopper to see what the product looks like before committing to touch or investigate them. Display on mannequins allows the shopper to view combinations of items and can aid multiple purchases, while folding can deter the shopper from investigation for fear of messing up a well-ordered display (Kerfoot, Davies, and Ward 2003).

Placing items on tables and creating space around them generates the perception of quality (Kerfoot, Davies, and Ward 2003), a strategy the Apple store has used well.

Wooden displays or shelves can prime natural associations, and depending on the finish may also connote exclusivity. In supermarkets, the use of wooden shelves can help cue a natural, fresh perception (Nassauer 2012).

In a restaurant, everything that is placed on the table in front of the diner can communicate a message about the quality of the food and or service that is to be expected (Wall and Berry 2007). The table also receives a large amount of visual attention and this is why brands will often work hard to ensure their message is displayed in the right way in this area.

In a supermarket, angling the shelf down so that products slide forward has been shown to lift sales by 3.5 percent in a category deodorant pilot (Glazer 2012).

Waiting Areas

When the shopper waits for service, the potential for customer dissatisfaction increases (Katz, Larson, and Larson 1991); in turn, this impacts present and future purchase behaviors (Hui, Dube, and Chebat 1997). However, before a shopper chooses to wait, they will estimate the length of wait and based on that assessment decide whether to leave or if they have not done so already, even enter the store (Grewal et al. 2003). The design of areas where the shopper either has to wait or has to look to assess wait times is, therefore, crucial.

Evidence of this comes from an intriguing UK study of petrol stations with convenience style shops that found that shoppers will actually take the time to browse if there are between two and five people in the queue, whereas if there are under two or over five people queuing, the shopper is more likely to join the queue immediately (Soars 2003).

Plates and Glasses

Beer drinkers apparently pace their consumption by watching the amount left in their glass. Glass design that makes it more difficult to judge the amount drunk (e.g., a flute versus a straight design) results in quicker consumption (Attwood et al. 2012; *The Economist* 2012a).

Larger plates and glasses also encourage additional consumption (Wansink 2010).

Point-of-Purchase and Decoration Variables

This includes elements like: point-of-purchase displays, signs, wall decorations, pictures, or product displays.

These areas are discussed in-depth in other chapters.

Human Variables

This includes elements like employee characteristics, employee uniforms, and crowding.

Employee Characteristics

Retail sales people are, as the name suggests, a powerful tool in generating sales. In the right environment, they have been shown to be more influential than other atmospheric variables in influencing sales (Hedrick, Oppewal, and Beverland 2006). A person's mood influences their shopping behavior and the small aspects of a retail sales person's behavior, whether they ignore you, talk to you, or smile at you, can affect shoppers' mood, and by virtue of this, their approach or avoidance behaviors (Baker, Grewal, and Levy 1992). These relatively fleeting service encounters also increase the likelihood of longer term shopper loyalty (Lemmink and Mattsson 2002).

In a fascinating example involving bank staff where training was offered to help them cross sell financial services in conjunction with point-of-sale material that promoted an extended range of products a 90-day pilot resulted in 142 new accounts representing $1.6 million in assets (Doepke 2008). In pharmacies where 25 percent of all sales can involve an interaction with store staff training sales assistants on new products will often make the difference between success and failure.

While the more retail sales people who actually greet shoppers, the higher the likelihood that those shoppers will perceive the store to offer higher service quality (Baker, Grewal, and Parasuraman 1994).

The atmospheric variables around these sales people can influence the shopper's expectations of service levels (Mitchell, Oppewal, and Beverland 2009). The surroundings in which these service encounters take place are called *servicescapes* and they have been shown to not only impact the shopper but the retail sales person as well (Bitner 1992). To this end, a more premium atmosphere, where the purchase may be more hedonic, will lift the service expectations of shoppers (Dhar and Wertenbroch 2000), whereas service expectations of service for more functional products are lower (Babin, Darden, and Griffin 1994).

Employee Uniforms

Retail service staff dressed in unprofessional attire negatively influence a shopper's satisfaction (Bitner 1990).

Crowding

Crowding is the most stressful part of any trip to the grocery store according to the shopper, followed by budgeting and then the actual decision of what to buy (IGD 2011b).

When shoppers experience crowding, they have a negative emotional reaction that reduces their satisfaction (Machleit, Eroglu, and Mantel 2000). In some instances experiencing crowding can also lead to emotional venting and confronting behavior (Whiting 2009).

Increased time awareness can also amplify the effect of crowding on the shopper, so finding ways to distract the shopper from the passing of time, such as playing continuous music when they are waiting, can temper dissatisfaction (Harrell and Hurt 1976).

Shoppers can of course also be distracted with impulse purchases while they wait in lines, at the register for example. Some recent interesting findings show that impulse decisions made while waiting in line in a school cafeteria can be nudged toward healthier snacks by simply removing the candy bars and substituting them with fruit (Just and Wansink 2009).

However, the introduction of the smartphone has meant that many shoppers who are waiting in line may be too busy with their social media or e-mail to be tempted by the racks of impulse products placed right in front of them (Edwards 2013).

Using Retail Theater

Despite the impact that retail theater can have on the shopper though, it is important to remember that customer service, easy shop-ability and a logical store layout, must be put in place before anything else is applied (Backstrom and Johansson 2006).

There is a lot of interesting retail theater information available and one way I have found useful to use it is as a lens to check your activation ideas. For example, I take this summary grid and ask if there is any way the idea could be improved with a retail theater element to increase shopper pleasure or lift their arousal.

Table 10.1 Retail Theatre Ideas Template

	Positive shopper impact	
Atmospheric element	**Ideas to increase pleasure**	**Ideas to lift arousal**
External variables • Exterior signs and walls • Exterior display windows • Entrances • Heights, sizes, and colors of buildings • Surrounding stores • Lawns and gardens • Addresses • Architectural style		
General interior variables • The flooring and carpeting • Color schemes • Lighting • Music • Scents • Movement space • Wall and ceiling composition • The temperature		
Layout and design variables • Space design and allocation • Placement of merchandise • Grouping of merchandise • Placement of equipment and cash registers • Waiting areas • Department locations • Traffic flow • Display racks • Digital interactivity		
Decoration variables • Point-of-purchase displays • Signs • Wall decorations • Pictures • Artwork • Product displays • Price displays • Mannequins		

Human variables		
• Employee characteristics • Employee uniforms • Crowding		

Top Tips

- Consider using a Hothouse to find activation ideas for your key shopper conversion opportunities.
- Create a set of examples of how retail theater is being used to influence the shopper in your market, use this as stimulus for your own activations.
- Use the checklist in this chapter to evaluate how well your existing activations are leveraging retail theater.

CHAPTER 11

The Key Points in This Chapter

- The path to purchase can also be used to gather insight into e-shoppers.
- When shopping online people find branded advertising messages the least intrusive.
- Digital technology in the retail setting can also influence shopper behavior and at the same time can provide a tangible benefit over e-shopping.

Part A: Digital Shopper Marketing

He had gathered the project team again to take them through the ideas that had been developed in the hothouse. Their creative agency had helped with the visuals and tidied up the concepts so that they were more ready for immediate execution. Simon presented the insight and idea and then Jamie talked about what barriers they would need to overcome with Shopmart in order to execute.

They had invited Reg along to the session too. Some of the ideas would involve capex investments from them as well as investment and a paradigm shift from Shopmart; Reg would be key in securing both. He had challenged them on the feasibility of the coffee cart idea given the resources required from Shopmart to make it work.

"Do we know how much coffee carts at the entrance of all of their stores are going to cost? How will we manage it? I like the idea, but how will it be executed?"

"Shopmart could manage it," Jamie had replied. "They are retailers after all. We'll train the baristas, provide the coffee at a good price and brand the cups. Never mind the goodwill, but turning every Shopmart into a café for their 40,000+ shoppers a week will mean great revenue!"

Reg shrugged in a noncommittal way, "I'm not sure, but I'm happy to hear what they say to it."

The discussion around the launch of Coffee Drops was the most controversial. It had been a great success in year one of its launch overseas but had declined by greater than 40 percent in the second year; the key question the team had was whether it would payback against the investment required to launch it.

"If we can get execution at the register, particularly along the express lanes, then we will win those top-up purchases and that could make the difference."

"With this stuff," said Reg waving his hand at the ideas that were lined up on boards "execution will be everything."

"What we have are some good ideas that will require a mind shift to execute; but the opportunity we clearly have is to find a better digital connection," finding this was going to be the next step.

"What became clear when we were reviewing the output from the Hothouse was that the link with digital wasn't strong enough. To illustrate, I want to do two things; first take those of you who haven't got the Starbucks app through it, and then secondly show you what Shopmart are doing with their club card."

The meeting was not intended as a brainstorming session, but it only took a few minutes after he had finished presenting how these two things worked before the ideas started to flow.

"Could we create an energy meter to help show the Home CEO when her energy is flagging?" asked one of the marketing team. "Somehow show this on the front screen of your phone so it can be seen in just a glance?"

"We could even link it with Weight Watchers, maybe even incorporate it somehow into their app. They are always saying that you need to watch out for these low energy periods because it's when you might eat something inappropriate." Jamie added.

"Shopping is an energy zapping exercise; I read somewhere that the average replenishment shopper walks just under one kilometer to finish their mission; maybe we could somehow turn this energy spent in Shopmart stores into a reward?" suggested Ben.

Jamie re-visited the coffee cart concept now that the conversation had turned to digital.

"And we could create their own coffee loyalty program, digital and plastic, and link it with their existing loyalty card!"

They circled back to the ideas which were displayed on backing cards in the room and started discussing digital links. At one point, when one of the agency team started talking about augmented reality and how it could be linked to a smartphone so that a shopper could look at the pack through their phone and then see additional information about how sustainable the products were, Reg started to laugh.

"They say the problem with most leaders is that they stop learning. I can see today I'm guilty of that and I'm not happy about it!"

As people spoke they began to pull out their own digital devices and explain their thoughts using examples from their own usage routines. This generated newer ideas again, and the agency guys pulled out sketch pads and began to write them down and draw diagrams explaining linkages across all of their ideas and how they could become more integrated campaigns.

"When we think of digital, I worry that it means that the days of selling from the register are fading fast. We know that the shopper is more likely to play with their phones here now than flick through magazines" said Simon.

"Because of this, I think we need a plan B for the Coffee Drops' launch."

"Well what if the register was the place where we targeted to have our digital conversations with the shopper? Supermarkets used to have those community noticeboards at the front of their stores didn't they? What about if we brought the digital community noticeboard into the register queue? Don't Shopmart have something in their strategy about giving back to the community?" This comment from the agency guy sparked an animated round of ideation.

This was the link that would win their advocacy for ideas like the coffee cart added Reg. "When we show that our ideas are designed to meet their shopper proposition, with our brands, we get a triple win."

The meeting continued for another hour until Reg announced that they had to finish because other people needed the boardroom. He summarized by saying that he thought all the ideas should be taken to Shopmart for discussion; "these feel like they can move the business forward."

"We have a week now to get everything together," said Jamie. "That should be plenty of time!"

Throughout the week the agency worked on the ideas, and Simon and Jamie prepared the presentation to integrate them with their category vision.

"Regardless of how Amy and Murray respond to these ideas, I reckon we've done a good job with this project!" added Jamie on e-mail sending back some slides for the selling deck.

"Until we get something in store these insights and actions are just fairytales!" Simon replied.

They were just finishing the C in their project management model; that was only half-way. They still had the E, R, and! to go and there were many good ideas that never got off the page to these stages.

"Yeah, but I can't remember the last time we actually took some ideas like this to a customer," Jamie wrote back.

Good ideas were like lightning, Simon remembered hearing once. A moment of illumination followed by a long period of darkness while work on the idea progressed. He had spent so much energy on this project that the thought of having to wait a prolonged period to execute something made him feel frustrated.

Part B: The E-Shopper

In 1999 *Time* magazine did two important things. The first was that it changed its annual Man of the Year prize to Person of the Year (even though women had won the award in the past); and secondly, they awarded it to an Internet pioneer for the first time, Jeff Bezos, the founder of Amazon. In the article that accompanied the award Bezos said; "online buying would ultimately be 10 to 15 percent of retail" (*Time* Magazine 1999).

He is not right; yet!

As of 2013 online buying, referred to in this chapter as e-shopping, represented 8 percent of all retail sales in the United States (Mulpuru 2013). While across Europe it is much lower, but upward of 10 percent for groceries now in the UK. However within the younger demographic, the use of online purchasing is growing (Capgemini 2012) so these numbers will continue to expand in the short term toward Mr. Bezos' prediction.

While online purchasing is still developing, digital is now involved in the execution and planning of up to a third of all physical store shopping trips (Brinker, Lobaugh, and Paul 2012). This use can be in the form of locating stores, checking promotions and prices through to preparing shopping lists (Neilsen 2012a). This figure is also expected to increase as access to broadband increases.

The objective of this chapter is not to convince you of the potential in e-shopping, but rather to focus on how shoppers use digital technology and what can be done with this to influence them.

The shopper is at the front of this discussion NOT the technology. As companies like Amazon, eBay, and Wal-Mart continue to stress, technology is a secondary consideration to the shopper (Guardian Professional 2012; Manjoo 2012).

As outlined in Chapter 6, winning on the path to purchase is fundamental to shopper marketing, and the digital path should be an equal thought—not an afterthought. Therefore, we will use the path to purchase with the same steps as our earlier model to understand e-shopper behavior. As with the earlier path, it is important to note that shoppers do not move through this path in a linear fashion; however, all shoppers will go through these steps at some point.

Mission

If they have purchased the product before, the shopper will know exactly where to go and will not need to spend much effort in searching for an appropriate web-shop or application. However, Google estimate that 70 percent of shoppers use search at some point in their purchase journey (Google 2011). What is also interesting is that it is often traditional media, like TV ads or retailer leaflets that drive shoppers online, often within the same week, to do further research (Sterling 2012).

One foundation idea that is important for all shopper marketers is that it is when shopping online that they find branded advertising messages the least intrusive (TNS Digital Life 2010).

It's also important to note that repeat e-shoppers are significantly more profitable (emarketer.com 2013); these shoppers can also be higher users of social media, streaming regular commentary on what they are buying and why (Bzzagent 2011). To this end, Bain & Co claim that shoppers who engage with companies over social media spend 20 to 40 percent more money with those companies than shoppers who don't (Barry et al. 2011). Therefore, it's in the interests of both retailers and suppliers to work together to try and create more satisfied and loyal e-shoppers.

Entering

In this step, the shopper enters the website or application.

The arrival at a web page or application front page is a little like the moment you look into a shop window; it either gets your attention or you move on. Clean, well-organized front pages resonate much more strongly with shoppers than those with flashing lights. To this end, a slow load time is the number one reason shoppers give for an unsatisfactory interaction with e-commerce (Scarpello 2012). While the more crowded a website is, the harder it will be for the shopper to process all the presented information (Mulvey 2013).

Personalization

Online buyers want personalization; they rate it as a critical component to the online shopping experience (Capgemini 2012). They are looking for personalization in these key areas (retailcustomerexperience.com 2010):

- Site recognizes me when I come back to visit.
- Remembers my personal preferences, for example, the types of books I like or clothes brands I prefer.
- Offers recommendations based on the items that I have already purchased.
- And top of their wish list for personalization is that the site automatically recalls billing and shipping information.

Retailer apps are a key way to provide personalization as they can be adjusted to the shopper's settings. They also have the added benefit of being faster and easier to launch. According to Deloitte, conversion to purchase is 21 percent higher for shoppers who use a retailer app (Brinker, Lobaugh, and Paul 2012). Retailer apps also enjoy the longest time spent shopping of all shopper-related apps (Cutler 2013) (though we hope this is because they are more interesting and not just harder to use!)

In Canada, Metro just launched what they are calling a digital eco-system that combines a website and an app. Shoppers can locate stores, view promotional leaflets, or have coupons ready to scan at the register on their smartphone. Online they can access menu planning tools, recipes, and video information (Planet Retail 2013d).

Loyalty Cards

Another area where personalization can be amplified is through loyalty schemes. In the United States, up to 90 percent of people are enrolled in at least one loyalty reward program (Bzzagent 2011). Smartphones are a much easier way of managing loyalty cards for the shopper. A good example of this can be found with the Walgreens app in the United States, where members scan their mobile device at the checkout to earn points and savings, and redeem rewards (Lawrence 2013).

In a recent experiment by Nielsen to explore the link between loyalty cards, coupons and retailer apps, shoppers used a retailer app that offered a range of coupons; they then chose coupons they were interested in which were automatically loaded onto their loyalty cards. When the shopper swiped their loyalty card at the register these coupons were activated. They found that shoppers who used the retailer app-coupon-loyalty card combination spent 66 percent more and had 44 percent more visits than shoppers who didn't use this combination. These same shoppers were also more likely to buy brands that were new to their household (Cameron, Gregory, and Battaglia 2012).

Trust

It is also important to establish credibility when the shopper first encounters the site, and then again later when they are entering their payment information. The use of trademarks like Cnet or Norton that people recognize can help achieve this; however, if they are over-emphasized they can create anxiety with the shopper (Dooley and Goward 2013).

Navigating

In this step, the shopper navigates the website or application to orientate themselves.

Hotspots

Just as there are hotspots on shelves in brick and mortar stores, they also exist on web pages or applications (Deherder and Blatt 2011; Google n.d.). Ads located above the fold (the first part of the screen you see) tend to perform better than those below the fold (another interesting finding is that: ads on a computer are seen quicker, and hold engagement longer than ads on an iPad) (Mediative and Tobii 2012). While ads placed near rich content and navigational aids usually do well because users are focused on those areas of a page.

When it comes to digital product display, just as with category management in brick and mortar stores, the order that products are displayed will impact the amount of attention they receive and ultimately their sales rate. Products that are seen earlier in the browsing process have a higher chance of ultimately being chosen (Breugelmans, Campo, and Gijsbrechts 2007).

Scanning

In this step, the shopper begins interacting within the area they have zoomed in on; in doing this, they may use the search function to find their products.

Unlike brick and mortar stores that can only present the shopper with one categorization of products at the shelf, digital has the opportunity to be more flexible. Providing the shopper with multiple filters so that they can narrow down their search can be very effective. As with shopping in-store, completing a quick and accurate browse of the segments available makes the shopper feel smart and good categorization facilitates this.

As the shopper begins browsing, the goal is to allow them to experience the product in the most immersive way possible, should they choose to explore further. Here is a list of things that facilitate this: (retailcustomerexperience.com 2010)

I. Product photography is clear and accurate

At a conference in London in 2011, Sainsbury's showed a case study where just showing what the bottle of beer inside the multipack looked like increased sales by 33 percent.

II. Advanced product viewing functionality

If the shopper is looking for fashion, then the ability to zoom in and look at the material as it is worn by an actual model is a minimum expectation (Kawaf 2013).

III. Demonstration of required assembly or installation

Anyone who has ever had to assembly children's toys or Ikea furniture will agree with this!

Although video has the potential to slow the site down, where video is used by the shopper they are more likely to convert to purchase (DeMarco 2013).

IV. Demonstrations of the product in use

One way of achieving this is through providing branded microsites within retailer websites. In a UK study, 23 percent of online shoppers have already used them (IGD 2012).

Online grocery Ocado in the UK recently trialed an interactive cartoon bear that appeared when the shopper purchased fish fingers. The activation was built with bird's eye and was designed to engage the shopper and gain greater stand out for their brand (Planet Retail 2012a).

V. Product reviews from actual customers

This is where peer reviews and social media can play a significant role in influencing purchase (Neilsen 2012b). Shoppers are becoming more skeptical of paid media at the same time that their willingness to use social media referrals is growing (Coca-Cola Retailing Research Council; The Integer Group 2012).

Customer reviews empower the shopper to feel smart. (And for men, who are often not the primary shopper in the household and therefore not as skilled or confident and undertaking it, helping them to feel this way is important.) Reviews on retailer websites are the number one source of social commentary that shoppers use at this step in their path to purchase. It is also a platform through which they regularly communicate (Esomar 2011). For this reason, retailer websites are good forums through which to stay connected with your shoppers.

Research also tells us that social media, whether connected to the retailer's website or not, also has the ability to encourage shoppers to try new brands and products (Ryan Partnership 2012). Digital retail sites therefore have to find ways to motivate shoppers to read and submit reviews to keep this valuable reference point fresh and relevant.

A recent study by Twitter found that users exposed to tweets from retailers were 40 percent more likely to buy from that retailer online than the average online shopper. Their learning from this finding was that exposure to tweets means that shoppers arrive at the retailers' website with a higher propensity to buy (Twitter 2012). While data from Levi Strauss indicates that products with more than 25 reviews have a return rate that is 45 percent lower (Pouy 2011).

VI. Product specifications are available

Particularly for men who want to know how products work. According to Saatchi Saatchi X, performance provides a kind of "emotional functionality." It helps men feel that their choice is more efficient, powerful, or technologically advanced (Goodall 2011).

Choosing

In this step, the shopper compares alternatives and selects something to purchase.

E-shoppers live with the belief that a better price exists; all they have to do is find it! They enact this belief by going to the store to try on clothes or explore products they are interested in, and then start searching for the best deal online, and they will often start that search in-store with their smartphone.

A recent study suggests that 29 percent of shoppers who use a smartphone to research a product while at any retail store end up purchasing the item from an online only retailer (prweb.com 2012). This phenomenon has been coined showrooming, and price differences of as little 2.5 percent or US$5 can encourage most shoppers to do it (Monteleone and Wolferseberger 2012).

One way they are doing this is by matching the best online price that the shopper can find. They are also offering promotions that are only available in-store through coupons that are directly sent to the shopper's smart phones through technologies like near-field communication. Near-field communication or geo-tagging works by trying to reach shoppers with messages while they are in the store deciding whether or not to buy. For some of us, this kind of communication may be invasive, but for others it adds to the entertainment of shopping in a real as opposed to virtual world.

Purchasing

In this step, the shopper makes payment for their product.

Favorites

A customer's favorites list is their future shopping cart. It predicts what they will buy.

Finding ways to make it easy for them to replenish, and asking the shopper to opt out of these recommendations, incorporating discounts, a top-sellers area and remembering customized delivery requirements, will make the purchase decisions quicker and easier and will be rewarded by repeat usage.

Payment

Internet users' attitudes about online shopping are not entirely consistent. They are willing to shop online because it is convenient and a time-saver, but they also do not like sending personal or credit card information over the Internet. This is one of the reasons why PayPal has become so popular and why they claim that merchants who offer their express payment service see an 18 percent growth in sales (Ipsos 2011).

Future mobile wallet solutions where you can pay using only your smartphone will further speed up and at the same time reduce the risk associated with payment. After all, who needs a wallet or a watch if you have a smartphone?

Shipping

Shipping charges are a key barrier to buying online, particularly as they often do not appear until the shopper is asked for their final purchase confirmation.

According to a recent Canadian study, nearly three-quarters of people agree that free shipping, with slower delivery, would encourage them to shop online. While nearly half of all Canadians suggested that, at the very least, online retailers should offer a greater variety of shipping options so they can select the speed and cost that fits their needs (The NPD Group 2010). To this end, an IGD study of UK shoppers actually found that delivery reliability (91 percent), slot availability (85 percent), and the delivery charge (75 percent) are important drivers of website choice (IGD 2012). To overcome delivery slot suitability for shoppers, many retailers are now offering collect services from the car parks outside their stores.

The words "free shipping" is very motivating to e-shoppers. Professor David Bell from Wharton University says that this is why approximately 60 percent of online retailers cite "free shipping with conditions" as their most successful marketing tool (Wharton 2006).

Abandoned Carts

Abandoned shopping carts are the number one thing all retailers could fix to grow sales.

There are no firm figures in the industry but a conservative estimate is that up to 60 percent of all carts are abandoned (Baymard Institute 2014).

To help reduce the number of abandoned shopping carts you can (Charlton 2012):

- Offer multiple payment methods of payment
- Remove distractions on the purchase page
- Keep form filling to a minimum
- Add reminders of price and delivery charges before the check-out so that it is not a surprise later
- Make it easy for customers to alter order details
- Show a progress indicator so that the customer knows where they are in the payment process
- Offer a stress-free returns policy

Execution Ideas

Because of this digital path to purchase behavior here are some recommendations to improve shopper marketing efforts:

- Be present in the online shops of your existing retail customers
- Consider offering them broader ranges than can be stocked in their stores
- If advertising or listing on a retailer site, do whatever you can to be in the hotspot (same as bricks and mortar!)
- Have search filters that match shopper decision criteria
- Ensure the shopper can get to your products to select them within three to four clicks
- Use as high definition media as possible to explain your product
- Take ownership of the explanatory content
- Make comparison easy
- Include the technical specifications
- Encourage social media comments and especially reviews
- Personalize for the shopper as much as possible
- Make sure PayPal is available

- Make sure there is fluency between the traditional advertising and the online advertising. This will help the shopper connect what they saw elsewhere with what they are searching for
- Understand the motivations and behaviors of shoppers that connect with you online, they are a recurring profit source
- Optimize your online advertising for mobile
- Understand how your brands are displayed on retailer apps, the earlier they are found within a category assortment the better
- Find a link between your brand and the retailers loyalty schemes
- Show comparative prices

Digital Theater In-Store

Digital technologies also open up possibilities for retailers to increase the pleasure or arousal of the shopper, and at the same time provide a tangible benefit over online shopping. These digital theater elements are developing at a rapid rate but below I have tried to list out some of the more interesting examples along the path to purchase.

Mission

Most online shopping is to replenish the home; penetration of smaller top-up baskets is less than through brick and mortar stores. To win a higher number of small basket purchases, the use of virtual store walls where shoppers can scan and buy items is growing. The first scaled grocery example of this came from Tesco in Korea. Many other examples have followed and it is now common practice to see these walls in busy thoroughfares like train stations. Results from the activations are limited; however, in trials I have been a part of, sales have been small.

Entering

As shoppers enter the store they will increasingly have the opportunity to check-in and begin earning loyalty points or receive instant coupons.

Target in the United States uses the Shopkick reward program in all its stores. If shoppers have the app on their smartphone (they don't even need to open the app to activate it) they receive points called "kicks" that can be redeemed for a variety of rewards. Bonnie Gross, Target Vice President of Marketing and Guest Engagement said of the program. "We've learned from our guests that they appreciate being rewarded for doing what they already love to do—shopping at Target" (Planet Retail 2012b).

Shopkick is just one reward program example; customer recognition upon entry will increase in coming years. The shoppers' history and preferences will be used to greet them with special offers. The same personalization they receive online will be available in bricks and mortar stores.

To facilitate the greater use of digital technologies by the shopper, many retailers are starting to offer free Wi-Fi that is available for a limited time each day for the shopper. Other retailers are starting to use the iBeacon system which is a Bluetooth Low Energy signaling system that detects shoppers on entry and facilitates communication with them while they shop (Planet Retail 2014a).

There are other analogue examples where shoppers can scan their loyalty card at a kiosk upon entry and receive personalized coupons or other information. At the Ukrop supermarket in the United States that has this, the shopper is promised deals that are unadvertised and are frequently changing (PR Newswire n.d.). Walmart's Sam's Club stores in the United States also have an interactive kiosk system in-store which sends eValues coupons to shoppers' smartphones. The Sainsburys UK loyalty program, Nectar is available on an app and provides shoppers with personalized offers, a store locator, and loyalty point information (Planet Retail 2011).

Perhaps most interesting of all is the Asda UK trial of a female hologram that greets shoppers and provides information on their 10 percent price guarantee! (Planet Retail 2012c).

Navigating

As the shopper navigates around the store they are being offered information through apps on their smartphones to help them find products. Google is facilitating this by mapping the inside of retail stores in the same way it has mapped streets. In France major retailers have already begun using this service (Planet Retail 2012d).

In the United States, retailer Meijer has an app called "Find-it" that helps the shopper find the location of more than 100,000 items. In addition, it also provides information on special offers in the store (Planet Retail 2011).

The humble shopping cart is also undergoing a renovation to help the shopper. At Whole Foods Market in the United States, a cart has been launched that is fitted with a tablet to offer you deals, product information and help with navigation, all tailored to your needs via the swipe of your loyalty card (Planet Retail 2012e).

There is also MediaCart, a shopping cart that has voice control to help you find products, a bar code scanner to help you check prices and self-checkout, it also reads your loyalty card to offer tailored deals (Media Cart n.d.). Hellman's Mayonnaise in Brazil also recently ran an activation with a retailer where they put screens on carts that alerted the shopper when they were near foods that would go well with their product. In one month, 45,000 people used the carts and sales for Hellman's rose 68 percent (Hellmanns Brasil n.d.).

Scanning

There are many digital tools being used to help the shopper as they browse and some of them like TV screens have been around for quite a while.

The Walmart Smart TV Network is present in all U.S. stores; screens are placed at the entry to greet the shopper and explain how the system works. Then there are more located at the shopper's eye-level in the category and positioned near the products that they are providing information for, and others still positioned at the end of each aisle. Walmart released data showing that the system increased sales by up to 28 percent, but also had a positive effect on total category sales (Planet Retail 2011).

As the cost of LCD screen continues to fall we may also see more point-of-sale material replaced by interactive surfaces. At an Albert Heijn store in Amersfoort in the Netherlands, screens with prices and product shots are being tested above fresh produce. While in the Real Future store in Tönisvorst, Germany screens are used to aid segmentation in a new interactive chiller cabinet. There are also interactive touchscreens that offer product details, recipes, and information on healthy eating (Planet Retail 2013a).

Tesco have also been trialing interactive screen in-store that shoppers can use to browse clothing lines available in-store as well as an extended range online. Product ratings, reviews, and suggested accessories are also available. The shopper can then order for collection in-store or home delivery (Planet Retail 2013b).

One of the more interesting interactive screen solutions to recently launch was the P&G SoloHelath kiosk. The kiosk is in-store and in seven minutes allows the shopper to assess their vision, blood pressure, weight, and body mass index for free. It also provides health recommendations and links to local doctors who might be able to help them (My SoloHealth Station n.d.).

Smartphone-enabled augmented reality is also coming to a supermarket near you. This technology adds further information like recommendations or coupons when something like a poster, pack on shelf, or beer coaster is viewed through an app. A restaurant chain in the United States uses this technology to entertain children with a video game when they view their placemat, while Bulmer's Cider used it to illustrate the perfect pour and their extended range of flavors (Taylor 2012).

Point-of-sale material near the shelf is also being digitized through the use of e-paper. This technology provides flashing animation that works for up to a year without having to change batteries. The launch of Cherry Cole Zero at Asda in the UK used epaper, and the manufacturer claims that it can deliver an uplift in sales of 25 percent versus paper-only point of sale material (Promotional Marketing 2013).

Choosing

As the shopper zooms in on products they are considering, technology is helping them make a final decision.

Clairol's "Find Your Color" kiosk helps achieve this by delivering recommended hair coloring and broader care and style products based on your answer to a set of questions. More impressive though is the virtual mirror that retailers like Walmart, Carrefour, and Superdrug are using to allow shoppers to see how cosmetics look on them before deciding whether or not to buy. The mirror takes a picture of the person who then scans the barcodes of the products they are interested in testing. The products are then automatically applied and the shopper can print the image, send it by e-mail, or post it on Facebook (Passariello 2010).

Similar mirrors exist that allow clothes shoppers to see what items look like on without having to actually undress in the changing room (Diesel Ginza Interactive Mirror n.d.). At the Burberry flagship store in London, when a shopper approaches a mirror having tried on a piece of clothing, the mirror transforms into a screen and shows how the item was made and what it looked like on the catwalk (Dacre and Urwin 2012). A Tesco store in the UK has a Kids StyleMe Mirror which overlays cloths on a picture of the shopper using a gesture-based interface (Planet Retail 2013b). Marks and Spencer are bringing digital to the fitting room with the launch of their body shape scanning technology. The scanner is similar to that used for airport security and is available to collect measurements of a fully clothed person and then provide recommendations on the best size fit (Planet Retail 2012f).

Lego's digital box allows shoppers to see what the Lego model will look like when they build it. While the eyewear chain OPSM in Australia has a concept store that allows shoppers to test products for glare and wind resistance in a simulator room as well as interactive mirrors (PRweb 2010).

Social Media can also help people select a product. Using the insight that "when women go shopping most of them feel insecure and need a second opinion. Although just one second opinion is not enough to make the right decision about what to buy" (Cardoso n.d.) the clothing retailer C&A in Brazil launched the Like Hanger that displays how many likes a garment has on their Facebook page. In the UK, the clothing store Uniqlo has launched Tweet counter where the price of clothing is reduced every time a shopper sends a tweet about the item (Whitehead 2010).

The information used most often by the shopper is actually that which is on the package itself, although only 10 percent of shoppers actually turn a product around to read the information that is on the back of the pack. QR codes on the pack allow the shopper to access extended information about the product. In China, Carrefour have started using QR codes on the fruit and vegetables to allow shoppers to view information on provenance, licenses of vendors, and other information on the farm where the products came from (Planet Retail 2013c). QR codes are also used on point-of-sale material to provide the same information. However, in my experience they are rarely used by the shopper in the store.

There are also a plethora of retailer apps to help shoppers select their products. Carrefour, Tesco, Migros, and Globus have apps to help the shopper choose wine. Manufacturers too have apps to help with things like meal creation, or medicine selection.

Purchasing

The purchasing decision occurs when the shopper places the products in the basket and walks away to finish their shopping and eventually pay. At this point, the shopper finishes shopping the category and will need a subsequent trigger like an off-location display with the categories products to revert to shopping mode.

Waiting at the check-out is something that no shopper likes. However new technologies mean that waiting may soon be a thing of the past. Technology that allows the shopper to scan their products as they shop and then place them directly into bags in their carts is becoming more commonplace. The shopper can scan their own products using their smartphone or handheld scanners provided by the store (Bishop 2012; Planet Retail 2012a). At the register, payment is made against the totals that have been scanned. Random checks are conducted for accuracy but the prevailing attitude from retailers is that the loss of revenue from any nonreporting scanners will outweigh the savings from reduced cashiers' salaries or shopper dissatisfaction with queues.

Retailers like Auchan in France are also introducing new proprietary mobile payments systems that also link to loyalty and couponing systems (Planet Retail 2012b). These payment systems will increasingly integrate with apps like Apple's Passport to open instantly as shoppers approach payment areas.

At Asda in the UK even this is not necessary with their new rapid scanning tunnel that scans products as they move along the register conveyor belt in 0.6 seconds (cashiers take an average of three seconds) (Poulter 2013). There are other examples of retailers equipping staff with iPads or other mobile technologies to process payments at any point in the store. The benefits of these systems are that they remove any barrier like a counter top between the assistant and the shopper, making for a more personal transaction while at the same time saving the shopper the hassle of queuing (Batchelor 2012) (One step retail solutions n.d.).

After payment technology is also helping edify the shoppers' purchase decisions. Tesco launched (and then retracted) a tool that allowed you to send them the number on your receipt; they would then analyze it and e-mail you back with how much you saved by shopping with them. Walmart is testing something similar; you upload a photo of your grocery receipt from a competitor in the last week and they come back to you on e-mail with a price comparison (Planet Retail 2012c).

A word of warning though: shopping is inherently a task-led process; shoppers are often in a hurry and looking to complete their mission with as little wasted time as possible. Any technology deployed in this environment has to make the trip simpler and quicker to finish; otherwise it runs the risk of becoming yet another element of the clutter they have to de-select.

Top Tips

- Collate digital shopper insights along the path to purchase in the same way that you have for physical behavior in a retail setting.
- Audit your existing digital shopper marketing against the recommendations in this chapter.
- Deploy digital retail theater to test and learn what can help the shopper make their trip simpler and quicker to finish.

CHAPTER 12

The Key Points in This Chapter

- Price helps shoppers make purchase decisions in two main ways; first it helps them understand the expected quality of a product relative to a consideration set, and second it helps them allocate their budget.
- It is rare that even half of all shoppers are able to accurately recall what they paid for a product even seconds after buying it. Absolute prices are not something we choose to clutter our memory with, instead we rely on the retail setting to help us understand magnitude differences in price between products.
- We do not process all of the numerical information in a price. We use shortcuts in reading and understanding prices in the same way we do with other elements of the marketing mix that confront us in stores. As a result retailers are able to influence shopper behavior with price frames.
- Shopper marketing helps with price communication by either amplifying the brand's benefits, or framing the price in a way that enforces the product's value to the shopper.

Part A: The Importance of Pricing to Shoppers

"Jamie, why are you proposing a 2 percent price increase when inflation is only running at 0.5 percent?"

Amy had called Jamie in to talk about the Big Beverage Company price increase, which she had just received.

"Amy, our beans come from all over the world, so it's not reasonable to hold us to local inflation only."

"The people who come to Shopmart expect to find fair prices though, and raising coffee more than the real value of their pay checks is going to affect sales," replied Amy.

"Look, we make our own private label, so I know what coffee costs and what you are making on each jar of your Grande Blend. It's way more than we make." She continued.

"So is this about the shopper or the profit that Shopmart makes?" he asked.

Amy paused, "Jamie, what does one gallon of milk cost?"

"Pardon?"

"What does one gallon of milk cost?"

Silence.

"The shoppers we have know how much one gallon of milk costs; they use it as a benchmark to evaluate other prices. So how much is it?"

Jamie didn't know, and he didn't want to embarrass himself by guessing.

"Amy it's not our intention to upset anyone. But we have cost increases for raw materials and things like trade discounts that we have to pass on" he said patiently, trying to calm the rising tension.

Amy then de-escalated things by explaining, "we see that promotional sales are increasing for all categories as shoppers get better at using digital sites to scan through leaflets for the best deals. The second biggest mission we have in our stores today is the cherry picker topping up on a few promotional offers. So price is even more of a sensitive issue with us now than it has been in the past."

This was a hot topic at the Big Beverage Company too; the increase of sales generated through a promotional discount had been increasing with all their customers in the last few years. They attributed it to the rise of the savvy shopper from the global financial crisis, a person characterized by a desire to do more to get value for the scarcer family financial resources. The rise of digital platforms to curate deals across the market had indeed helped this shopper, but so had expanding numbers of products on promotion in retailers' stores.

Amy was still single, but her background was lower middle class. This, together with the everyday struggles of her sister, a stay at home mom who was raising two children on her husband's blue-collar wage, kept her tuned in to the importance of price as a marketing tool. And if that wasn't enough, at Shopmart, it was not unusual for their monthly team meeting to be interrupted by a pop quiz from her manager, Murray where they had to guess the price of leading products in a category like cake mixes or spices.

"Our price image supports our position in the market," Murray would often say after they had corrected each other's answers, and shared their disparaging results. "It's part of our brand and right at the top of why shoppers choose one retailer over another."

"It has to be a triple win Jamie, Shopmart, the Big Beverage Company and the shopper; that's what Project Java is supposed to be about isn't it?"

Where does this end? thought Jamie. We already give them over 20 percent in discounts and rebates and on top of that they make 15 percent margin on the retail price; if it keeps growing at the rate it is has been these last couple of years, one day that figure will be close to 40 percent. Can the Big Beverage Company even survive with that much profit erosion?

"I agree," replied Jamie but with just enough of a pause to indicate that he wasn't completely convinced.

"So I see how you win from this, but let's now discuss what we can do for the shopper and then after that, Shopmart. If we get the shopper bit right then that helps us both."

"Well we are going to hold the old promotional price for at least three months."

"That's a start," she replied.

"And we have some ideas on what we can do for Christmas too."

"Good, because Murray will want to know how we have resolved this before we show him any of the Project Java plans."

Part B: Shoppers' Interaction with Pricing

The focus of this section is shopper-facing prices, not the more prosaic topic of price negotiations with retailers.

The Role of Price

Price helps shoppers make purchase decisions in two main ways: first it helps them understand the expected quality of a product relative to a consideration set, and second it helps them allocate their budget.

Price is what is scarified in order to obtain the product; for this sacrifice to be acceptable it must be, at a minimum, equal to the product's benefits. When this occurs, the shopper sees a level of value that is satisfactory relative to the pain of paying.

Value = Benefits – Price

The shopper sees value therefore when benefits exceed price (Chen, Monroe, and Lou 1998).

Benefits include things like: the intrinsic quality of the product, the extrinsic attributes like packaging or purchase location, or hedonic elements like the self-expression associated with the product's consumption.

When the shopper is in-store and in the choosing step on their path to purchase, the calculation of value is an iterative process as they compare extrinsic elements (unless there is the chance to experience the intrinsic) of the products relative to the consumption and occasion needs they have (Jones 2012; Zeithaml 1988).

This process of comparison will occur even if the shopper has prior experience with the products, as the cues that signal product benefits change over time as new claims are made by the manufacturer, for example, "dishwashing liquid that now contains grease eating enzymes!" (Zeithaml 1988).

At this moment, if the balance between benefits and price is not right, the product can be quickly de-selected. Shopper marketing helps at this moment by either amplifying the brand's benefits, or framing the price in a way that enforces the product's value to the shopper.

Price Knowledge

When you ask a group of shoppers why they chose the particular store that they are visiting, price is never the first answer; instead they are more likely to cite location, convenience, or assortment as the key driver of their choice.

When we look at the shopper decision tree for a given category we also see price, or its twin—value—feature as tertiary considerations. This is true despite the relatively low cost associated with a few seconds of extra search to compare prices.

Not only is it a lower level decision-making factor at the store and category levels, but is also something we have a limited ability to accurately recall.

There is research to suggest that more affluent shoppers search prices less because they do not believe the costs are worth the return (Zeithaml 1988), while for shoppers who have lower incomes and tighter budgets price is more of a concern and as a result is more likely to be accurately recalled (McGoldrick and Marks 1987; Wakefield and Inman 1993).

What is also interesting is some of the emerging insights around price sensitivity online versus in-store for groceries. It seems that online grocery shoppers are less price sensitive when they buy online, a fact supported by research (Chu, Chintagunta, and Cebollada 2008), and the ad hoc comments from many European retailers.

Price Recall

From Italy to Hong Kong, when you stop shoppers just moments after buying products like beer, tampons, or baby powder, it is rare that even half of them are able to accurately recall what they paid for the product. However, they may be slightly better at telling you if it was more or less expensive than a comparable product (Dickson and Sawyer 1990; McGoldrick and Marks 1987). This tends to be the case as shoppers are better at recognizing a relatively good deal when they compare prices.

It seems that absolute prices are not something we choose to clutter our memory with, even if they have been a key factor in our purchase decision. Instead we rely on the retail setting to help us understand magnitude differences in price between products (Vanhuele and Drèze 2002) and on our underlying knowledge of the range of prices we expect to find in the category given our prior purchases (Monroe and Lee 1999).

It's not only after purchase that we have poor recall of prices; when we investigate price knowledge just before people set off on a shopping mission, we also find limited accuracy of the specific prices that will make up the majority of their baskets, though there are exceptions and caveats, which we will discuss later. Instead, it is price expectations of the given retailer that will often influence store choice decisions.

I suspect this is why I have yet to interact with a retailer in the capacity of product supplier, who doesn't consider price to be "very important for us." It seems to be the ubiquitous focus of retail commercial teams the world over. And this focus is disproportionately focused on promotional prices.

Promotional Prices

When we get a deal we feel both a sense of excitement and a sense of being a smart shopper (Chandon, Wansink, and Laurent 2000), the type of person who makes good decisions in both retail stores and life!

But it's not the size of the deal that's important; it's the relativity of the deal that's important. In this way the psychological impact of saving a $1 off of a $2 item is much greater than saving $1 off a $10 item (Chen, Monroe, and Lou 1998; Gendall et al. 2006; Grewal and Marmorstein 1994).

For retailers, the lift in volume caused by price promotions represents purchases that they hope are incremental to their total category sales. Their thinking is that shoppers use multiple stores, so try and win the purchase when they are walking down their aisle by incentivizing it via a price discount. The prevalence and ongoing use of price discount suggests that they believe in the effectiveness of this strategy.

But the way a retailer's overall price image is formed in the shopper's mind would appear to be much more complex than just the prices they have. Their advertising above and below the line, product range, retail theatre, pricing tickets, and service level all play a role in forming their price image (Zielke 2007).

Anchoring

I have often been in meetings with Walmart managers and heard them refer to the category's "opening price." This is the product with the lowest regular price in the category, and it is normally the private label. Their belief was that it was this price that was the anchor for the rest of the category.

Price anchors are the reference point that influences the shopper's perception of all other prices.

Price anchors can also be more general, average prices established through what the shopper regularly experiences in-store, and used to evaluate which sale prices are high, low, or neutral (Urbany, Bearden, and Weilbaker 1988).

There seems to be no agreement in the industry on what prices shoppers use to anchor their evaluations (Biswas, Wilson, and Licata 1993). Instead, it seems that when deciding whether or not to buy, shoppers have acceptable price ranges for products, when the price is within this range they buy and when it is outside they don't buy (Ariely, Loewenstein, and Prelec 2003). To this end, small changes around these reference price ranges produce no change in the shoppers' price perception (Monroe and Lee 1999).

Price Framing

Framing refers to the way that the price information is provided to the shopper. Here are some examples:

- Buy one get one free
- Was $2, now $1
- For a limited time only
- While stocks last
- 2 for the price of 1
- 50 percent off
- $1 plus shipping costs

Price framing is important because, despite the pervasiveness of prices in our daily life, we do not process all of the numerical information in the price. We use shortcuts in reading and understanding prices in the same way we do with other elements of the marketing mix that confront us in stores (Striving and Winer 1997).

When a shopper sees both a regular and promoted price together, the regular price is the reference frame from which the shopper can calculate perceived value. The more credible the reference price, the greater the impact (Urbany, Bearden, and Weilbaker 1988). While when it comes to cheap items, they actually prefer savings communicated as discounts rather than in currency terms, but the opposite is preferred for more expensive items (Chen, Monroe, and Lou 1998).

Behavior

Retailers are able to influence shopper behavior with price frames, some of the key framing elements they can use are listed below.

Price endings and beginnings

Shoppers read prices from left to right and when comparing products pay less attention to left digits that are the same for the products under consideration. When this occurs, they use the digits toward the right as the basis for their price comparisons (Poltrock and Schwartz 1984).

When the left most numbers are different though, shoppers will use them as the basis for their initial comparison.

Here is an example:

Option A: $79 $93, Option B: $75 $89

When tested many people report option A as being most different (Monroe and Lee 1999).

When a "9" is placed at the end of price in some markets like the United States, it will act as a sale sign and announce a deal to the shopper (Anderson and Simester 2003). In fact, research also suggests that shoppers have a preference for odd over even numbers. To this end, pricing below the nearest round number, for example, $1.99 instead of $2.00, produces better sales results for frequently purchased household products. This effect works when the left most digits are different and when the two prices are close in value, as in the example above (Thomas and Morwitz 2005).

This effect is produced because as shoppers we seem to trick our perception of magnitude by primarily referring the left most digit in price and rounding numbers down (Asamoah and Chovancová 2011; Thomas and Morwitz 2005).

A casual stroll through the aisle of the supermarket in most countries will give you an impression of the most popular price ending number. In my experience, you are most likely to see 0, 5 or 9.

Unit prices

Unit pricing refers to the presence on the price ticket of a relative price for a rounded quantity of the product. For example, a pack of 30 baby diapers might have a price of $21.95 and a unit price 0.73 cents per diaper. These unit prices are provided in the hope that they help the shopper make quicker judgments on the product's value.

There is some evidence to suggest that unit prices can actually lower the grocery expenditure of the household over time (Mortimer and Weeks 2013). However, there are also findings that indicate that shoppers find unit pricing confusing and don't use it (Mitchell, Lennard, and Mcgoldrick 2003). To this end, a study on unit pricing in Australia identified the fact that 60 percent of people would prefer unit prices to be more prominent and therefore easier to identify and read (choice.com.au 2011).

Colors

In another interesting test, it was found that males perceive greater saving when prices are shown in red versus black! (Puccinellia et al. 2013).

Physical distance between prices

Another interesting finding is that when it comes to the display of the standard shelf price, for example, $7 versus the sale price $5, a greater horizontal separation between these prices leads to higher discount perceptions. It seems that our internal "magnitude representations" is impacted by the space between the two prices (Coulter and Norberg 2009).

Font size

Another interesting example of this magnitude effect can be seen in pricing font size. When the regular price is in a larger font than the sale price, people perceive the sales price as small in comparison to when the sale price is written in a larger font than the regular price. It seems that font size helps the shopper distinguish between the regular and sale prices more quickly, which in turn impacts their perception of the size of the discount (Coulter and Norberg 2009).

Retailer leaflets

When you look at the front page of a retailer's leaflet, the products you see are most likely being sold at very small to negative margin when all operational costs are fully allocated. These are the items often referred to as loss leaders or signpost items that build traffic.

In some of the Asian and European markets that I have worked in, large jars of coffee, beer, and diapers are products that build traffic by causing shoppers to switch from their primary store to a secondary, less used store. The shopper will often be able to accurately recall the price for these products and will use them to form an expectation of all products within the store (Anderson and Simester 2003; Desai and Talukdar 2003; Helbling, Leibowitz, and Rettaliata 2011).

As such the retailer needs to offer competitive prices on these products as a way of ensuring the shopper that a trip to their store will provide the base-level value that they need to justify the visit. Once they are in the door, the hope is that they will fill their basket to the extent that the retailer makes net profit on their visit.

What they don't want is a "cherry picking" shopper who comes only on a specific need mission for the specials. Unfortunately though, the growth in online sites that provide across market summaries of what is on promotion at key retailers are driving up this specific need mission.

As the use of basket-level data to understand the profit from each transaction becomes more prevalent, my belief is that the use of loss leaders will decline significantly.

Words

Pricing messages displayed on point-of-sale material at the shelf, like "guaranteed price matching" can also help improve the shopper's perception of the store's overall pricing scheme (Anderson and Simester 2003).

Research has also shown that words can be used to reframe the price for larger items into smaller increments that our brains are better at processing. For example, a $1,200 a year gym membership will appear more attractive when it is advertised at $100 a month. In the same way, adjectives can moderate the price to reframe it; in tests "a small $5 fee" receives a response rate 20 percent higher than "a $5 fee" (Hayes 2012).

When messages like "limited to five bottles per shopper" are used to imply scarcity, the shopper will often respond favorably to the promotion, as long as the associated deal is plausible (Inmann, Peter, and Raghubir 1997).

Sale signs

Fact: the presence of a sale price in-store, without a price discount, has been shown to increase sales (Inman, McAlister, and Hoyer 1990).

The simple shelf flag that announces the price offer is often enough to capture the shopper's attention and trust. The fact that they have found motivating deals using these signs in the past re-enforces their relevance for finding deals in the future. However, when sale signs are placed on more than 30 percent of the products within the category, their effectiveness drops (Anderson and Simester 2003).

In this way, price promotions can improve the convenience and speed of shopping (Chandon, Wansink, and Laurent 2000).

Free versus percent off

Shoppers prefer getting something for free versus getting something cheaper. Paying for something means parting with our money while getting something free is a gain, not a loss, of our hard earned cash!

It also seems that we prefer double discounts, for example, 20 percent off plus another 25 percent versus a single discount of 45 percent (The Economist 2012b).

The task orientation of shopping and the strain that retail stores place on our cognitive abilities mean that shoppers often neglect base prices when processing percentage change information.

The interpretation of a percentage change requires a quick calculation on the standard price that is being changed; for example, a price discount presented as a 33 percent price reduction on a $1 can of beans (saving of 0.33 cents), and a bonus pack may be presented as 33 percent extra free on the same can.

When given a choice, we have a preference for more free versus a price discount, even when the economics of both offers is the same (Chen et al. 2012).

As an interesting aside, larger packs of familiar branded products also tend to be consumed faster due in part to the fact that we perceive that they have a lower unit cost per consumption; so, bonus packs can also play a role in shortening the interval between purchases (Wansink 1996).

Bundling

Price bundle promotions are where two products are offered to the shopper and a discount is provided if both are purchased.

These kinds of promotions have been shown to decrease price sensitivity and increase purchase likelihood while at the same time differentiating the offer. They can be especially useful for new products as the bundling with an existing product helps cue the new product's benefits (Stremersch and Tellis 2002).

Smaller bundles of two or three products tend to be viewed more favorably than larger bundles; this is most likely because the discount is easier to perceive given the cognitive demands of shopping (Krishna et al. 2002).

Premiums

Premiums such as a free hair brush or make-up kit can work better than price discounts for hedonic products (Chandon, Wansink, and Laurent 2000).

However, premiums can detract from value if they are not aspirational enough.

Shopper-Led Pricing Strategy

Promotional Price Strategy

Price promotions are the most maligned element of the marketing mix; as commercial people, we both love and hate them. They lift sales, encourage pantry loading in the home and by virtue of this, increase consumption as well as helping new products find first time buyers; but they also increase the shopper's price sensitivity to the regular price, reduce baseline sales, impact profit and can damage the long-term equity of the brand.

Yet, since the global financial crisis of 2008, the percentage of sales of products across Europe and Asia that are brought on promotion by the shopper has increased.

Price promotions have to be treated with the same strategic mind-set that is brought to other elements of the marketing mix and not simply be treated as a short-term tactic.

Some of the elements that need to be considered when creating a promotional strategy that is shopper-centric are discussed below.

- Profits
  It is a universal truth that you sell more at lower prices; of course to achieve this, the shopper must realize that you are offering a lower price than normal through appropriate in-store price frames. What isn't a universal truth though is that you will make more profit at lower prices.

  It is true that promotions encourage some shoppers to switch from their last purchased brand, or even last shopped retailer, but this often comes at a cost. This is lost profit given away at the lower promotional price to shoppers who would have purchased at the regular price anyway. To this end, research in the United States in 1999 found that a 5 percent increase in promotional depth or frequency can decrease profit margin 0.3 percent to 0.5 percent (Jedidi, Mela, and Gupta 1999).
- Elasticity
  Elasticity differs dramatically by category; for example, baby toiletries have much smaller sales lifts than does coffee.

  There is also a lot of energy spent trying to understand the source of incremental volume; for example, does it come from existing shoppers or from those that regularly buy other brands. Unfortunately, the results of these analyses are often spurious.

When evaluating store level scan data you may often find that stores in lower demographic areas produce lower promotional lifts for branded products. At first this may feel counter-intuitive; shouldn't lower income households buy more when prices drop? The answer is, not if the lower price means they still have to trade up from a lower priced item like a private label that they buy regularly. This finding was also reported by researchers who summarized that demographic variables have a much greater impact on elasticity than store-level competitive variables (Hoch et al. 1995).

- Stockpiling
  Household panel data confirms that stockpiling (or pantry loading as it is often called) of a given product can be driven by actions such as promotional prices or multipack offers. In turn, pantry loading in the home can lead to increased consumption, particularly of snacking foods in expandable consumption categories if it is readily available and visible to the household consumers (Chandon and Wansink 2002; Chandon and Wansink 2011).

  One explanation for increased consumption of what we pantry load is that we value these products less (Gourville and Soman 1998), but I think it is just more likely that we consume what we see! (Wansink 2010).

Creating Promotional Strategy

When creating a promotional strategy these are the key questions that need to be answered:

- What is the goal of the promotion?
- Which products to promote?
- Which channels to promote in?
- The frequency of your promotions?
- The depth (% discount) you want to offer?

I normally try and summarize the strategy in a table as per the example in Table 12.1 like this:

Table 12.1 *Example promotional strategy*

Product:	Baron Juice 1 liter glass bottle				
Goal:	Encourage shoppers on main shop missions, to lift home inventory for home consumption				
Competitive benchmark:	Lardy Juice 1 liter glass bottle				
Retail formats	**Frame**	**Promotional price**	**Frequency per year**	**% Elasticity (Estimate) (%)**	**ROI (Estimate)**
Hypermarkets	% Discount	1.99	6	120	3.1
	Buy 1 get 1 free	–	1	250	1.8
Supermarkets	% Discount	1.99	4	80	2.5
Convenience	% Discount	2.29	2	50	1.9
	50% More free	–	1	180	1.8
Traditional trade	% Discount	2.19	4	50	1.9

Executing Promotional Strategy In-Store

When it comes to executing the promotional strategy, you can also consider the following:

- Do not promote products that target a similar need or usage occasion at the same time.
- Ensure there is a defined gap between promotions.
- Prioritize certain price promotion frames; for example:
  - Buy one get one free
  - Two for the price of 1
- Ensure promotional price tickets:
  - have the regular price in a smaller font than the promotional price
  - ensure that the regular price and promotion price are separated by the width of the regular price
  - show the % discount
  - show the unit price
  - use a red font

Regular Price Strategy

It may be stating the obvious but price will significantly influence the profit of a supplier to the extent that a 1 percent price increase can lift profit by 8.7 percent, assuming no loss of volume (Baker, Kiewell, and Winkler 2014).

However, any shopper marketing activities involving price must be handled with care, as misleading claims can and will receive significant shopper backlash. After all, shoppers want to feel smart and anything you do that has the opposite effect can have a lasting impact, particularly given the social media platforms that allow for fast dissemination of anything the shopper deems unfair (Bertini and Gourville 2012).

When it comes to setting the regular shelf price strategy these are the key questions that need to be answered:

- Where does my brand equity (not gross profit!) allow me to price?

For example, at mainstream level below market leader.

- What are my pricing benchmarks at product level within the brand?
- Is the benchmark at a pack or unit level?
- Are the benchmarks within the shoppers' consideration set, and therefore something they could compare at shelf?

For example, using Listy mouthwash:

External: 15 to 20 percent premium per mL versus Plax

Internal: Base = Original and Coolmint to entice entry level shopper, Tier 1 = Tartar Control +10 percent to 15 percent per mL to Base, Tier 2 = Whitening +25 percent to 30 percent to Base

- How do larger packs communicate value?

  For example, in baby toiletries, larger packs (e.g., 750 mL) should always be at a 10 percent to 20 percent discount per mL to the next smallest pack (e.g., 500 mL).

  However, in other categories like beer, multipacks are often priced at a premium because of the convenience of having a heavy purchase packaged in a box with an easy carry handle.
- What is my pricing strategy?

  For example:

  Highest price per mL in the segment, to re-enforce equity as most efficacious mouthwash. Larger packs offering a discount on smaller packs to encourage trade up and volume in home.

Top Tips

- Understand the role that price plays in your Shopper Decision Tree.
- Create a promotional strategy that is shopper-centric and test different price frames to understand the impact they can have on shopper behavior.
- Create a trade standard on the way pricing information should be presented to the shopper in your category.
- Use the checklist in this chapter to create price strategy.

CHAPTER 13

The Key Points in This Chapter

- Packaging is the only guaranteed shopper marketing material in the store.
- Packaging sits next to the competition, so it is rarely considered in isolation. The design of the packaging can influence whether or not a shopper notices it on shelf.
- The shopper understanding that is incorporated into packaging design should help the shopper quickly and accurately understand: *Who Am I, What Am I*, and *Why Am I Good for You.*

Part A: Execution in the Real World

It was 8 a.m. and the shopping center was empty. The cafe was the only shop open; it was not the ideal place to meet Amy's boss Murray. A Monday morning "pow-wow" had been Murray's request though; "to discuss the Project Java proposal in-store."

"Please bring Reg," he added as a final line in his short e-mail, and so here they were drinking tepid cappuccinos, waiting for Murray and Amy to arrive.

They had presented to Murray the prior Wednesday, and he sent the note late the next day. That meeting had been cut short by an unnamed emergency that had taken him from the room a few slides before the end, and the abrupt close meant there was no discussion on whether or not to proceed with Project Java's actions. When Jamie had approached Amy later for feedback, she was none the wiser as the emergency had kept Murray away from his desk on Thursday and Friday.

"Amy just texted," said Jamie looking up. "She says they will be here in 15 minutes."

Reg had been his philosophical self about the meeting request, "if it was a 'no,' you would know by now. I'd say he just wants to test our commitment in a real world situation like this," and he lifted his hands to indicate the uninspiring surrounds they found themselves in.

Ben fidgeted with his phone, the daily sales SMS had just come through and the numbers were below expectations. Volume was down— again, but so were the net sales per kg, so they couldn't even bridge the gap with higher profit product.

"Let's head back into the store," said Reg "and go through the path to purchase one more time; this time in reverse. Let's start at the shelf and move backward to the entrance."

"I've got a quick call to make," said Ben. "Sales," he said motioning to his phone. They left him with the bill and a pained look on his face.

Simon led them from the coffee aisle back to the power aisle and then into the bakery and around the perimeter to the fresh department at the entrance. In each area of the store they passed through, Reg wanted to know what they thought the shoppers' key task would be, and therefore what would have the most chance of capturing their attention.

"Navigation signage, visuals and prominent display of the signpost brand have the best chance of helping with key task fulfillment. Anything that can be understood in 0.01 seconds helps. Things like this don't," and he pointed to a set of Tetley Tea shelf wobblers dangling below the brand on the shelf.

"So all that stuff we do to interrupt the shopper?"

"Interruption marketing is OK, but it doesn't help with task fulfillment. Not unless it's done in a way that is connected to the task. So I think that's OK," pointing to a display unit of crackers that was placed next to a circular cheese case.

"If you think about our coffee category vision, and the way we are proposing to activate it in-store, well part of that is definitely interrupting the shopper. In a sense, that is why we are going to place things in their way, but we want to do it in a way that is connected to the different missions they are on."

Reg made a ponderous "hmmmm" and was about to speak when Jamie announced that Amy and Murray had arrived.

They greeted each other at the entrance, Reg instigating the obligatory question about performance. Amy then appeared with the store manager, a harried, nervous looking man who they sensed had not been warned of their visit. He shook everyone's hand, nodding as Amy introduced him. He smiled through his discomfort and after a few minutes of awkward introduction to the store and its performance, extracted himself.

"So, I asked you to be here today to hear a little more about your plans in the real world environment. Twenty-five years of retail experience tells me that brands grow because of what is done out there," motioning outside the store, "and then executed in here, but your plans are to do much more in here with us. We're better merchants than we are communication partners, so let's discuss it slowly, with the person who pays my wages, our shoppers, in mind."

Reg nodded, "thanks for the chance to do that. This kind of thinking is new for us too, so we want to make sure you're on board before we invest." The slight emphasis on the word invest conveying the message that money, not just hopes, was backing this up.

Amy took over, "so why don't we start this just outside the store and follow the shopper along and talk about the plans."

"Actually," said Reg "if it's OK, can we start with a coffee from this little place?" pointing at the cafe. "This kind of cafe is the most common type of outlet for the general population; it will show us what we're up against in winning more in your stores."

"Let's get it take away then," replied Murray checking his watch, "I only have 90 minutes."

"No problem."

In the short time Simon had been with the Big Beverage Company, he had learned many things about general management from watching Reg. His clear, direct feedback style, the moment to set up objectives for meetings before discussion started, and his way of managing by walking-around, to get quick unsolicited information about the drivers behind performance. But perhaps the most subtle and effective trait he had noticed, and was now trying to adopt, was the simple way he primed people before engaging with them. If the catalyst for this project had been a trip to Starbucks by Murray and Amy, then its continuation would spring from the knowledge that most cafe coffee was not good, and was therefore a profit source that Shopmart could and should access.

While they waited for their order, Simon pulled out some Hot Shot product samples from his bag. "I got these last week," handing them across to Amy. "They're from Canada where they have a range of six now; this is the best seller and that one the new product."

Amy turned them around, moving away from the shadow cast by Simon and Jamie to get a better view.

"They must be displayed in the outer packaging; this wouldn't work on the shelf would it?"

"They are, but I only have a picture of that," he pulled a sheet of A4 paper from his bag.

Jamie leaned across Amy's shoulder to see the image. It was a pixelated shot of the die-line and not the actual pack assembled and sitting on the shelf.

"Looks pretty drab to me!" They both looked at Simon for confirmation. At that point, Ben appeared and handed them each a coffee.

"I'll get a better example to share." And he quickly packed away the image and the samples before they further deflated, and thereby primed, the mood heading back into the store.

Over the next hour, they moved around the store at a slow pace; "nothing at all like the shopper!" Amy reminded them at one point. In the coffee aisle, they watched from a discreet distance as a middle-aged woman in her gym sweats deliberated for an interminable 90 seconds over two types of filter coffee. Murray was stoic as the lady oscillated, but Amy was more enthusiastic, muffling a cheer as she placed the chosen jar in her cart. "That's not unusual," added Simon. "Dwell time in coffee is one of the longer ones in the store."

The most contentious conversations were in the fresh area, where the discussion was firstly about the role of beans and whether operations could manage them among the potatoes and apples. Murray was skeptical but willing to try the idea. "They're not as fragile as stone fruits and lettuce, but wastage will be a concern, as will be handling. We also need to make sure the scent doesn't overpower the rest of the department."

It then turned to coffee carts and whether they were possible at the store entrance beside the fresh area. "The list of barriers they would need to overcome was a long one," warned Murray; "but if that's the standard we're up against," pointing back to the café, "then we would be silly not to at least pilot it." Reg promised that he would stay very close to the details on their side, including the analysis of what the impact is to the other cafes close-by; "we want this to be incremental, not a PR issue." Murray nodded. "From your point of view though, anything we can do to improve the overall delivery of coffee to the consumer has to help." It was Reg's turn to nod, "yes, we want to build more passion for coffee culture." Simon smiled at the sound of the category vision.

The session ended at the entrance to the store. "Reg," said Murray, "if you're willing to pay for the trial and move forward on the launch with us first, then I'm willing to support a pilot of the structural changes to the category and store."

"Done," replied Reg.

"Amy, pick five stores spread across the state and take a summary to the monthly operations meeting."

"No thanks, not until you get some results," this time looking at Simon and Jamie as well, "until then it's just a good idea." And they shook hands.

Part B: Packaging

Packaging is the only guaranteed shopper marketing material in the store. It is the silent sales person that sits on the shelf every moment of every day selling the benefits of your brand to shoppers. Through the elements of its design it imparts value on the actual product it contains and helps transform its economic value.

The focus of this chapter is the packaging that faces shoppers and how they interact with it, and based on this understanding, implications for packaging design.

The objective of shopper facing packaging is to sell a product (Rundh 2009; Vitalija Butkeviciene 2008). To be able to do this, it must:

1. Attract attention
2. Provide the necessary information to the shopper
3. Differentiate the product among its competitive set

This is important because packaging is inherently comparative in nature in that it sits next to the competition. For this reason, it is rarely considered in isolation. This differentiates it from many other types of advertising that are often viewed apart from their competitors.

However, shoppers spend only a few seconds comparing products or even looking at the package they are buying and, perhaps because of this, 70 percent of shoppers reported having purchased a wrong product within the last year (Ahern 2010; Young 2005).

Shoppers Recognize Products Using Color and Shape

Shoppers recognize products using color and shape, they use them as a shortcut to de-select what is not relevant and conversely to find what they are searching for (Morton 2004; Rundh 2009; Scamell-Katz 2012; Scott Young 2009a; Young 2004; 2008).

Some examples of colors and shapes that you might be familiar with are:

- The red and white Marlboro pack
- The absolute vodka bottle shape
- The Coke white font on a red background

This is one of the reasons why changes to a pack's color and shape can affect sales. In fact, industry research shows that only 10 percent of pack changes increase sales while 20 percent decrease sales (Packaging News 2011; Young 2010). In the United States, PepsiCo discovered this in 2009 when they changed the packaging for their market leading juice brand Tropicana. On January 8, their new pack started to appear in stores; the orange color on the new pack was quite different, the branding had been reduced and the benefit claim "100 percent Orange Juice" significantly increased.

However, by February 23, the company announced that it would be moving back to the old packaging. Why? They had lost 2 percent of sales or about $35 million in the two months the new product had been on the shelves (Young and Ciummo 2009).

The learning: shopper confusion at the shelf happens when multiple pack equity components are changed at once.

Even Coca Cola, one of the world's great packaging owners recently made this mistake! In 2011 they introduced over a billion white polar bear cans to replace their red can as part of a World Wildlife Fund campaign to highlight the threat to the bears' habitat.

Unfortunately, people confused this new polar bear can for the silver Diet Coke can. As a result their complaint line was flooded with calls, the most serious of which came from diabetics who drank the full sugar red can liquid by mistake (*Daily Mail* 2011).

Polar bear can replaces red can   Shoppers think they are buying diet coke

In my experience, using eye tracking tests, about a half to one-third of the products in a category are not seen by the shopper when scanning the category for even the briefest of moments, so being seen is the primary objective of packaging.

Because of this, use packaging to maximize visibility first before considering any other issue!

(But remember that shelf space return for retailer is a critical consideration, so vertical orientation is often better than horizontal)

And then think about shop-ability as a secondary consideration.

Shop-ability is one of those made-up business words that you won't find in the dictionary. It means the ease with which a shopper can differentiate products within a range. As a brand line is extended and new benefits introduced, the ability of the shopper to quickly differentiate between products is essential, particularly if there are products within the range that are more premium. To this end, it is important that products within a range have a consistent layout in terms of the variables, which we will discuss in this chapter (Synovate BrandLife 2011; Young 2008).

Shoppers Are Drawn to Packaging Elements That Cause the Greatest Contrast from the Products Around Them (Jonathan Asher 2011)

A great example of using contrast to highlight your product comes from Coke and the *birth of the contour bottle.*

"Bottlers worried that the straight-sided Coca-Cola bottle was easily confused with imitators. A group representing the Company and bottlers asked glass manufacturers to offer ideas for a distinctive bottle. A design from the Root Glass Company of Terre Haute, Indiana won enthusiastic approval in 1915 and was introduced in 1916. The contour bottle became one of the few packages ever granted trademark status by the U.S. Patent Office. Today, it's one of the most recognized icons in the world—even in the dark!" (Coca Cola Company n.d.)

In recent times, products that have succeeded thanks in part to strong contrast on the shelf from their competitors are Pringles Chips in the iconic cylinder and Garnier Hair Care which was launched in bright green to stand out from its predominately white competitors.

However, when trying to attract the shopper through contrast, it's important to know that shoppers have an internal category code when it comes to products within a given category; deviation from this has the potential to cause confusion (Block 1995).

Because of this, decide whether you want to create contrast from your brand footprint or the category code using color and shape.

In this context, contrast can be defined as using opposing design elements from those presently used in the category.

The difficulty with using contrast is that it must not be so strange within the category that it fails to convert increased attention into shopper consideration.

The Form (Shape, Color, and Label) of a Product Provides Information to the Shopper Around Suitability

A product's form (shape, color, and label) communicates information to shoppers more quickly than the individual components of its packaging. It creates the initial impression and generates inferences regarding other product characteristics such as durability, value, technical sophistication, ease of use, sex role appropriateness, and prestige (Block 1995). In this way, visual elements transfer nonverbal information (Vitalija Butkeviciene 2008).

When it comes to form, shoppers prefer proportion and unity (Veryzer 1993), while there is some research to suggest that the most preferred shape by shoppers is rectangles (Raghubir and Greenleaf 2006). This is important if you are trying to design a product that breaks the category code to capture attention.

An interesting side about package size is that shoppers are less responsive to package size changes than to package price. A Nielsen study in 2007 concluded that "the demand elasticity with respect to package size is approximately one-fourth of the magnitude of the demand elasticity with respect to price" (Cakir and Balagtas n.d.).

When packaging shape is able to attract more attention than those around it, it is also perceived as containing greater volume than same-sized packs that receive less attention! (Folkes and Matta 2004)

Because of this, understand both the consumer and the usage occasion that the package will meet and make sure that your packaging is appropriate.

In my experience, packages that are designed to call out the target usage occasion stand the best chance of being chosen by shoppers who are under time and cognitive pressures.

Shoppers Scan Three to Four Messages on the Front of the Pack If Selecting It

Shoppers read three to four messages on the front; these predominantly follow the pattern of: branding—product descriptor—main visual—primary claim. They start at the dominant visual element, which is often the branding (though in developing markets where branding is less developed it might be the main visual) (Asher 2010; Asher 2011b; Asadollahi and Givee 2011; Scott and Vincenzo 2009b).

Viewing time, if selected, is rarely longer than seven seconds (Scott and Vincenzo 2009b), while less than 10 percent of shoppers turn packaging around to view the back (Asher 2011b). The latter statistic is always surprising given the increase in interest for nutritional information that is often reported by academics and research houses (Vijaykumar et al. 2013). The gap between interest in nutritional information and actual examination of the pack in-store is most likely driven by the fact that 59 percent of shoppers find the nutritional information confusing (Grant 2012). However, the recent trend bringing nutritional information to the front of the pack may help in increasing awareness and understanding of this kind of information (Asher 2011).

The net weight of the product is not typically something they scan either, instead they rely on the size of the pack and the picture on the front for guidance (Lennard et al. 2001). When it comes to the picture, shoppers believe that packages with a higher number of units in the main visual, for example, 15 pretzels versus three, actually have a higher product quantity inside (Madzharov and Block 2010). While when it comes to size, there is research to suggest that shoppers purchase fewer of a taller, versus shorter pack with the same quantity. In a twist to this finding, researchers also found that the shopper believed that bottles contained less than a can with the same volume (Yang and Raghubir 2005).

Unfortunately, many of us fall into the trap of placing more information on the front of the pack in the hope that it will win a shopper; however, the reality is that as additional information is added it dilutes the impact of the other elements (Young 2005).

Because of this, prioritize the front panel and the four key visual elements; do not rely on the back panel.

The four key visual elements are the: brand, descriptor, main visual, and key claim.

For viewing simplicity, it is also better to arrange the four elements so that they can be seen in cascading order, in a single visual sweep that can be completed within one second (which equates to three eye fixations) (Steffens, Egner, and Scheier 2003).

It is my belief that in the future a fifth visual element will become important also, and that is the sustainability message. Today, only 25 percent to 30 percent actually see the environmental message even if they select the product, but this will change significantly (Asher 2011a). Retailers like Tesco and Walmart are actively requesting that suppliers put in place plans to reduce the layers of packaging, while manufacturers are moving toward sustainability messaging like carbon foot printing on labels or how recyclable it is (IGD 2011a). Shoppers are increasingly looking for sustainability messages, and they would prefer them to be consistent across retailers. Where a tie break between product preferences exists, this issue may very well decide which product is selected.

Remember that claims will not compensate for unappealing packaging design so the goal has to be to capture attention so that the shopper will see your product and then scan toward your key claim.

Also, understand the visual equities and their meaning to the shopper. Design should be grounded in an awareness of the key visual elements and what the shopper associates with them. So, for example, if you have a crown on the front of your product, understand what that crown stands for and why it is useful for the shopper.

The main visual will communicate information about the brand equity positions and the sensory experience of consumption; as a result, it will influence the core brand beliefs and should be chosen very carefully (Underwood and Burke 2001; Underwood and Klein 2002).

I have always had a preference for visuals that convey energy (e.g., rising steam) or movement (the crunch from flying cookie chips) and increasingly neuroscience-based case studies are finding that these packs have high emotional engagement with the shopper (Young 2011).

Images and their placement on the package can also be used to infer the weight of the product. Our tendency to associate things on the ground as heavy and things in the air as light, applies to pack images such that if we see a cookie, for example, floating on the pack we may assume that it is relatively light. We also associate products that are more to the right of a pack to be heavier, while a package that shows a scenic vista will also be inferred as heavier by the shopper (Kahn and Deng 2011).

However, the size of this visual is not necessarily as important; the eyes can process pictures so quickly that size doesn't matter says Michel Wedel, professor of consumer science at the University of Maryland's Robert H. Smith School of Business (Glazer 2012).

If It Is a Sub-Brand Put the Claim in the Name

For sub-brands, a claim in a name is important. This will allow the shopper to more quickly navigate through the range. Good examples include: Diet Coke, Benylin Dry Cough, or Miller Lite.

It is important to get the balance in size right between the parent brand name and the sub-branding line. As a guide, the parent brand should always help the shopper find the product and the sub-brand assist with shopability and therefore choice across the range.

Shoppers Recall Packaging More Readily When Words Are on the Right and Pictures Are on the Left

Research shows that we absorb visual information more readily from the left side and verbal information from a right side. Under conditions of rapid perception, for example, scanning packs while walking along the aisle in a supermarket, the positioning of the elements in a pack design make the difference between identifying and missing the item concerned (Brewer 2000).

Because of this, words should be on right-hand side of packs, and pictures should be on the left.

The Majority of Shoppers Who Touch Products Go On to Buy

In many of the shopper studies I have been involved with, the correlation between touch at the main shelf and eventual purchase is very high. However, this correlation drops when the shopper touches products on display away from the main shelf.

Because of this, try to find ways to invite the shopper to touch the product.

An interesting execution of this idea came from Heineken in 2011 where they introduced the new touch can. Filip Wouters, vice president of marketing for Heineken, said at the time that, "the innovative ink technology creates a unique texture that is immediately noticeable and creates a more enjoyable drinking experience for our consumers through the sense of touch. The new design stands out better on shelf, in the cold box and on display" (BarBizMag 2011).

The Environment Around the Packaging: Lighting, Shelving, and so on Influence How It Is Perceived

The atmosphere around the product, as discussed in Chapter 9, will also influence purchase. This is particularly true for prestige products as the atmospherics serve as informational cues (Morton 2004).

Because of this, understand the environment that your product will be viewed in and compensate accordingly. Think about:
1. *Lighting.*
2. *The fact that products are often turned around so that their label is not facing the front.*
3. *The way that tertiary packaging can hide branding.*
4. *And the height from the ground the product is likely to be displayed at.*

Shoppers look for a connection between the packaging and what is inside

Humans have a subconscious desire for continuity and by linking the product at hand with the place or ingredients or contributors from which it is made, you help them connect what's outside with what's inside (Block 1995; Winnett and Pohlmann 2011; Young 2004).

Because of this, try to find ways to bring the inside to the outside.

A great example of this is Domestos Sink & Pipe Unblocker 500 mL. The packaging illustrates what the product does.

Despite the risks associated with packaging changes, it is something that many companies still practice. The primary drivers of this decision seem to be either:

A. To try and win a second glance from the shopper who de-selects and does not regularly buy the product.

Figure 13.1 Domestos Sink & Pipe Unblocker

Source: Ocado: The online supermarket.

B. Building equity against a new or under-performing dimension.

C. Reducing cost by downsizing.

To safeguard against packaging failure, I always use this scorecard to evaluate the new design.

Packaging Scorecard

Who am I?: Catching the eye and expressing the brand equity

- If the objective is interruption: how strong is the packaging contrast to the rest of the brand or category?
- If the objective is to help the shopper: how well does the packaging help shop-ability?
- Regardless of the objective: how strong is the contrast to identify the key visual element?
- Are the words to the right and the main visual to the left?

What am I?: Communicating the contents

- Do the four key visual elements flow in sequence on the front panel? (branding, product descriptor, main visual, primary claim)
- If I turn around the pack, what is the most noticeable visual? Is this what the shopper would be looking for?
- If it is multilingual packaging, then is copy minimized and one language prioritized? Are the languages grouped together?
- If shelf ready packaging is being used, does it help increase visibility or overcome a purchase barrier?
- If it is a sub-brand, then is the product claim in the descriptor?
- Is the packaging easy for the shopper to take down from the shelf and place in their basket?

Why am I right for you?: closing the sale

- Is there a single, coherent claim on the front panel?

- How unique is the primary claim relative to the rest of the category?
- If the packaging provides a functional benefit, like handling, storage, opening, re-closing, dispensing or improved sustainability, then is this evident to the shopper without the need for copy claims?
- If the packaging is for traditional stores, then are the seal tamper proof and the best before date clear?
- Is the packaging maximized to provide GMROI for the retailer?

Top Tips

- Understand the color and shape combination the shopper uses to identify key products.
- Use the packaging scorecard in this chapter to gather a selection of good and bad packaging examples from different categories.
- Use the packaging scorecard in this chapter to both evaluate your existing design and inform new design.
- Ensure that packaging design is co-created with shopper and consumer marketing teams.

CHAPTER 14

The Key Points in This Chapter

- The energy for shopper marketing is maintained by capturing learning. When this learning is captured together with retail partners it creates a return force that generates momentum for more ambitious targets, new activations, and execution.

Part A: Celebrating

The convention center was like a cavernous tribal council, with tables of ten populated by the vast Shopmart supplier community. It was the Annual Supplier of the Year awards, with all money raised going to the state's largest children's hospital. That, and the promise of entertainment from one of the country's oldest and most enduring rock stars, had led to what Amy described as "record attendance!"

The awards had a long and illustrious history. Started as a way to reward better supply and service when Shopmart had only a small share of the industry, they had grown in importance as their market share had risen. The skeptics viewed them as a reward for increased investment, but the more pragmatic saw them as a good benchmark on how your offer compared within industry.

"We don't just sell brands," Reg liked to remind them. "We sell a value bundle to the customer that includes distribution support, innovation, trade marketing, equipment, and some of the best marketing in the country."

It was early in the evening and the chinking of knives and forks on porcelain coupled with the unsteady din of conversation made it difficult to talk with people more than two chairs apart. Jamie was on Simon's left.

"Cheers," he said raising his glass to Simon.

His son Rory had spent the first three months of his life connected to a terrible array of tubes and cables in the same children's hospital that tonight was supporting. There had been problems with his heart; valves that didn't function with the tempo and cadence that was expected. His wife had been stoic throughout the ordeal, but Jamie was a tangle of emotion at the best of times and had struggled.

"Come on you lot, money for raffle tickets please!" said Jamie as each table had an allotment to sell and given Jamie's connection to the hospital he had nominated himself table captain.

As money was extracted from wallets, Murray shuffled onto the stage to begin the official proceedings.

There were well over 20 awards to be presented throughout the evening; the name of each was printed on the reverse side of the table menu. They were designed to cover all sizes of suppliers and categories, as well as functions like supply chain, IT, and of course the main one: commercial. There was one grand prize, and that was the one Jamie thought they had a chance at winning: The Supplier of the Year. He was alone in his optimism though; they had only just rolled their planogram out to all stores, while the coffee cart and fresh beans pilot had been extended to 20 stores. They had just run their first shopper marketing campaign too—Energy for the Home CEO—and while the results had been promising, data were not yet available for a full analysis.

Murray was not the most dynamic speaker; he squirmed like a toddler waiting for the toilet and was quite happy to have the general welcome over and the night's MC replace him.

The awards got started; as there was no orchestra to cut off effusive acceptance speeches, they dragged on well into dessert. In the quiet that followed the applause after each prize, Reg was at his droll best, entertaining them all with an easy socialness. The winter months had not been good for sales; they were well behind last year's level with little luck of closing the gap in the months that remained. As performance had declined, Project Java had grown in prominence; Reg was now using it with his seniors as an example of what could be done to "grow the baseline in hard times." Simon was even asked to present the plan to the regional president.

"No promises," said Reg when talking to him about the opportunity; "but we're thinking about increasing our focus on shopper marketing," emphasizing the phrase to indicate that he now accepted it as a function separate from trade marketing, "so do a good job, as you don't know where this could lead."

When dessert had been cleared away, the Shopmart CEO Roger Darley appeared on stage with the MC. A storied veteran who had started his journey to the top from the shop floor, he was well liked and respected as a businessman of high ethics and community values. When towns were flooded or wild fires rampant, he would often be seen in the background distributing food and blankets, and then later when the situation was stable he would lead the efforts to raise money to re-build. In the era of rock-star CEOs, he was a reminder of the gentler and more humble style of leadership.

As he spoke, Jamie tightened the knot on his tie and brushed the breadcrumbs from his jacket in anticipation of being called to the stage to receive the Supplier of the Year award. When the name was called though it was not theirs, it was a dairy supplier from the far south of the country. They all clapped as an ebullient team of mixed gender and age from the table to their right hugged and high-fived their way to the stage. The Shopmart CEO explained that they had won for their innovation in packaging, supply chain efficiency, and focus on category development in-store.

When the acceptance speech was finished and the obligatory photos taken, the MC appeared to close the formal part of the evening and announce the imminent performance of the band, "it's going to get loud!" she warned with a screech.

"That might be my cue to retire to the back-bar," announced Reg. "I can see a few other old commercial travelers scattered around who might like to commiserate over a few drinks." He said it with a cheeky smile though.

Before he could leave though, Murray arrived at their table with Amy.

"Having fun?" asked Amy. Jamie smiled through his disappointment and rose to greet her.

"Just wanted to tell you that we didn't consider you this year," said Murray shaking hands with Reg and nodding to the others at the table.

"We thought so" said Reg.

"Right now we have promising signs but not a full roll out."

"But keep it up," he said looking at Simon and Jamie, "and you'll be right in it next year."

"Thanks," they both said.

Murray leaned closer to speak to Reg and so Amy moved toward Jamie to ask after Rory. Jamie updated her using the word "my son," and for Simon it was both a wonderful and heart-breaking sound.

Simon's phone beeped and he looked down to find a text from his wife, "????"

"Not this year." he tapped back.

"And thanks for the updated packaging," said Amy turning to Simon. "It looks so much better!"

"I'm glad you like it; took a lot of work to get approval on that one believe it or not. Getting people to think from the shopper back, takes time."

Amy smiled, "well, at least we're on our way now."

"Yeah, you're right," he said with a tired smile.

Part B: RACER!

The R at the end of RACER! stands for the recommendation on what to roll out. The Big Beverage Company and Shopmart have made some decisions regarding this, but are testing further in other areas before proceeding.

The exclamation point at the end RACER! though is perhaps the most important; it is where you announce the learning and the journey you have undertaken together to senior management of both companies so that everyone knows progress is being made.

The energy that this creates should return you to the A step, where you align again on an objective for expanded trials. This loop is important as it entrenches the learning and creates a growth platform with the retailer that is distinct from price promotions and trading terms growth. To this end, IGD in Europe recently found that 79 percent of retailers are looking to suppliers to develop greater capability in turning shopper insight into activation, whereas over half of retailers are looking for suppliers to develop bespoke shopper programs for each of their store formats (Walters 2013).

The Energy from Learning

The energy for shopper marketing is maintained by capturing learning. When this learning is captured together with your retail partners, it creates a return force that generates momentum for more ambitious targets, new activations, and execution.

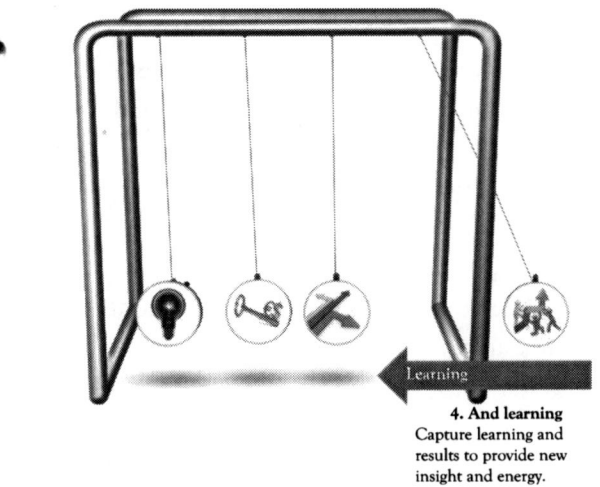

4. And learning
Capture learning and
results to provide new
insight and energy.

Business is a race to learn faster than your competition not simply the race to market as it was in the 1990s and 2000s when the range in grocery stores expanded exponentially. This race requires learning to be curated from markets and geographies beyond the ones you work within as well.

This learning then needs to be captured and made available for others to build upon. The most effective way I have found of doing this is to create a path to purchase guidelines. These guidelines are physical or digital collections of insights, learnings, and execution standards gathered over time from multiple locations.

Taking the time to capture these examples and learnings is also a way to ensure investment in finance and other resource is maximized. The consumer marketing community has been very good at this for many years, and now it is the time for shopper marketing to do this as well.

The Final Word

Shopper marketing is indeed something that can be used as a coalescing force for retailers and manufacturers, but it is also something that can be undertaken without retailer involvement and as a guiding principle, rather than new activity, for customer and trade marketing teams. It is way of working that helps improve the effectiveness of materials that are placed in front of the shoppers who ultimately dictate the success of all organizations.

Shopper marketing is the next evolution of trade marketing, and this reinvention is already well underway across the world. The retail space has been a medium strong enough to build brand equity for a long time now, but only in recent times have retailers moved beyond single generic strategies for their categories and become interested in the shopper as a source of competitive advantage. This has created the oxygen for shopper marketing to grow.

It is both an art and a science and becoming a popular area for job growth. I just searched for the term "shopper" in the job section on LinkedIn.com and returned 8,960 jobs (whereas there were 24,761 jobs listed under the search term "trade marketing"). Whether or not this number grows over time will be influenced by the performance of the people doing this job today! My hope is that this small book in some way will help shopper marketers everywhere, and (because I love meeting a KPI) the number of people practicing shopper marketing will steadily grow over time.

References

Ahern, D. 2010. "Winning the On-Shelf War." Webinar March 11, 2010. http://www.pmalink.org

Ailawadi, K.L., and K.L. Keller. 2004. "Understanding Retail Branding: Conceptual Insights and Research Priorities." *Journal of Retailing* 80, no. 4, pp. 331–42.

Allen, J., F.F. Reichheld, B. Hamilton, and R. Markey. 2005. *Closing the Delivery Gap.* Bain & Company.

Alter, A.L., and D.M. Oppenheimer. 2009. "Uniting the Tribes of Fluency to Form a Metacognitive Nation." *Personality and Social Psychology Review* 13, no. 3, pp. 219–35.

Anderson, E., and D. Simester. 2003. "Mind Your Pricing Cues." *Harvard Business Review,* September, pp. 96–103.

Andersson, P.K., P. Kristensson, E. Wastlund, and A. Gustafsson. 2012. "Let the Music Play or Not: The Influence of Background Music on Consumer Behaviour." *Journal of Retailing and Consumer Services* 19, no. 6, pp. 553–60.

Areni, C.S., and D. Kim. 1993. "The Influence of Background Music on Shopping Behavior: Classical Versus Top-Forty Music in a Wine Store." *Advances in Consumer Research* 20, no. 1, pp. 336–40.

Areni, C., and D. Kim. 1994. "The Influence of In-Store Lighting on Consumers' Examination of Merchandise in a Wine Store." *International Journal of Research in Marketing* 11, no. 2, pp. 117–25.

Areni, C.S., D.F. Duhan, and P. Kiecker. 1999. "Point-of-Purchase Displays, Product Organization, and Brand Purchase Likelihoods." *Journal of the Academy of Marketing Science* 27, no. 4, pp. 428–41.

Ariely, D., G. Loewenstein, and D. Prelec. February 2003. "'Coherent Arbitrariness': Stable Demand Curves Without Stable Preferences." *The Quarterly Journal of Economics* 118, no. 1, pp. 73–106.

Armel, K.C., A. Beaumel, and A. Rangel. June 2008. "Biasing Simple Choices by Manipulating Relative Visual Attention." *Judgment and Decision Making* 3, no. 5, pp. 396–403.

Asadollahi, A., and M. Givee. 2011. "The Role of Graphic Design in Packaging and Sales of Product in Iran." *Contemporary Marketing Review* 1, no. 5 pp. 30–34.

Asamoah, E.S., and M. Chovancová. 2011. "The Influence of Price Endings on Consumer Behavior: An Application of the Psychology of Perception." *Acta Universitatis Agriculturae et Silviculturae Mendelianae Brunensis* LIX 3 no. 7, pp. 29–38.

Asher, J. November 2010. "Effective Packaging: An Essential Tool for Success." Retrieved June 7, 2012 from http://www.prsresearch.com/fileUploads/Effective_Packaging_PL_Buyer_Nov_2010.pdf

Asher, J. 2011a. "Battling the Backlash." *Brand Packaging*, August, pp. 18–19.

Asher, J. March 2011b. "Healthier Package Design." Retrieved June 7, 2012 from http://www.prsresearch.com/fileUploads/Healthier_Package_Design_Pack_Design_Mag_March_2011_edit.pdf

Atalay, S.A., O.H. Bodur, and D. Rasolofoarison. 2012. "Shining in the Center: Central Gaze Cascade Effect on Product Choice." *Journal of Consumer Research* 39, no. 4, pp. 848–66.

Attwood, A.S., N.E. Scott-Samuel, G. Stothart, and M.R. Munafo. 2012. "Glass Shape Influences Consumption Rate for Alcoholic Beverages." *PLoS One* 7, no. 8, p. e43007.

Babin J.B., M.D. Hardesty, and A.T. Suter. 2003. "Color and Shopping Intentions: The Intervening Effect of Price Fairness and Perceived Affect." *Journal of Business Research* 56, no. 7, pp. 541–51.

Babin, B.J., W.R. Darden, and M. Griffin. 1994. "Work and/or Fun: Measuring Hedonic and Utilitarian Shopping Value." *Journal of Consumer Research* 20, no. 4, pp. 644–56.

Backstrom, K., and U. Johansson. 2006. "Creating and Consuming Experiences in Retail Store Environments: Comparing Retailer and Consumer Perspectives." *Journal of Retailing and Consumer Services* 13, no. 6, pp. 417–30.

Baker, J., D. Grewal, and M. Levy. Winter 1992. "An Experimental Approach to Making Retail Store Environmental Decisions." *Journal of Retailing* 68, no. 4, p. 445.

Baker, J., D. Grewal, and A. Parasuraman. 1994. "The Influence of Store Environment on Quality Inferences and Store Image." *Journal of the Academy of Marketing Science* 22, no. 4, pp. 328–39.

Baker, W., D. Kiewell, and G. Winkler. 2014. "Using Big Data to Make Better Pricing Decisions." *McKinsey Quarterly*.

BarBizMag. 2011. "New Heineken Can Has Contemporary Look." BarBizMag. com

Barry, C., R. Markey, E. Almquist, and C. Brahm. 2011. *Putting Social Media to Work*. Bain & Company.

Bassett, R., B. Beagan, and G.E. Chapman. 2008. "Grocery Lists: Connecting Family, Household in Grocery Store." *British Food Journal* 110, no. 2, pp. 206–17.

Batchelor, C. 2012. "Retail: Knowing Your Stock Is the Key to a Busy Shop." *Financial Times*, February 24.

Bawa, K., J.T. Landwehr, and A. Krishna. 1989. "Consumers Response to Retailers' Marketing Enviornments: An Analysis of Coffee Purchase Data." *Journal of Retailing* 65, no. 4, pp. 471–95.

Baymard Institute. March 12, 2014. "Cart Abandonment Rate Statistics." Retrieved March 15, 2014 from http://baymard.com/lists/cart-abandonment-rate

Bell, J., and K. Ternus. 2006. *Silent Selling: Best Practices and Effective Strategies in Visual Merchandising.* United Kingdom: Fairchild Books.

Bellizzi, J.A., A.E. Crowley, and R.W. Hasty. 1983. "The Effects of Colour in Store Design." *Journal of Retailing* 59, no. 1, pp. 21–45.

Bertini, M., and J.T. Gourville. 2012. "Pricing to Create Shared Value." *Harvard Business Review* June, pp. 96–104.

Betancourt, R.R., and D. Gautschi. 1992. "The Demand for Retail Products and the Household Production Model New Views on Complementarity and Substitutability." *Journal of Economic Behavior and Organization* 17, no. 2, pp. 257–55.

Biner, P.M., D.L. Butler, A.R. Fischer, and A.J. Westergren. 1989. "An Arousal Optimization Model of Lighting Level Preferences: An Interaction of Social Situation and Task Demands." *Environment and Behavior* 21, no. 1, pp. 3–16.

Bishop, B. February 7, 2012. "'Mobile-izing' Grocery Shopping." Bricks Meets Clicks. http://www.brickmeetsclick.com/mobile-izing-grocery-shopping

Biswas, A., E.J. Wilson, and J.W. Licata. 1993. "Reference Pricing Studies in Marketing: A Synthesis of Research Results." *Journal of Business Research* 27, no. 3, pp. 239–56.

Bitner, M.J. April 1990. "Evaluating Service Encounters: The Effects of Physical Surroundings and Employee Responses." *Journal of Marketing* 54, no. 2, pp. 69–82.

Bitner, M.J. 1992. "Servicescapes: The Impact of Physical Surroundings on Customers and Employees." *Journal of Marketing* 56, no. 2, pp. 57–71.

Black, D., N.J. Clemmensen, and M.B. Skov. 2009. "Shopping in the Real World: Interacting with a Context-Aware Shopping Trolley." *Proceedings of MIRW 2009.* Universität Oldenburg. BIS-Verlag.

Block, P.H. July 1995. "Seeking the Ideal Form: Product Design and Consumer Response." *Journal of Marketing* 59, no. 3, pp. 16–29.

Bone, P.F., and S. Jantrania. 1992. "Olfaction as a Cue for Product Quality." *Marketing Letters* 3, no. 3, pp. 289–96.

Bordier, A. 2011. *International Customer Strategy and Channel Trends.* IGD.

Borin, N., and P. Farris. Summer 1995. "A Sensitivity Analysis of Retailer Shelf Management Models." *Journal of Retailing* 71, no. 2, pp. 153–71.

Breen, P. May 5, 2011. Case Study: Walgreens Makes the Best of Intentions. *In Store Marketing Institute.*

Breugelmans, E., K. Campo, and E. Gijsbrechts. 2007. "Shelf Sequence and Proximity Effects on Online Grocery Choices." *Marketing Letters* 18, no. 1–2, pp. 117–33.

Brewer, R.R. 2000. "The Verbal and Visual Components of Package Design." *The Journal of Product and Brand Management* 9, no. 1, pp. 56–70.

Brinker, M., K. Lobaugh, and A. Paul. 2012. "The Dawn of Mobile Influence." deloittedigital.com   http://www2.deloitte.com/us/en/pages/consumer-business/articles/dawn-of-mobile-influence-retail.html

Broniarczyk, S.M. 2006. "Product Assortment." In *Handbook of Consumer Psychology*. Austin, TX: Psychology Press.

Bruner, G.C. October 1990. "Music, Mood, and Marketing." *Journal of Marketing* 54, no. 4, pp. 94–104.

Bullmore, J. March 2005. "Why Is a Good Insight Like a Refrigerator?" WPP. Retrieved August 7, 2012 from http://www.wpp.com/wpp/marketing/marketresearch/why-is-a-good-insight-like-a-refrigerator.htm

Bultez, A., and P. Naert. Summer 1988. "S.H.A.R.P.: Shelf Allocation for Retailers' Profit." *Marketing Science* 7, no. 3, pp. 211–31.

Buss, D. 2011. "Better Understanding of Shopper's Journey Helps Procter & Gamble Boost Brand Sales." *CPG Matters*, May. http://www.cpgmatters.com/instoremarketing0511.html/

Bzzagent. 2011. *From Loyalty to Advocacy with Social Shoppers*. Boston, MA. http://www.dunnhumby.com/sites/default/files/filepicker/2100/dunnhumby_Advocacy.pdf

Cakir, M., and J.V. Balagtas. n.d. "Consumer Response to Package Downsizing: An Application to the Chicago Ice Cream Market." Retrieved May 5, 2014 from http://ageconsearch.umn.edu/bitstream/123980/2/Cakir_Balagtas_ConsumerResponsetoPackageDownsizing.pdf

Cameron, D., C. Gregory, and D. Battaglia. 2012. "Nielsen Personalizes the Mobile Shopping App: If You Build the Technology, They Will Come." *Journal of Advertising Research* 52, no. 3, pp. 333–38.

Capgemini. 2012. "Digital Shopper Relevancy." https://www.capgemini.com/thought-leadership/digital-shopper-relevancy-2012

Cardoso, C. n.d. "Fashion Like." Retrieved March 18, 2014 from http://cargocollective.com/caiocardoso/C-A-Fashion-Like

Carpenter, J.M., and M. Moore. 2006. "Consumer Demographics, Store Attributes, and Retail Format Choice in the US Grocery Market." *International Journal of Retail & Distribution Management* 34, no. 6, 434–52.

Celsi, R.L., and J.C. Olson. 1988. "The Role of Involvement in Attention and Comprehension Processes." *Journal of Consumer Research* 15, no. 2, pp. 210–24.

Chandon, P., W. Hutchinson, and E. Bradlow. 2005. "Is Unseen Really Unsold? Measuring the Value of Point of Purchase Marketing with EyeTracking Data." *IC1 Conference*. http://www.insead.edu/facultyresearch/research/doc.cfm?did=2691

Chandon, P., J. Hutchinson, E. Bradlow, and S. Young. 2009. "Does In-Store Marketing Work? Effects of the Number and Position of Shelf Facings on Brand Attention and Evaluation at the Point of Purchase." *Journal of Marketing* 73, no. 6, pp. 1–17.

Chandon, P., and B. Wansink. 2002. "When Are Stockpiled Products Consumed Faster? A Convenience—Salience Framework of Postpurchase Consumption Incidence and Quality." *Journal of Marketing Research* 39, no. 3, pp. 321–35.

Chandon, P., and B. Wansink. 2011. "Is Food Marketing Making Us Fat? A Multi-Disciplinary Review." *8: Foundations and Trends in Marketing* 5, no. 3.

Chandon, P., B. Wansink, and G. Laurent. 2000. "A Benefit Congruency Framework of Sales Promotion Effectiveness." *Journal of Marketing* 64, no. 4, pp. 65–81.

Charlton, G. December 4, 2012. "10 Tips for Improving Ecommerce Checkouts." https://econsultancy.com/blog/11240-10-tips-for-improving-ecommerce-checkouts

Chebat, J.-C., and P. Filiatrault. 1993. "The Impact of Waiting in Line on Consumers." *The International Journal of Bank Marketing* 11, no. 2, pp. 35–40.

Chebat, J.-C., C.G. Chebat, and D. Vaillant. 2001. "Environmental Background Music and In-Store Selling." *Journal of Business Research* 54, no. 2, pp. 115–23.

Chen, H., H. Marmorstein, M. Tsiros, and A.R. Rao. 2012. "When More Is Less: The Impact of Base Value Neglect on ConsumerPreferences for Bonus Packs Over Price Discounts." *Journal of Marketing* July 76, no. 4, pp. 64–77.

Chen, S.-F.S., K.B. Monroe, and Y.-C Lou. 1998. "The Effects of Framing Price Promotion Messages on Consumers' Perceptions and Purchase Intentions." *Journal of Retailing* 74, no. 3, pp. 353–72.

Chernev, A. 2003. "When More Is Less and Less Is More." *Journal of Consumer Research* 30, no. 2, pp. 170–83.

choice.com.au. 2011. "Supermarket Pricing System Needs Birthday Boost." http://consumersfederation.org.au/wp-content/uploads/2011/12/UP-Survey-Report-FINAL.pdf

Chu, J., P. Chintagunta, and J. Cebollada. 2008. "A Comparison of Within Household Price Sensitivity Across Online and Offline Channels." *Marketing Science* 27, no. 2, pp. 283–99.

Chui, M., and T. Fleming. November 2011. "Inside P&G's Digital Revolution." *McKinsey Quarterly.*

Chung, C., T.M. Schmit, D. Dong, and H.M. Kaiser. 2007. "Economic Evaluation of Shelf-Space Management in Grocery Stores." *Agribusiness* 23, no. 4, pp. 583–97.

Chung, S.-W., and K. Szymanski. 1997. "Effects of Brand Name Exposure on Brand Choices: An Implicit Memory Perspective." *Advances in Consumer Research* 24, pp. 288–94.

Claus Ebster, M.G. 2011. *Store Design and Visual Merchandising.* New York City, NY: Business Expert Press.

Coca Cola Company. n.d. "History of Bottling." Retrieved April 10, 2014 from http://www.coca-colacompany.com/our-company/history-of-bottling

Coca-Cola Retailing Research Council; The Integer Group. 2012. "Untangling the Social Web: Insights for Users, Brands and Retailers."

Cody, S. January 15, 2011. "Consumers, Media, Advertising, Theory and Philosophy: The Aesthetics of the Human Face in Advertising." sachacody. blogspot.hu. Retrieved March 12, 2013 from http://sachacody.blogspot. hu/2011/01/aesthetics-of-human-face-in-advertising.html

Concordia University. 2012. "Closer Look at Consumers' Gazes." Concordia: Concordia University. http://www.concordia.ca/cunews/main/stories/2012/ 07/30/closer-look-at-consumers-gazes.html

Conroy, P., and S. Bearse. 2006. "The Changing Nature of Retail: Planting the Seeds for Sustainable Growth." Deloitte Development LLC.

Cornelius, B., M. Natter, and C. Faure. 2009. "How Storefront Displays Influence Retail Store Image." *Journal of Retailing and Consumer Services* 17, no. 2 , pp. 143–51.

Coulter, K.S., and P.A. Norberg. 2009. "The Effects of Physical Distance Between Regular and Sale Prices on Numerical Difference Perceptions." *Journal of Consumer Psychology* 19, no. 2, pp. 144–57.

Cutler, K.-M. January 25, 2013. "Time Spent in Retailers' Mobile Apps Grows More Than Five-Fold in a Year, Flurry Finds." techcrunh.com. http:// techcrunch.com/2013/01/25/mobile-shopping-apps/

D'Andrea, G., E.A. Stengel, and A. Goebel-Krstelj. 2004. "6 Truths About Emerging- Market Consumers." *Strategy+Business* 34, pp. 58–69.

Dacre, K., and R. Urwin. 2012. "Burberry Flagship Store Lands in Regent Street." *London Evening Standard*, September 13.

Daily Mail. 2011. "Coca-Cola Ditches Holiday-Special Snow White Can and Brings Back Red Again after Frosty Reception by Customers Mistaking It for Diet Coke." December 2.

Deherder, R., and D. Blatt. 2011. *Shopper Intimacy.* NJ: FT Press.

DeMarco, T. April 3, 2013. "Why Product Videos Will Soon Be Worth a Thousand Pictures, and How to Scale." Retrieved March 15, 2014 from http://blog.bazaarvoice.com/

Desai, K.K., and D. Talukdar. 2003. "Relationship Between Product Groups' Price Perceptions, Shopper's Basket Size, and Grocery Store's Overall Store Price Image. *Psychology and Marketing* 20, no. 10, pp. 903–33.

Dhar, R. Febraury 16, 2012. "The Irrational Consumer: Four Secrets to Engaging Shoppers." Retrieved May 5, 2013 from: http://www.huffingtonpost.com/ravi-dhar/psychology-shopping_b_1280341.html

Dhar, R., and K. Wertenbroch. 2000. "Consumer Choice Between Hedonic and Utilitarian Goods." *Journal of Marketing Research* 37, no. 1, pp. 60–71.

Dickson, P.R., and A.G. Sawyer. 1990. The Price Knowledge and Search of Supermarket Shoppers." *Journal of Marketing* 54, no. 3, pp. 42–53.

Diesel Ginza Interactive Mirror. n.d. *Diesel Ginza Interactive Mirror®*. Retrieved March 18, 2014 from https://www.youtube.com/watch?v=QU5DrVu2gdg

Doepke, R. July 1, 2008. "Think Like a Retailer: The First Step in Improving Cross-Sell Is to Create a Dynamic Space Where Customers Want to Linger, Browse and Shop for New Products. (Fundamentals: Cross-Selling). ABA Bank Marketing.

Donovan, R.J., J.R. Rossiter, G. Marcoolyn, and A. Nesdale. 1994. "Store Atmosphere and Purchasing Behaviour." *Journal of Retailing* 70, no. 3, pp. 283–94.

Donovan, R., and J. Rossiter. Spring 1982. "Store Atmosphere: An Environmental Psychology Approach." *Journal of Retailing* 58, no. 1, p. 34–57.

Dooley, R., and C. Goward. 2013. *Neuromarketing Meets Conversion Optimization: Brainy Profit Boosters.* http://www.slideshare.net/chrisgoward/neuromarketing-meets-conversion-optimization-brainy-profit-boosters

Drèze, X., S.J. Hoch, and M.E. Purk. 1994. "Shelf Management and Space Elasticity." *Journal of Retailing* 70, no. 4, pp. 301–26.

Dubé, L., and S. Morin. 2001. "Background Music Pleasure and Store Evaluation: Intensity Effects and Psychological Mechanisms." *Journal of Business Research* 54, no. 2, pp. 107–13.

Edwards, J. 2013. "How Mobile Phones in Supermarkets Are Killing the Magazine." *Business Insider*, Febraury 11.

Edwards, S., and M. Shackley. 1992. "Measuring the Effectiveness of Rretail Window Display as an Element of the Marketing Mix." *International Journal of Advertising* 11, no. 3, pp. 193–202.

Emarketer.com. March 11, 2013. "Online Retailers Move Past Discounts to Earn Deeper Customer Loyalty." http://www.emarketer.com/Article/Online-Retailers-Move-Past-Discounts-Earn-Deeper-Customer-Loyalty/1009719

Esomar. 2011. *A New World Order in Shopper Marketing.* Brussels.

Folkes, V., and S. Matta. 2004. "The Effect of Package Shape on Consumers' Judgments of Product Volume: Attention as a Mental Contaminant." *Journal of Consumer Research* 31, no. 2, pp. 390–401.

Frade, A. 2009. *Case Study - Instant Lottery.* TNS.

Franzen, G. 1994. *Advertising Effectiveness: Findings from Empirical Research.* Henley on Thames, UK: N.T.C. Publications.

Garcia, C., V. Ponsoda, and H.E. Aranz. 2000. "Scanning Ads: Effects of Involvement and of Position of the Illustration in Printed Advertisements." *Advances in Consumer Research* 27, pp. 104–09.

Garlin, F.V., and K. Owen. 2006. "Setting the Tone with the Tune: A Meta-Analytic Review of the Effects of Background Music in Retail Settings." *Journal of Business Research* 59, no. 6, pp. 755–64.

Gendall, P., J. Hoek, T. Pope, and K. Young. 2006. "Message Framing Effects on Price Discounting." *Journal of Product and Brand Management* 15, no. 7, pp. 458–65.

Ginthner, D. n.d. *Lighting: Its Effect on People.* University of Minnesota.

Glazer, E. 2012. "The Eyes Have It: Marketers Now Track Shoppers' Retinas." *Wall Street Journal,* July 12.

Goodall, S. 2011. "How to Connect with the Heart and Mind of the Male Shopper." *Ad Age,* March 29.

Google. 2011. "Beyond Last Click: Understanding Your Consumers' Online Path to Purchase." Google. http://services.google.com/fh/files/blogs/google_clickstream_whitepaper.pdf

Google. n.d. "Best Practices for Ad Placement." Google Adsense. Retrieved March 15, 2014 from https://support.google.com/adsense/answer/1282097?rd=2

Gourville T.J., and D. Soman. 2005. "Overchoice and Assortment Type: When and Why Variety Backfires." *Marketing Science* 24, no. 3, pp. 382–95.

Gourville, J.T., and D. Soman. 1998. "Payment Depreciation: The Behavioral Effects of Temporally Separating Payments from Consumption." *Journal of Consumer Research* 25, no. 2, pp. 160–74.

Grant, J. Febuary 2012. "Food Labeling Confusion Weighs on Consumers Around the World." CPGmatters.com. http://www.cpgmatters.com/International021612.html

Grewal, D., and H. Marmorstein. 1994. "Market Price Variation, Perceived Price Variation, and Consumers' Price Search Decisions for Durable Goods." *Journal of Consumer Research* 21, no. 3, pp. 453–60.

Grewal, D., J. Baker, M. Levy, and G.B. Voss 2003. "The Effects of Wait Expectations and Store Atmosphere Evaluations on Patronage Intentions in Service-Intensive Retail Stores." *Journal of Retailing* 79, no. 4, pp. 259–68.

Guardian Professional. November 22, 2012. "How Innovation Can Unlock Shoppercentric." guradian.com

Harrell, G.D., and M.D. Hurt. 1976. "Buyer Behavior Under Conditions of Crowding: An Initial Framework." *Advances in Consumer Research* 3, no. 1, pp. 36–39.

Hauser, J.R., and B. Wernerfelt. 1990. "An Evaluation Cost Model of Consideration Sets." *Journal of Consumer Research* 16, no. 4, pp. 393–408.

Hawley, K.J., W.A. Johnston, and J.M. Farnham. 1994. "Novel Popout with Nonsense Strings: Effects of Predictability of String Length and Spatial Location." *Perception & Psychophysics* 55, no. 3, pp. 261–68.

Hayes, M. September 8, 2012. "Using Behavioral Economics,Psychology, and Neuroeconomics to Maximize Sales." shopify.com Retrieved July 11, 2014 from www.shopify.com/blog/6563013-using-behavioral-economics-psychology-and-neuroeconomics-to-maximize-sales#axzz2NKYim6cf

Hedrick, N., H. Oppewal, and M. Beverland. 2006. "Store Atmosphere Effects on Customer Perceptions of the Retail Sales Person." *Asia-Pacific Advances in Consumer Research* 7, pp. 96–97.

Helbling, J., J. Leibowitz, and A. Rettaliata. 2011. "The Value Proposition in Multichannel Retailing." *McKinsey Quarterly*.

Heller, L. August 29, 2006. "Innovative Merchandising Needed to Capture Declining Shelf Space." foodnavigator-usa.com http://www.foodnavigator-usa.com/Suppliers2/Innovative-merchandising-needed-to-capture-declining-shelf-space

Hellmanns Brasil. n.d. "Hellmann's Recipe Cart." Youtube. Retrieved May 11, 2015 from https://www.youtube.com/watch?v=CT_Uc4PZBqQ&index=117&list=LLsQKeaHjMFl6uRvSDSt-vIQ

Hirsch, A. 1995. "Effect of Ambient Odors on Slot Machine Usage in a Las Vegas Casino." *Psychology and Marketing* 12, no. 7, pp. 585–94.

Hoch, S.J., B.-D. Kim, A.L. Montgomery, and P.E. Rossi. 1995. "Determinants of Store-Level Price Elasticity." *Journal of Marketing Research* 32, no. 1, pp. 17–29.

Hoffman, A.L. 2011. "Effect of Signage and Suggestive Selling on Sales of Healthy Food Options in a University Setting." Retrieved September 26, 2012 from http://opensiuc.lib.siu.edu/theses/665

Hoffman, D.K., and J.E. Bateson. 1997. *Essentials of Services Marketing.* 2nd ed. South-Western College Pub.

Hoffman, J.E. 1998. *Attention*, viii, 407. Hove, England: Psychology Press/ Erlbaum (UK) Taylor & Francis.

Hoffman, K.D., and L.W. Turley. 2002. "Atmospherics, Service Encounters and Consumer Decision Making: An Integrative Perspective." *Journal of Marketing Theory and Practice* 10, no. 3, pp. 33–47.

Hoyer, W.D. 1984. "An Examination of Consumer Decision Making for a Common Repeat Purchase Product." *Journal of Consumer Research* 11, no. 3, pp. 822–29.

Hoyt, C. 2007. "What's that Sound." *The Hub*, March–April.

Hugh, P. 2009. *The Cognitive Psychology of Shopping and Its Application to In-Store Marketing.* Phillips Foster and Boucher Inc.

Hui, M.K., L. Dube, and J.-C. Chebat. 1997. "The Impact of Music on Consumers' Reactions to Waiting for Services." *Journal of Retailing* 73, no. 1, pp. 87–104.

IGD. 2011a. "Category Management and Shopper Marketing." IGD.

IGD. 2011b. "Environmental Sustainability–How to Engage Shoppers."

IGD. 2011c. "What Shoppers Want." IGD.

IGD. 2012. "ShopperVista Report, September 2012." IGD.

IGD. 2013. "Category Management and Shopper Marketing Survey." IGD.

IGD ShopperVista. 2011. *Influencing the Shopper In-Store.* United Kingdom: IGD.

Inman, J.J., L. McAlister, and W.D. Hoyer 1990. "Promotion Signal: Proxy for a Price Cut?" *Journal of Consumer Research* 17, no. 1, pp. 74–81.

Inmann, J., A.C. Peter, and P. Raghubir. 1997. "Framing the Deal: The Role of Restrictions in Accentuating Deal Value." *Journal of Consumer Research* 24, no. 1, pp. 68–79.

Institute of Grocery Distribution. n.d. "Glossary." igd.com. Retrieved February 12, 2013 from http://www.igd.com/Category_Management_Glossary

Ipsos. 2011. "Eight in Ten (83%) PayPal Merchants Say Sales Have Increased Since Offering Popular Payment Method." http://www.ipsos-na.com/news-polls/pressrelease.aspx?id=5153

Itti, L. 2005. "Models of Bottom-Up Attention and Saliency." *Neurobiology of Attention.* San Diego, CA: Elsevier.

Jedidi, K., C.F. Mela, and S. Gupta. 1999. "Managing Advertising and Promotion for Long-Run Profitability." *Marketing Science* 18, no. 1, pp. 1–22.

Johnson, S.C. 2009. "Call to Action: Rethinking Shopper Behavior in the New Transformational Economy." Information Resources, Inc.

Jonathan A. May–June 2011. "Unseen is Unsold." Retrieved June 7, 2012 from http://www.prsresearch.com/fileUploads/UnseenisUnsold_BP.pdf

Jones, R.P. 2012. *Shopper Value: A Framework and Examination of the Impact of Importance, Shopping Context and Shopping Social Situation* [Doctoral Dissertations]. Tennessee: University of Tennessee.

Just, D.R., and B. Wansink. 2009. "Smarter Lunchrooms: Using Behavioral Economics to Improve Meal Selection." *Choices: The Magazine of Food, Farm and Resource Issues.*

Kahn, B.E., and X. Deng. 2011. "Effects on Visual Weight Perceptions of Product Image Locations on Packaging." In *Sensory Marketing: Research on the Sensuality of Products*, ed. A. Krishna. Hoboken, NJ: Taylor and Francis.

Kahn, B.E., and B. Wansink. 2004. "The Influence of Assortment Structure on Perceived Variety and Consumption Quantities." *Journal of Consumer Research* 30, no. 4, pp. 519–32.

Kahneman, D. 2011. *Thinking, Fast and Slow.* New York: Farrar, Straus and Giroux.

Kamaşak, R. 2008. "The Impact of Shelf Levels on Product Sale." *Ç.Ü. Sosyal Bilimler Enstitüsü Dergisi* 17, no. 2, pp. 219–30.

Karolefski, J. November 8, 2007. "Crayola Connects with Consumers Using New Assortments, Merchandising." retailwire.com http://www.retailwire.com/discussion/12557/cpgmatters-crayola-connects-with-consumers-using-new-assortments-merchandising

Katz, K.L., B.M. Larson, and R.C. Larson. 1991. "Prescription for the Waiting-in-Line Blues: Entertain, Enlighten, and Engage." *Sloan Management Review* 32, no. 2, pp. 44–53.

Kawaf, F. 2013. "The Role of Web Atmospherics and Consumers Emotions in Online Fashion Shopping Experiences." *Later Stage Doctoral Research*.

Kerfoot, S., B. Davies, and P. Ward. 2003. "Visual Merchandising and the Creation of Discernible Retail Brands." *International Journal of Retail & Distribution Management* 31, no. 3, pp. 143–52.

Kim, K., and J. Meyers-Levy. April 2008. "Context Effects in Diverse-Category Brand Environments: The Influence of Target Product Positioning and Consumers' Processing Mind-Set." *Journal of Consumer Research* 34, no. 6, pp. 882–96.

Kök, A.G., M.L. Fisher, and R. Vaidyanathan. 2009. "Assortment Planning: Review of Literature and Industry Practice." In *Retail Supply Chain Management*, International Series in Operations Research & Management Science, 99–153.

Kollat, D.T., and R.P. Willett. 1967. "Customer Impulse Purchasing Behavior." *Journal of Marketing Research* 4, no. 1, pp. 21–31.

Kotler, P. Winter. 1973. "Atmospherics as a Marketing Tool." *Journal of Retailing* 49, no. 4, pp. 48–64.

Krajbich, I., C. Armel, and A. Rangel. 2010. "Visual Fixations and the Computation and Comparison of Value in Simple Choice." *Nature Neuroscience* 13, no. 10, pp. 1292–98.

Krishna, A., R. Briesch, D.R. Lehmann, and H. Yuan. 2002. "A Meta-Analysis of the Impact of Price Presentation on Perceieved Savings." *Journal of Retailing* 78, no. 2, pp. 101–18.

Lamberton, C.P., and K. Diehl. 2013. "Retail Choice Architecture: The Effects of Benefit- and Attribute-Based Assortment Organization on Consumer Perceptions and Choice." *Journal of Consumer Research* 10, no. 3, pp. 393–411.

Lans, R.V., R. Pieters, and M. Wedel. 2008. "Competitive Brand Salience." *Marketing Science* 27, no. 5, pp. 922–31.

Lawrence, A. 2013. *How Mobile Is Reshaping Retailing*. IGD.

Lemmink, J., and J. Mattsson. 2002. "Employee Behavior, Feelings of Warmth and Customer Perception in Service Encounters." *International Journal of Retail & Distribution Management* 30, no. 1, pp. 18–33.

Lennard, D., V.-W. Mitchell, P. McGoldrick, and E. Betts. 2001. "Why Consumers Under-Use Food Quantity Indicators." *The International Review of Retail, Distribution and Consumer Research* 11, no. 2, pp. 177–99.

Li, Z. May 3, 2011. "Gambling Stinks: Food Odors Could Encourage Punters at Casinos in Macau." http://travel.cnn.com/hong-kong/visit/macau-casinos-may-smell-green-tea-and-cooked-rice-103348

Luce, M.F., J.R. Bettman, and J.W. Payne. 1997. "Choice Processing in Emotionally Difficult Decisions." *Journal of Experimental Psychology: Learning, Memory, and Cognition* 23, no. 2, pp. 384–405.

Lutz, K.A., and R.J. Lutz. 1978. "Imagery-Eliciting Strategies: Review and Implications of Research." *Advances in Consumer Research Volume* 5, no. 1, pp. 611–20.

Machleit, K.A., S.A. Eroglu, and S.P. Mantel. 2000. "Perceived Retail Crowding and Shopping Satisfaction: What Modifies This Relationship?" *Journal of Consumer Psychology* 9, no. 1, pp. 29–42.

Macinnis, D.J., and L.L. Price. March 1987. "The Role of Imagery in Information Processing: Review and Extensions." *Journal of Consumer Research* 13, pp. 473–91.

Madzharov, A.V., and L.G. Block. 2010. "Effects of Product Unit Image on Consumption of Snack Foods." *Journal of Consumer Psychology* 20, no. 4, pp. 398–409.

Manjoo, F. 2012. "Walmart's Evolution from Big Box Giant to E-Commerce Innovator." *Fast Company*, November 26.

Martin, T.W. 2009. "Want to Save? Put It on the List." *The Wall Street Journal*, May 5.

McCann, P. 2012. "Finding Faster Growth: New Customers." TNS Global. Retrieved Febraury 13, 2013

McGoldrick, P.J., and H.J. Marks. 1987. "Shoppers' Awareness of Retail Grocery Prices." *European Journal of Marketing* 21, no. 3, pp. 63–76.

McKoon, G., and R. Ratcliff. 1986. "Automatic Activation of Episodic Information in a Semantic Memory Task." *Journal of Experimental Psychology:Learning, Memory, and Cognition* 12, no. 1, pp. 108–15.

Medford, C. 2014. "Seeing Water Differently." *Category Management and Shopper Marketing*.

Media Cart. n.d. Retrieved March 16, 2014 from http://www.mediacart.com/

Mediative and Tobii. 2012. "The Effectiveness of Display Advertising on a Desktop PC vs. a Tablet Device." http://www.mediative.com/the-effectiveness-of-display-advertising-on-a-desktop-pc-vs-a-tablet-device/

Meurs, L.V., and M. Aristoff. March 2009. "Split-Second Recognition: What Makes Outdoor Advertising Work?" *Journal of Advertising Research* 49, no. 1, pp. 82–92.

Milliman, R.E. Summer 1982. "Using Background Music to Affect the Behavior of Supermarket Shoppers." *Journal of Marketing* 46, no. 3, pp. 86–91.

Milliman, R.E. 1986. "The Influence of Background Music on the Behavior of Restaurant Patrons." *Journal of Consumer Research* 13, no. 2, pp. 286–89.

Mitchell, D.J., and B.E. Kahn. 1995. "There's Something in the Air: Effects of Congruent or Incongruent Ambient Odor on Consumer Decision Making." *Journal of Consumer Research* 22, no. 2, pp. 229–38.

Mitchell, N., H. Oppewal, and M. Beverland. 2009. "Great Expectations: The Power of Store Atmosphere and Merchandise Effects on Customers' Perceptions of a Retail Salesperson." ANZMAC. Retrieved April 2, 2013 from http://www. duplication.net.au/ANZMAC09/papers/ANZMAC2009-426.pdf

Mitchell, V.-W., D. Lennard, and P. Mcgoldrick. 2003. "Consumer Awareness, Understanding and Usage of Unit Pricing." *British Journal of Management* 14, no. 2, pp. 173–87.

Mogilne, C., T. Rudnick, and S.S. Iyengar. 2008. "The Mere Categorization Effect: How the Presence of Categories Increases Choosers' Perceptions of Assortment Variety and Outcome Satisfaction." *Journal of Consumer Research* 35, no. 2, pp. 202–15.

Monroe, K.B., and A.Y. Lee. 1999. "Remembering Versus Knowing: Issues in Buyers Processing of Price Information." *Journal of the Academy of Marketing Science* 27, no. 2, pp. 207–25.

Monteleone, J.P., and J. Wolferseberger. 2012. "Showrooming & the Price of Keeping Buyers In-Store." GroupM Next. http://www.scribd.com/doc/103349382/GroupM-Next-White-Paper-Showrooming-and-the-Price-of-Keeping-Buyers-In-Store#scribd

Morales, A.B. 2005. "Perceptions of Assortment Variety: The Effects of Congruency Between Consumers' Internal and Retailers' External Organization." *Journal of Retailing* 81, no. 2, pp. 159–69.

Morrin, M., and S. Ratneshwar. 2000. "The Impact of Ambient Scent on Evaluation, Attention, and Memory for Familiar and Unfamiliar Brands." *Journal of Business Research* 49, no. 2, pp. 157–65.

Mortimer, G., and C.S. Weeks. 2013. "The Effect of Consumer Education on Unit Price Usage : An Early Exploratory Study." In *Conference of the European Institute of Retailing and Services Studies*. Philadelphia, PA.

Morton, A.-L.H. November 5, 2004. "Beyond the Bubbles: Identifying Other Purchase Decision Variables Beyond Country of Origin Effect that Make Australians Buy Champagne." Queensland University of Technology. Retrieved June 19, 2012 from http://eprints.qut.edu.au/1182/

Mulpuru, S. 2013. "US Online Retail Sales to Reach \$370B By 2017; €191B in Europe." *Forbes*, March 13.

Mulvey, J. 2013. "'Brain Friendly' Website Design Attracts More Viewers." *BusinessNewsDaily*, March 7.

My SoloHealth Station. n.d. "My SoloHealth Station." Retrieved March 18, 2014 from https://mysolohealthstation.com/products/overview/

Nassauer, S. 2012. "Food Fight in the Produce Aisle." *The Wall Street Journal*, October 20. Retrieved August 10, 2012 from http://online.wsj.com/article/SB10001424052970203752604576640923370662418.html

Nedungadi, P. 1990. "Recall and Consumer Consideration Sets: Influencing Choice Without Altering Brand Evaluations." *Journal of Consumer Research* 17, no. 3, pp. 263–76.

Neilsen. 2012a. How Digital Influences How We Shop Around the World. Neilsen. http://www.nielsen.com/us/en/insights/reports/2012/how-digital-influences-how-we-shop-around-the-world.html

Neilsen. 2012b. Mobile Devices Empower Today's Shoppers In-Store and Online. http://www.nielsen.com/us/en/insights/news/2012/mobile-devices-empower-todays-shoppers-in-store-and-online.html

North, A.C., D.J. Hargreaves, and J. McKendrick. 1999. "The Influence of In-Store Music on Wine Selections." *Journal of Applied Psychology* 84, no. 2, pp. 271–76.

Oakes, S. 2000. "The Influence of the Musicscape Within Service Environments." *Journal of Services Marketing* 14, no. 7, pp. 539–56.

One Step Retail Solutions. n.d. "Case Study Video 1." Retrieved March 16, 2014 from http://teamworkretailusa.com/

Ocado: The online supermarket. n.d. Domestos Sink & Pipe Unblocker 500ml https://www.ocado.com/webshop/product/Domestos-Sink--Pipe-Unblocker/28894011

Packaging News. July 8, 2011. "Drinks: The Search for a Refreshing New Look." Packaging News. Retrieved June 19, 2012 from http://www.packagingnews.co.uk/markets/drinks/the-search-for-a-refreshing-new-look/

Park, C.W., E.S. Iyer, and D.C. Smith. 1989. "The Effects of Situational Factors on In-Store Grocery Shopping Behavior: The Role of Store Environment and Time Available for Shopping." *Journal of Consumer Research* 15, no. 4, pp. 422–33.

Passariello, C. 2010. "Electronic Mirrors Sell Lipstick and a Makeover." *The Wall Street Journal*, August 27.

Path to Purchase Institute. June 28, 2012. "How Can Behavioral Economics Help Develop P-O-P Messaging Strategy?" Webinar.

Payne, J.W. 1976. "Task Complexity and Contingent Processing in Decision Making: An Information Search and Protocol Analysis." *Organizational Behavior and Human Performance* 16, no. 2, pp. 366–87.

Peck, J., and T.L. Childers. 2003. "To Have and to Hold: The Influence of Haptic Information on Product Judgments." *Journal of Marketing* 67, no. 2, pp. 35–48.

Pieters, R., and M. Wedel. 2007. "Goal Control of Attention to Advertising: The Yarbus Implication." *Journal of Consumer Research* 34, no. 2, pp. 224–33.

Planet Retail. 2011. Retail Technology Trends.

Planet Retail. December 7, 2012a. "AUCHAN to Introduce New m-Commerce System 7/12/12." *Planet Retail.*

Planet Retail. September 26, 2012b. "French Retailers Pilot Google Instore Mapping." *Planet Retail.*

Planet Retail. August 21, 2012c. "MARKS & SPENCER Touring Body Shape Scanner." *Planet Retail.*

Planet Retail. June 11, 2012d. "OCADO Pioneering a Virtual Gondola End." *Planet Retail.*

Planet Retail. May 24, 2012e. "TARGET Rolls Out Shopkick Reward Programme." *Planet Retail.*

Planet Retail. May 18, 2012f. "WALMART Asda Mulls Over Virtual Assistants." *Planet Retail.*

Planet Retail. August 24, 2012g. "WALMART Launches Online Receipt Comparison Tool." *Planet Retail.*

Planet Retail. September 3, 2012h. "WALMART Tests New iPhone Self-Checkout System." *Planet Retail.*

Planet Retail. April 13, 2012i. "WHOLE FOODS MARKET Trials Smart Shopping Cart." *Planet Retail.*

Planet Retail. March 12, 2013a. CARREFOUR China introduces QR codes for fresh produce. *Planet Retail.*

Planet Retail. September 16, 2013b. "METRO (CAN) Introduces Online Shopper Tools." *Planet Retail.*

Planet Retail. March 1, 2013c. "METRO GROUP Pilots Interactive Chiller Cabinet in Real Future Store." *Planet Retail.*

Planet Retail. January 24, 2013d. "TESCO Trialling Digital Shopper Interfaces." *Planet Retail.*

Planet Retail. January 8, 2014. "US Grocers Roll Out Apple iBeacon." *Planet Retail.*

Poltrock, S.E., and D.R. Schwartz. 1984. "Comparative Judgments of Multidigit Numbers." *Journal of Experimental Psychology: Learning, Memory, and Cognition* 10, no. 1, pp. 32–45.

Popai. 2012. "2012 Shopper Engagement Study." USA: POPAI.

Porcheddu, D., and A. Venturi. 2011. "Choices from Identical Options in a Virtual Shopping Aisle." *The Open Business Journal* 4, no. 1, pp. 36–45.

Poulter, S. 2013. "Does This Conveyor Belt Scanner Mean the End of the Checkout Girl?" *Mail Online*, July 3.

Pouy, G. 2011. "The Future of Commerce: Real ROI Inside" http://www.slideshare.net/gregfromparis/the-future-of-commerce-real-roi-inside

PR Newswire. n.d. "Ukrop's Super Markets Launches the Savings Spot." Retrieved March 16, 2014 http://www.prnewswire.com/news-releases/ukrops-super-markets-launches-the-savings-spot-58040797.html

Promotional Marketing. 2013. "Cherry Coke Zero Launched with Innovative Epaper POS." *Promotional Marketing*, June 5.

PRweb. July 20, 2010. "Luxottica Unveils Future of Retailing at Revolutionary New Concept Store." Retrieved March 18, 2014 from http://www.benzinga.com/pressreleases/10/07/n384652/luxottica-unveils-future-of-retailing-at-revolutionary-new-concept-store

prweb.com. 2012. "Walmart, Target and Best Buy Are Losing Sales to Amazon from Consumers Who Conduct In-store Product Research with Their Mobile Devices." http://www.prweb.com/releases/2012/3/prweb9291383.htm

Puccinellia, N.M., R. Chandrashekaran, D. Grewal, and R. Suri. 2013. "Are Men Seduced By Red? The Effect of Red Versus Black Prices on Price Perceptions." *Journal of Retailing* 89, no. 2, pp. 115–25.

Quinn, T. 2012. "Examining C-store Shoppers from Pump to Register." *Conveinence Store News*, January 27.

Raghubir, P., and E.A. Greenleaf. 2006. "Ratios in Proportion: What Should the Shape of the Package Be?" *Journal of Marketing* 70, no. 2, pp. 95–107.

Rahman, O. 2012. "The Influence of Visual and Tactile Inputs on Denim Jeans Evaluation." *International Journal of Design* 6, no. 1, pp. 11–25.

Ramo, J.C. 1999. "Jeffrey Preston Bezos: 1999 Person of the Year." *Time Magazine,* December 27.

Reichheld, F. 2001. *Prescription for Cutting Costs.* Boston, MA: Bain & Company.

Retail Customer Experience. November 9, 2010. "The Five Online Commerce Features that Create Loyalty." retailcustomerexperience.com. http://www.retailcustomerexperience.com/articles/the-five-online-commerce-features-that-create-loyalty/

Riegelsberger, J., M.A. Sasse, and J. McCarthy. 2004. "Trust at First Sight? A Test of Users' Ability to Identify Trustworthy E-commerce Sites." *People and Computers XVII — Designing for Society*, pp. 243–59.

Rodriguez, S. 2013. "Apple Granted U.S. Trademark for Its Retail Store Design." *L.A. Times*, January 29.

Rompay, T.J., K. Tanja-Dijkstra, J.W. Verhoeven, and A.F. van Es. April 19, 2011. "On Store Design and Consumer Motivation: Spatial Control and Arousal in the Retail Context." *Environment and Behavior* 44, no. 6, pp. 800–20.

Rossiter, J.R. 1982. "Visual Imagery: Applications to Advertising." *Advances in Consumer Research* 9, no. 1, pp. 101–6.

Rottenstreich, Y., S. Sood, and L. Brenner. 2007. "Feeling and Thinking in Memory-Based Versus Stimulus-Based Choices." *Journal of Consumer Research* 33, no. 4, pp. 461–69.

Ruiz G., L.M. n.d. "Design and Implementation of a System for Examination of Shopping Lists." www.dfki.de. Retrieved May 5, 2013 from http://www.dfki.de/iui/bms/folien/LinaRuiz-Masterseminar.pdf

Rundh, B. 2009. "Packaging Design: Creating Competitive Advantage with Product Packaging." *British Food Journal* 111, no. 9, pp. 988–1002.

Ryan Partnership. 2012. A Tectonic Shift in Shopping Behavior: Ryan Digital Retail Study 2012.

Scamell-Katz, S. 2012. *The Art of Shopping: How We Shop and Why We Buy.* London: LID Publishing, Inc.

Scarpello, L. December 14, 2012. "Which Retailers Deliver the Best Mobile Shopping Experiences?" popai.com https://www.popai.com/industry-news-blog/which-retailers-deliver-the-best-mobile-shopping-experiences?A=WebApp&CCID=22451&Page=6&Items=1

Schmidt, M. 2012. "Retail Shopping Lists: Reassessment and New Insights." *Journal of Retailing and Consumer Services* 19, no. 1, pp. 36–44.

Schwartz, M.B. 2007. "The Influence of a Verbal Prompt on School Lunch Fruit Consumption: A Pilot Study." *International Journal of Behavioral Nutrition and Physical Activity* 4, no. 1, p. 6.

Scott, Y., and A. Jonathan. August 2009a. "Designing for Retail Realities." Brand Packaging. Retrieved June 19, 2019 from http://www.brandpackaging.com/articles/designing-for-retail-realities

Scott, Y., and C. Vincenzo. July 2009b. "Package Viewing Patterns." Research Global Design. Retrieved June 7, 2012 from http://www.prsresearch.com/fileUploads/Package_Viewing_Patterns.pdf

Sen, S., L.G. Block, and S. Chandran. 2002. "Window Displays and Consumer Shopping Decisions." *Journal of Retailing and Consumer Services* 9, no. 5, pp. 277–90.

Shapiro, S., D.J. MacInnis, and S.E. Heckler. 1997. "The Effects of Incidental Ad Exposure on the Formation of Consideration Sets." *Journal of Consumer Research* 24, no. 1, pp. 94–104.

Simonson, I. 1999. "The Effect of Product Assortment on Buyer Preferences." *Journal of Retailing* 75, no. 3, pp. 347–70.

Simonson, I., and A. Tversky. 1992. "Choice in Context: Tradeoff Contrast and Extremeness Aversion." *Journal of Marketing Research* 29, no. 3, pp. 281–95.

Smith, P.C., and R. Curnow. 1966. "'Arousal Hypothesis' and the Effects of Music on Purchasing Behavior." *Journal of Applied Psychology* 50, no. 3, pp. 255–56.

Soars, B. 2003. "What Every Retailer Should Know about the Way into the Shopper's Head." *International Journal of Retail & Distribution Management* 31, no. 12, pp. 628–37.

Sorensen Associates Inc. 2004. "How They Shop the Supermarket: An Electronic Study of Shopper Behavior During Purchases of One Million Items from a Suburban Supermarket." http://shopperscientist.com/resources/sorensen-white-papers/HowTheyShop-2003.pdf

Sorensen, H. 2009. *Inside the Mind of the Shopper: The Science of Retailing.* Upper Saddle River, NJ: Pearson Prentice Hall.

Sorensen, H. October 19, 2010a. "Tell 'em Where to Go; Tell 'em Which to Buy! (The "Path-to-Purchase" Ought to Be a U-Turn)."TNS Global. Retrieved May 4, 2015 from http://blogs.tnsglobal.com/retail_shopper/2010/10/tell-em-where-to-go-tell-em-which-to-buy-the-path-to-purchase-ought-to-be-a-u-turn.html

Sorensen, H. March 27, 2010b. "The 'Path-to-Purchase' Is Often a U-Turn." shopperscientist.com. http://www.shopperscientist.com/2010-03-27.html

Spangenberg, E.R., A.E. Crowley, and P.W. Henderson. April 1996. "Improving the Store Environment: Do Olfactory Cues Affect Evaluations and Behaviors?" *The Journal of Marketing* 60, no. 2, pp. 67–80.

Spangenberger, E.R., B. Grohmann, and D.E. Sprott. 2005. "It's Beginning to Smell and Sound a Lot Like Christmas: Interactive Effects of Ambient Scent and Music in the Retail Setting." *Journal of Business Research* 58, no. 11, pp. 1583–89.

Speier, C., J. Valacich, and I. Vessey. 1999. "The Influence of Task Interruption on Individual Decision Making: An Information Overload Perspective." *Decision Sciences* 30, no. 2, pp. 337–60.

Spiggle, S. 1987. "Grocery Shopping Lists: What Do Consumers Write?" *Advances in Consumer Research* 14, no. 1, pp. 241–45.

Spring, M.B., and M.C. Jennings. 1993. "Virtual Reality and Abstract Data: Virtualizing Information." *Virtual Reality World* 1, no. 1. http://www.sis.pitt.edu/spring/papers/abstdat_vr.pdf

Steffens, G., S. Egner, and C. Scheier. 2003. "Tracking Consumer Attention at the Point-of-Sale." *Retailing/Category Management*, Dublin.

Sterling, G. January 6, 2012. "Google's Toy Study Exposes Complex Consumer Purchase Path." Marketingland. http://marketingland.com/googles-toy-study-exposes-complex-consumer-purchase-path-2720

Street, R. 2013. "Post-Recession Shoppers Are Changing Their Attitudes to Brands." SymphonyIRI Group.

Stremersch, S., and G.J. Tellis. 2002. "Strategic Bundling of Products and Prices: A New Synthesis for Marketing." *Journal of Marketing* 66, no. 1, pp. 55–72.

Striving, M., and R.S. Winer. 1997. "An Empirical Analysis of Price Endings with Scanner Data." *Journal of Consumer Research* 24, no. 1, pp. 57–67.

Summers, T.A., and P.R. Hebert. 2001. "Shedding Some Light on Store Atmospherics: Influence of Illumination on Consumer Behavior." *Journal of Business Research* 54, no. 2, pp. 145–50.

SymphonyIRI Group. 2012. "Merchandising Trends: Driving Consumption Through Shopper Marketing." http://supermarketnews.com/site-files/supermarketnews.com/files/uploads/2012/01/T_T%20January%202012%20Merchandising.pdf

Synovate BrandLife. 2011. Packaging & Product Design Specialty Foods: Asian tofu.

Taphouse, Z. 2014. "Re-Igniting Peoples Passion for Tea." *Category Management and Shopper Marketing.*

Taylor, L., and E. Sucov. 1974. "The Movement of People Toward Lights." *Journal of the Illuminating Engineering Society* 3, no. 3, pp. 237–41.

Taylor, P. 2012. "Advertisers Embrace Augmented Reality." *Financial Times*, June 11.

Thaler, R. 1980. "Toward a Positive Theory of Consumer Choice." *Journal of Economic Behavior and Organization* 1, no. 1, pp. 39–60.

The Economist. 2012a. "The Psychology of Discounting Something Doesn't Add Up." *The Economist*, June 30.

The Economist. 2012b. "What Sort of Glass You Drink from Predicts How Fast You." *The Economist*, September 1.

The Hartman Group. 2012. *The New Path to Purchase: Meet the Constant Consumer.* The Hartman Group.

The Hartman Group. 2013. *Shopper Tactics: The Mythology of the Shopping List.* Bellevue, WA: The Hartman Group.

The NPD Group. August 14, 2010. "Consumers Begin Shopping Long Before Entering a Store." Retrieved March 15, 2014 from http://www.befoundmore.com/canadians-browsing-not-shopping-online/

Thomas, A., and R. Garland. October 1996. "Susceptibility to Goods on Promotion in Supermarkets." *Journal of Retailing and Consumer Services* 3, no. 4, pp. 233–39.

Thomas, M., and V. Morwitz. 2005. "Penny Wise and Pound Foolish: The Left-Digit Effect in Price Cognition." *Journal of Consumer Research* 32, pp. 54–64.

TNS. 2010. "POSM Efficiency and Shopper in Depth Understanding." TNS.

TNS Digital Life. 2010. "Drivers of Online Behaviour." Kantar Group.

Tobii. n.d. "Package design & shelf placement - Leading Eye Tracking Technology." Japan Consumer Marketing Research Institute. Retrieved June 25, 2012 from http://www.jmr-marketing.com/user/580/Shelf_placement/

Treisman, A. November 1986. "Features and Objects in Visual Processing." *Journal Scientific American* 255, no. 5, pp. 114–25.

Turley, L.W., and R.E. Milliman. 2000. "Atmospheric Effects on Shopping Behavior: A Review of the Experimental Evidence." *Journal of Business Research* 49, no. 2, pp. 193–211.

Tversky, A., and D. Kahneman. 1974. "Judgment under Uncertainty: Heuristics and Biases." *Science* 185, no. 4157, pp. 1124–31.

Twitter. 2012. "Tweets in Action: Retail." Kantar Media.

Underhill, P. 1999. *Why We Buy: The Science of Shopping.* New York: Simon & Schuster.

Underwood, R.L., and N.M. Burke. 2001. "Packaging Communication: Attentional Effects Product Imagery." *Journal Product and Brand Management* 10, no. 7, pp. 403–22.

Underwood, R.L., and N.M. Klein. 2002. "Packaging as Brand Communication: Effects of Product Pictures on Consumer Responses to the Package and Brand." *Journal of Marketing Theory and Practice* 10, no. 4, pp. 58–68.

Urbany, J.E., W.O. Bearden, and D.C. Weilbaker. 1988. "The Effect of Plausible and Exaggerated Reference Prices on Consumer Perceptions and Price Search." *Journal of Consumer Research* 15, no. 1, pp. 95–110.

Vaccaro, V., V. Yucetepe, G. Torres-Baumgarten, and M.-S. Lee. September 2008. "The Relationship of Music-Retail Consistency and Atmospheric Lighting on Consumer Responses." *Review of Business Research* 8, no. 5, pp. 214–221.

Valenzuela, A., and P. Raghubir. 2009. "Product 'Position'-ing: Implications of Vertical and Horizontal Shelf Space Placement." *Advances in Consumer Research* VIII, pp. 22–23.

Vanhuele, M., and X. Drèze. 2002. "Measuring the Price Knowledge Shoppers Bring to the Store." *Journal of Marketing* 66, no. 4, pp. 72–85.

Veryzer, R.W. 1993. "Aesthetic Response and the Influence of Design Principles on Product Preferences." *Advances in Consumer Research Volume* 20, eds. L. McAlister and M.L. Rothschild, 224–28. Provo, UT: Association for Consumer Research.

Vijaykumar, S., M.O. Lwin, J. Chao, and C. Au. 2013. "Determinants of Food Label Use among Supermarket Shoppers: A Singaporean Perspective." *Journal of Nutrition Education and Behavior* 45, no. 3, pp. 204–12.

Vitalija Butkeviciene, J.S. 2008. "Impact of Consumer Package Communication on Consumer Decision Making." Kauno Technologijos Universitas. Retrieved June 20, 2012 from http://www.ktu.lt/lt/mokslas/zurnalai/inzeko/56/1392-2758-2008-1-56-57.pdf

Vivid brand. n.d. "Diet Coke." Retrieved June 9, 2013 from http://www.vividbrand.com/coke-lite/

Vlahos, J. 2007. "Scent and Sensibility." *The New York Times*, September 9.

Volkow, N., G. Wang, J. Fowler, J. Logan, M. Jayne, D. Franceschi, C. Wong, S.J. Gatley, A.N. Gifford, Y.S. Ding, and N. Pappas. 2002. "'Nonhedonic' Food Motivation in Humans Involves." *Synapse* 44, no. 3, pp. 175–80.

Vul, E., and D.I. MacLeod. July 2006. "Contingent Aftereffects Distinguish Conscious and Preconscious Color Processing." *Nature Neuroscience* 9, no. 7, pp. 873–74.

Wakefield, K.L., and J.J. Inman. 1993. "Who Are the Price Vigilantes? An Investigation of Ifferentiating Characteristics Influencing Price Information Processing." *Journal of Retailing* 69, no. 2, pp. 216–33.

Wall, E.A., and L.L. Berry. 2007. "The Combined Effects of the Physical Environment and Employee Behavior on Customer Perception of Restaurant Service Quality." *Cornell Hotel and Restaurant Administration Quarterly Volume* 48, no. 1, pp. 48–59.

Walters, I. 2013. "Building Customer Engagement Capability." IGD Special Analysis.

Wang, H., and C. Chi. 2009. "The Impact of Revenue Sharing Contracts on a Retailer's Shelf-Space and Pricing Decisions." *Management and Service Science, 2009. MASS '09. International Conference on*, pp. 1–4. IEEE.

Wansink, B. 1996. "Can Package Size Accelerate Usage Volume?" *Journal of Marketing* 60, pp. 1–14.

Wansink, B. 2010. *Mindless Eating: Why We Eat More Than We Think*. New York: Bantam Books.

Wedel, M., and F. Pieters. 2000. "Eye Fixations on Advertisements and Memory for Brands: A Model and Findings." *Marketing Science* 19, no. 4, pp. 297–312.

Wedel, M., and R. Pieters. 2008. *Eye Tracking for Visual Marketing*. Hanover, MA: Now Publisher.

Wells, W.D., and L.A. Sciuto. 1966. "Direct Observation of Purchasing Behavior." *Journal of Marketing Research* 3, no. 3, pp. 227–33.

Wharton. April 19, 2006. "How the Offer of 'Free Shipping' Affects On-line Shopping." Retrieved March 15, 2014 from http://knowledge.wharton. upenn.edu/article/how-the-offer-of-free-shipping-affects-on-line-shopping/

White, C. 2012. "The Smell of Commerce: How Companies Use Scents to Sell Their Products." *The Independent*, September 22.

Whitehead., J. 2010. "Uniqlo's U.K. Twitter Campaign Looks to Be a Perfect Fit for Retailer." *AdAge*, September 7.

Whiting, A. 2009. "Push, Scream, or Leave How Do Consumers Cope with Crowded Retail Stores?" *Journal of Services Marketing* 23, no. 7, pp. 487–95.

Wilson, S. January 2003. "The Effect of Music on Perceived Atmosphere and Purchase Intentions in a Restaurant." *Psychology of Music* 31, no. 1, pp. 93–112.

Winnett, C., and A. Pohlmann. 2011. "Neuromarketing: Understanding the Subconscious Drivers." NeuroFocus, The Nielsen Company.

Wolfe, J.M. 2005. "Guidance of Visual Search by Preattentive Information." *Neurobiology of Attention*, pp. 101–04.

WPP. 2012. "Shopper Decisions Made In-Store by OgilvyAction." WPP. Retrieved Febraury 13, 2013 from http://www.wpp.com/wpp/marketing/ consumerinsights/shopper-decisions-made-instore.htm

Yang, S.S. September 2012. "Eye Movements on Restaurant Menus: A Revisitation on Gaze Motion and Consumer Scanpaths." *International Journal of Hospitality Management* 31, no. 3, pp. 1021–29.

Yang, S., and P. Raghubir. 2005. "Can Bottles Speak Volumes? The Effect of Package Shape on How Much to Buy." *Journal of Retailing* 81, no. 4, pp. 269–82.

Young, S. Winter 2004. "Breaking Down the Barriers to Packaging Innovation." *Design Management Review* 15, no. 1, pp. 68–73.

Young, S. 2005. "Five Principles for Effective Packaging Research." *Brand Packaging*, January–Febreauy.

Young, S. 2008. "Designing for the Shopper." *Brand Packaging*, April.

Young, S. January 2010. "Winning at the Two Moments of Truth." Retrieved June 7, 2012 from http://www.prsresearch.com/fileUploads/Winning_at_ the_two_moments_of_truth.pdf

Young, S. 2011. "Neuroscience Explains the Emotional Buy." *BrandPackaging*, July.

Young, S., and V. Ciummo. 2009. "What Can We Learn from Tropicana?" *Brand Packaging*, August.

Zeithaml, V.A. July 1988. "Consumer Perceptions of Price, Quality, and Value: A Means-End Model and Synthesis of Evidence." *Journal of Marketing* 52, no. 3, pp. 2–22.

Zielke, S. 2007. "Measurement of Retailers Price Images with a Mulitple Item Scale." *The International Review of Retail, Distribution and Consumer Research* 16, no. 3, pp. 297–316.

Index

OTHER TITLES IN OUR CONSUMER BEHAVIOR COLLECTION

Naresh Malhotra, Georgia Tech, Editor

- *Fashion Marketing: Influencing Consumer Choice and Loyalty with Fashion Products* by Caroline Le Bon
- *Store Design and Visual Merchandising: Creating Store Space That Encourages Buying, Second Edition* by Claus Ebster and Marion Garaus
- *Consumer Experiences and Emotion Management* by Avinash Kapoor

Announcing the Business Expert Press Digital Library

Concise e-books business students need for classroom and research

This book can also be purchased in an e-book collection by your library as

- a one-time purchase,
- that is owned forever,
- allows for simultaneous readers,
- has no restrictions on printing, and
- can be downloaded as PDFs from within the library community.

Our digital library collections are a great solution to beat the rising cost of textbooks. E-books can be loaded into their course management systems or onto students' e-book readers.
The **Business Expert Press** digital libraries are very affordable, with no obligation to buy in future years. For more information, please visit **www.businessexpertpress.com/librarians**. To set up a trial in the United States, please email **sales@businessexpertpress.com**.

CPSIA information can be obtained
at www.ICGtesting.com
Printed in the USA
FFOW02n2056080917
39789FF